THE COMMER STORY

Geoff Carverhill

The Crowood Press

First published in 2002 by
The Crowood Press Ltd
Ramsbury, Marlborough
Wiltshire SN8 2HR

© Geoff Carverhill 2002

All rights reserved. No part of this publication may be reproduced or transmitted in any form or by any means, electronic or mechanical, including photocopy, recording, or any information storage and retrieval system, without permission in writing from the publishers.

British Library Cataloguing-in-Publication Data
A catalogue record for this book is available from the British Library.

ISBN 1 86126 491 7

Photographic Acknowledgements
The author and publishers would like to thank the following organizations and individuals for supplying the photographs used in this book: Norman Lawrence, Cyril Corke, Ken Cain, Fred Lewis, Arthur Ingram, Peter Daniels, Pamela Watson Lee, The Museum of British Road Transport at Coventry, The National Motor Museum at Beaulieu, The Tank Museum Bovingdon, Renault V. I. Ltd, Chas. K. Bowers & Son, *The Commercial Motor* magazine, Luton Borough Council Libraries and Museum Service, and Avon Fire Brigade. Renault Dunstable photos 1994 and 2001 by the author.

Typeface used: Bembo.

Typeset and designed by
D & N Publishing
Baydon, Marlborough, Wiltshire.

Printed and bound in Great Britain by Bookcraft, Midsomer Norton.

Contents

Introduction and Acknowledgements		4
Foreword *by Robin Dickeson*		5
1	Dogs that Bite with a Click: The Early Years	6
2	The Twenties	27
3	Karrier Joins Commer: The Thirties	37
4	The War Effort	61
5	The Export Drive	79
6	Dunstable: A New Era	105
7	The TS-3 Engine	125
8	Rootes and the Pentastar: The Sixties	141
9	The Chrysler Takeover	173
10	Recession and Demise: The French Phase	195
Bibliography		222
Index		223

Introduction and Acknowledgements

Why Commer? Well it's like this: I was in a pub one day with my good friend and fellow jazz fanatic Peter Courtney discussing the finer points of trumpeter Miles Davis' career, when Peter mentioned that his father Eric had worked for Commer Cars in Luton for a number of years during the war and now wanted to write about his life and times at Commer, and asked whether I would help him. Being an automotive fanatic, I said 'Yes'. Apart from the fact that Eric Courtney is a first-class raconteur, it became clear to me that there was a book here, so in early 1994 I started to delve into the history of Commer. I made contact with Robin Dickeson, the Communications Manager at Renault V.I. Ltd, who immediately saw the project as being a worthy one and offered his assistance and access to Renault archives. My contact with Robin was timely in as much as the Dunstable plant was about to close, and it was he who persuaded me to continue the story beyond Commer to its final conclusion, to include Dodge and Renault.

In writing the book, I have deliberately not gone into overly technical aspects of the vehicles, but at the same time have endeavoured to exemplify important technical innovations, such as the TS-3 engine. The style of the book is intended to give an insight into how these innovative vehicles helped us deliver goods, clean streets, transport passengers, fight fires and generally enhance our daily lives, as well as evoke an age when people, and in some cases several generations, dedicated the whole of their working lives to one company … accomplishments in an age that the likes of us will never see again!

I have done my best to make sure the book is as factually accurate as possible. I have been able to correct some mistakes and misunderstandings that have been perpetuated in previous potted histories of Commer: spellings of names, model types and dates of company incorporation, for example. To straighten out certain other facts I sought the assistance of experts like Geoff Lumb of Huddersfield, who has been studying the history of Karrier for over forty years. Most of the pre-Rootes' section about Karrier is from Geoff himself, or from his books and magazine articles on Karrier. I have deliberately not included photographs of pre-Rootes' Karriers (with the exception of early Karrier-Cars) as the Karrier history is a book in itself, and a job best left to Geoff Lumb.

Special thanks are due to past employees of Commer, Karrier and Dodge, who gave me their time, entrusted me with valuable photographs, and recalled important aspects of their working lives: the great A.J. Smith, Roland Browne, Peter Lewis, Fred Lewis, Eric Courtney, Norman Lawrence, Bill Holmes, John Milnns, Roland Golby, Don Kitchen, John Horley, David Streeton, David Bryant, Geoff Booth, Cyril Corke, Brian Bateman, Roger Jenkins, Ken Cain, Norman Smith, Pamela Watson Lee and present employees at Renault Trucks Ltd. Such information would have been virtually impossible to obtain from other sources.

Thanks also go to Peter Daniels who runs the Commer Car Archive and Register, who checked early chapters of the manuscript and computer enhanced some of the early photographs originally lent to me by Norman Lawrence. Thanks especially to Barry Collins at The Museum of British Road Transport in Coventry, who supplied many of the Rootes' era photographs; Annice Collett, Marie Tiéche, Malcolm Thorne and Jonathan Day at The National Motor Museum at Beaulieu, for allowing me to raid their archives and coffee jar; David Fletcher at The Tank Museum at Bovington; and Eric Courtney for providing the Shuff cartoons.

Don Kitchen deserves a special mention for not only providing technical information on the TS-3 engine, but also for meticulously checking and re-checking the chapter. There were many others who pointed me in the right direction concerning certain aspects of the book: the late Pat Kennett; Peter Wallage; Geoff Portas; journalist and writer Will Hutton; Simon Redley (who interviewed Gerry Marsden) and Sir Geoffrey Chandler, who was chairman of the National Economic Development Council during the seventies and gave me his time and a first-hand insight into the political climate during that period. Last but not least, thanks to my ever patient wife, Sue, for proofreading every word of the manuscript.

This book is dedicated to all the Commer 'old boys'. It is after all, their story.

Geoff Carverhill
Cogenhoe, Northampton, March 2002

Foreword

The Commer story is a complex one, woven around changes of ownership and factories, and a very wide range of frequently innovative products. In this book Geoff Carverhill takes the unusual step of looking at least as much at the people as at the cars, vans and trucks they made. Frequently industrial histories tell us about this or that piece of exciting engineering, without ever telling us much about the people involved. This book is different.

It has become a management-speak cliché to say that a company is no more than the sum of its people. But all too often, companies are less than that sum. People get complacent, opportunities get missed and then the rest is history. And so are they.

Over the years I'm sure the team who worked for Commer, Karrier, Dodge and Renault in Luton and Dunstable made their share of mistakes. They'd not be human if they hadn't. And of course some of us prove our humanity all too frequently. Geoff Carverhill has captured much of that humanity and its trials and triumphs. He shows many of the people who were part of the complex history of the company. Too often people such as these are simply forgotten, but this book will help ensure that those people are less likely to disappear into the fog of history.

I joined the then 1,000-strong team at what was then Renault Truck Industries, Dunstable in 1989. Even then the writing had been on the wall there for more than a decade. For UK-owned truck building in general, the seeds of disaster had already been sown by poor managers and short-sighted politicians over many years.

This book traces some of the landmarks on a road to decline and for the site at Dunstable, inevitable closure. It is not a sad story; more, it is almost a natural tale, perhaps like the biography of a person from childhood through to adolescence, adulthood and inevitable death. That biography is itself made up of biographical fragments, the snapshots of the men and women who were the company. I was privileged to work with some, most of them refreshingly ordinary and all very individual. Some were quite extra-ordinary. Most were, and many still are, genuinely proud of the part they played in the story.

I saw the final years, and found myself explaining mass redundancies on radio and television, and in the press, and then saw a resurgence of confidence as a much smaller and now Volvo-owned team imported an increasingly impressive range of trucks and vans from France and slowly turned the company around.

Ironically, as the Renault renaissance lifts hearts in the team at Renault Trucks, UK, commercial vehicle building is also turning around, with some quite spectacular growth. Even more ironically, Renault has a real role in that change too. A joint project with General Motors is building increasingly large numbers of vans in Luton for sale behind Renault, Vauxhall, Opel and Nissan badges all across Europe. But for Dunstable the opportunities passed by and won't come back.

The memories captured in this book will now be much slower to pass. The Commer story deserved to be told and Geoff Carverhill has told it well.

Robin Dickeson
Development Manager – Commercial Vehicle Manufacturers – Society of Motor Manufacturers and Traders

1 Dogs that Bite with a Click: The Early Years

The motor van with two men will do the work of three large horse vans and six men.
Commer Cars publicity brochure, 1911

Around the end of the nineteenth century, the transition from horse-drawn to horseless transport was starting to be made. The earliest mechanically propelled commercial vehicles produced in Britain were steam-driven lorries and passenger-carrying vehicles. These were used from about 1831 until the 'Red Flag Act' was brought about in 1850. With the repeal of the Act in 1896, new encouragement was given to the pioneer vehicle builders who were striving to meet the needs of a new breed of potential customers in the exciting new 'motor age'.

A number of problems were facing designers, however. Apart from the bad condition of roads in Britain, which necessitated vehicles having strong tyres, wheels and suspension systems, the drivers of motor vehicles often had little experience with any form of motorized transport, many being ex-draymen or horse-bus drivers. Therefore, engineers who could build vehicles that were easier to drive and maintain would enable the new motor companies to offer products with a wider appeal.

One such engineer who was attempting to address some of these problems was Charles M. Linley, who designed an ingenious new gearbox. The gearbox was simple and uncomplicated but allowed much easier gear changes than other gearboxes of the period.

The Linley gearbox differed from the normal 'crash' type gearboxes. It was a constant mesh gearbox and changes were made by means of dog clutches that 'pre-selected' the gears. It bore little resemblance, though, to the pre-selector type gearboxes that would be in use some twenty years later.

The advantages of a vehicle with a gearbox that could be operated more easily and with less resultant damage to the gears appealed to a widely travelled electrical engineer and entrepreneur named Julian A. Halford, who, when the Linley gearbox was brought to his attention, decided to form a small syndicate with Linley and some business colleagues with a view to building a vehicle in which to test the new gearbox. A workshop was set up in Taybridge Road, off Lavender Hill in Clapham, South London, near to where Linley lived, and work commenced on the new vehicle, a 4-tonner with upright steering and iron-tyred wheels.

In 1903, the new prototype vehicle was put on the road and, after lengthy trials, the new gearbox was declared a resounding success. It was decided that a company should be formed for the manufacture of motor vehicles featuring the Linley gearbox.

On 22 September 1905, with a nominal capital of £20,000, a company was registered, its directors and shareholders being the original group that had backed the trials two years earlier: namely, Harry Charles Baillie Underdown, Frank H. Mitchell and Horatio G. Hutchinson. Julian Halford was to be the managing director and Charles Linley the works manager. Although Linley was not a director of the company, he did become a shareholder. In January 1906, an agreement was made between Linley and the company to sell the 'drawings and specifications for building his motor lorry' for £750, payment being in the form of £300 worth of preference shares and £450 worth of ordinary shares. The name chosen for the new venture was 'Commercial Cars Limited'.

Very soon it was realized that much larger premises would be needed in order to produce vehicles in volume, so land was acquired at Biscot Road, Luton, in Bedfordshire. The area enjoyed a fog-free environment as well as cheaper rates than in London, and was relatively close to Halford's home at Hill End Farm, in the Hertfordshire village of Sandridge, just south of Harpenden. The 3½ acre (1.4ha) site at Luton was also ideally situated adjacent to the London main-line railway. The erection of a purpose-built factory occupying 1½ acres (0.6ha) commenced in early 1906.

Building progressed at a rapid rate and by June the factory was nearing completion. The front of the factory contained primarily offices. The works behind the offices was divided up into three bays. The main bay was utilized as stores, to include 'rough' stores, 'finished' stores and 'non-standard' stores. The rough stores contained a large cold-sawing machine powered by a 10hp motor. The same bay also included the engine erecting shop, into which engines would be brought from the machine shop and lowered into position on the chassis. The second bay was for chassis and gearbox

(Left) The first Commer Car: built in the workshops in Taybridge Road, Clapham, in 1903, but photographed at the back of the Luton factory some years later. This is the little vehicle that signalled the start of a ninety-year lineage of commercial vehicle manufacturing.

(Right) The original tinsmiths' shop. The photo is dated 1905, so it is possible that it was taken at Biscot Road, or at a makeshift premises prior to the new factory being completed in 1906.

assembly and the third bay contained a variety of machine tools: lathes, grinders and drilling machines. The milling and gear-cutting machine shop was a separate department. The whole of the interior was gas lit and gas warm-air heaters would take the chill off the workforce during the winter months. The engine testing shop was built outside and could accommodate up to eight engines at a time. Petrol tanks and engine bonnets were fabricated in the adjacent sheet metal room. Machined parts awaiting assembly were case-hardened in another part of the factory.

The foresight of Julian Halford and the finance management skills of Harry Underdown combined with the engineering talent of Charles Linley made for an excellent team who were determined to make their new company a success. They were certainly off to a good start with a very well fitted-out factory that would enable them to be as self-sufficient as possible. By July 1906, the factory was ready to start manufacturing a new range of commercial vehicles, that subsequently would be known as 'Commer Cars'.

The first vehicle produced was a 36hp 4-cylinder SC type omnibus chassis and was officially announced to the press in the August of 1906. The vehicle was sold to one of the new London bus companies. The company's products were more suited, however, to provincial passenger operation, and this is where their marketing emphasis remained.

1907: the Heavy Vehicle Trials

Halford was never slow to seize any opportunity to expound the virtues of Commer Cars, either by editorial in *The Commercial Motor* magazine, by publishing testimonials from satisfied customers, or by advertisements.

An ideal opportunity to publicize the company presented itself in 1907 prior to the first Heavy Vehicle Trials, which were organized by the RAC. The company entered a Commer Car in the 3ton class and provided service vehicles (a small van and a bus) for press and officials. Halford decided that in order to prove the reliability of the Commer Car and its gearbox he would have seals put on the gearbox before the trials in September, and have them broken at the International Commercial Vehicle Motor Show which was to be held at Olympia in London in March 1908.

On 5 July 1907, Halford sent a letter to the Editor of *The Commercial Motor* requesting the seals be attached by a member of the magazine's technical staff prior to the trials; they duly obliged. The Commer Car performed flawlessly during the 880 mile (1,415km) test and was awarded the Silver Medal and much acclaim from press and public alike.

The vehicle was kept in daily service by Thomas Lipton Ltd right until the event of the Show when the seals would be broken and the gearbox inspected. Since the seals had been attached, the vehicle

This HC-type builders' lorry dates from 1907 to 1910. It was powered by the smaller output 4-cylinder 24 to 26hp engine and could carry payloads of up to 2½ton, plus body. A similar vehicle was available on a shorter wheelbase, fitted with a 2-cylinder 16 to 18hp motor, designed for 30cwt loads.

had covered nearly 7,000 miles (11,260km). Mr J.W. Orde, the secretary of the RAC, had inspected the seals to make sure they had not been tampered with and at precisely midday, on the first Saturday of The Commercial Vehicle Motor Show they were then broken by a representative of *The Commercial Motor*. Upon inspection, the gearbox was found to be in excellent condition, with 'practically no signs of wear ... with the teeth of the gear wheels and faces of the clutches in perfect condition', stated *The Commercial Motor*.

As a result of this proof positive of the reliability of Commer Cars, the company had a flood of orders for its vehicles, enabling it to expand its range of vehicles considerably. In addition to the SC type, an LC 30cwt chassis with a 16–18hp 2-cylinder engine was introduced in July 1907, followed by the HC 4-cylinder 24–26hp model capable of payloads of 2–2½ton. In October 1908, a 6-cylinder BC type fire-engine chassis was added to the range.

The variety of different chassis that the company offered complemented the range of body types that were available. A customer could choose from: a tilt van; a box van on platform, tipping, fixed or removable sides; a 'County' motor

The company had a high-profile approach to advertising and publicity during the early days, as this front cover of The Commercial Motor *from 1908 exemplifies. The illustration shows the Station Omnibus supplied to the Rt Hon. The Earl Brownlow.*

The Linley Patent Change-Speed Gearbox

The unique design of the Linley gearbox was Commer Cars' principal advantage over its competition. The box was designed to allow easier gear changing, with less noise, whilst reducing the possibility of damage to gear teeth. Gear wheels were always in mesh and gears were 'pre-selected' by means of spring-loaded dog clutches. When the dog clutches were placed in the 'ready' position and the clutch pedal depressed (or the engine throttled down), the springs forced the dog clutches into mesh and the drive was transferred to the selected gear. A change speed lever mounted just below the steering wheel operated a worm drive and camshaft, which locked any one of the gear wheels by means of the dog clutches.

The claim that the box enabled drivers to make 'silent gear changes' was not altogether correct. Instead of the sound of drivers 'crunching' gears, as with a conventional crash-type gearbox, gear changes on the Linley box would be announced by a metallic clicking sound, but the company assured customers that there was no need for alarm with the publicity slogan 'DOGS THAT BITE WITH A CLICK!'

Two views (above and left) and a sectional drawing (below left) of a 3-speed Linley gearbox of around 1910–11.

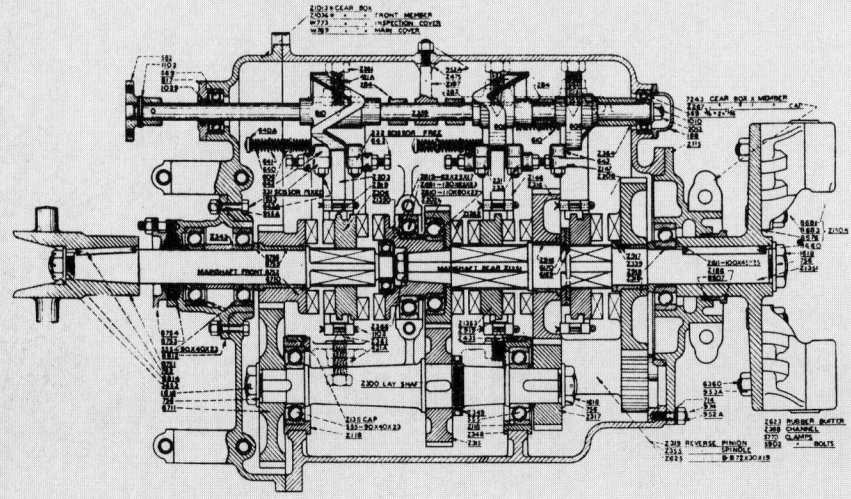

coach; charabancs; or a single-deck motor bus. The HC and LC models were also available as a private station bus and estate lorry as well as a 'Norfolk Convertible Country House and Estate Car' version. The Norfolk was displayed in the company's new London showroom at Craven House, Kingsway and took pride of place on the company stand at the Commercial Vehicle Motor Show in November 1908.

Sales of the versatile Norfolk car were brisk, as was the case with most of the new Commer Cars' range. In April of 1908, a night shift had to be put on at the factory in order to cope with the volume of orders on the books. In May, new buildings were added: a coppersmiths' shop; a test house; a repair shop; a body shop; and a paint shed.

The rapid expansion of the company and its rise to become a respected name in commercial vehicle manufacturing was quite unprecedented. Much of it was due, no doubt, to the marketing abilities of Halford.

In December 1908, two months after the birth of his second son, Halford resigned. His role at Luton had been fulfilled but although his new business ambitions were to take him to America he would continue to be of service to the company, with its proposed expansion into export markets. On 9 March 1910, he sailed from Southampton aboard the White Star liner *Oceanic* for New York.

Halford's place was taken by Underdown, as chairman and managing director. Mitchell was appointed general manager and Linley remained works manager until 1912. Aldersey Taylor became sales manager.

1909: 'Cost-Effective' Commers

In March 1909, four double-deck motor buses, the first to have covered-in top decks, were delivered to Widnes to provide a service from the transporter bridge to the town.

The order for the buses came as a result of a trial at Widnes by T.S. Allen of Manchester, who operated a Commer Car bus with Dodson double-deck open-top bodywork. It commenced running on 1 September 1907 and covered some 40,000 miles (64,360km) during the eighteen-month trial period. The operators were particularly impressed by the small amount of wear and tear on the Shrewsbury and Challiner tyres, only three sets being used during the trial. Virtually no repairs or parts were needed except for the replacement of a set of worn-out drive chains. On the August Bank Holiday of 1908, 2,748 penny fares were taken, and the average weekly number of passengers during the eighteen months was about 6,500.

Running costs during the first twelve months of the test were calculated by the operators to be 7.56d per mile, the total mileage for the

In 1909, a single-deck WP1 bus was put into service to link Leagrave residents with the tramways' system in Luton. Some time after the service had established itself, one of the drivers, Richard Rowell, courted the kind of controversy that the company had taken great pains to avoid in the early days. Rowell was summoned at Luton magistrates' court for driving 'in a manner dangerous to the public' and for passing a tramcar at a dangerous speed, estimated to be 'between 20 and 25mph.' The defence elicited from the tram driver that it was impossible to drive the Luton trams at more than 12mph; in fact 'that was all they could get out of them!' Rowell was fined 12s. 6d. and the summons for exceeding the limit was dismissed.

A 1908–09 36hp SC-type charabanc. This particular model was known as a 'Grassington' large garden seated charabanc with side entrance, to seat thirty-three passengers. It is shown outside the Hartshead Hotel, Skipton, North Yorkshire.

year being 22,800. Petrol costs were put at £158.7s.7d; tyres at £123; wages £162; repairs £84.13s; insurance £50 and depreciation (at 20 per cent), £122.

The publicity department at Biscot Road also published examples of running costs for its vehicles. A 'BC' 1½ton lorry, for example, taking the usual criteria of tyre costs, petrol at 9d per gallon, lubricants and maintenance, insurance, depreciation at 15 per cent and driver's wages of £1.15s.0d, was said to cost £6 per week to run, assuming that the vehicle covered 350 miles each week!

The company was also making efforts to 'sell' the idea of motor traction to would-be buyers. Horse transport and railway transport were still important economic considerations, but the advantages of motor transport were quickly becoming obvious. 'Speed of delivery is greater than with horse traction and in many cases, railway goods transport' stated the Commer Cars' publicity brochure.

A double-deck SC 36hp Commer Car bus operated by the Lancashire & Yorkshire Railway in the Liverpool to Southport and Chorley to Bamber Bridge areas, taken around 1908.

'Provided that a van of proper design is employed, the motor van with two men will do the work of three large horse vans, spare horses and six men.' When compared to railway transport, the motor van would also in many cases prove to be a better bet. A good example of the cost-effectiveness of motor transport was shown in a comparative cost exercise carried out by a loyal customer of Commer Cars, Waring and Gillow Ltd, the London-based furnishings company. Waring's operated a fleet of eight Commer Car pantechnicons as well as an Argyll delivery van and a Gillet steam van.

In April 1910, a 4ton Commer Car lorry and rubber-tyred trailer carrying 5ton of furniture was put on three set routes: from Edgware, Middlesex to Reading, Berkshire and back, a distance of 140 miles (225km); Highgate to Rayleigh in Essex, some 105 miles (169km); and London to York, some 400 miles (644km). The costs of each trip were recorded and compared to estimated costs of completing the same journeys by rail and horse-van. In all three cases, the motor van showed the lowest running costs. As an example, the costs for the 140 mile journey from Edgware to Reading were: £5.1s.6d by motor van; £15 by horse-van; and £7.14s.8d by railway. Only motor van and railway were compared for the London to York trip!

Armed with this kind of information, many transport managers now no longer questioned which method of transport to choose to move their goods around, but merely which motor lorry to choose. For those not wanting to tie up capital in motor vehicles, there was an alternative. In June 1909, a subsidiary company was formed, Commercial Car Hirers Ltd, under the supervision of managing director J.C. Moth. The purpose of the company was to offer vehicles for contract hire, with or without a driver, to transport goods or run temporary bus services. This arrangement was ideal for those without a constant need for a motor vehicle.

Run from a former horse-tram shed in Junction Road, Holloway, the business grew to become the main Commer Cars spares and repairs depot in London. In February 1911, the company transferred the repairs side to Parkhurst Road, Holloway, when they acquired the business and premises of S.S. Nevil, a motor engineer and repairer. In 1909, Nevil had been the assistant works manager at Biscot Road, so the acquisition of his business and creation of Commercar Repairs Ltd, with Nevil in charge, seemed to be a mutually beneficial move.

As well as depots in Glasgow and Birmingham, a north of England sales and service centre was opened in October 1911 at Deansgate, Manchester.

Commer Cars 'Booming'

Many transport fleets would have two or three different makes of vehicle, such was the choice

Commer Car Station Buses at London's Charing Cross Station around 1910–11.

(Above) A general view of the machine shop, taken about 1910. The forest of drive belts and overhead shafting and pulleys shows how power was transmitted to the machines in the early days.

Another part of the machine shop at Biscot Road (1910).

now available. The London & North Western Railway Co., for example, chose to use Thornycroft chassis for use at their Leeds depot, as well as various Commer Car chassis. They also chose Commer Cars over rival makes for their fleet of station buses.

Meanwhile, Dennis introduced a 'commodious and luxurious' country-house bus to compete with the Norfolk estate car and could offer chassis for lorry, passenger or municipal vehicle as serious alternatives to many of the models offered by Commercial Cars Ltd. The Guildford-based company was similar in size, had similar manufacturing capabilities to those of Commercial Cars, and was able, in many cases, to compete on price with an equivalent Commer Car.

Despite the intense competition, the company continued to prosper and enjoy a full order book. Orders received during January and February 1910 exceeded those received during the first three months of 1909. From 1 June to 20 October, output more than equalled that of the whole of 1909! Successive increases of business yet again necessitated an extension to the factory over a five-month period in 1910. It was also decided that the talents of Aldersey Taylor could be used to better effect as a travelling sales representative.

His place as sales manager at Biscot Road was taken by R. Barry Cole. In December 1910, despite interruptions of sales due to a general election and the holiday season, the company reported a record year for sales.

New Export Markets

The sales success of 1910 was due, in part, to newly found export territories. In addition to its exports to British colonies, the company was exporting literally all over the world. As with the home market, many repeat orders were being placed as well as orders from completely new sources. Typical examples in 1910 were a 2ton chassis with a 12-seater charabanc body and a 32hp 4ton chassis and lorry body for Sydney, Australia; two 7ton tipping wagons for Russia; one 3ton chassis for the Philippines and a 30cwt wagon for Messrs Aalgaarde Uldvarefabriker, of Stavanger, Norway. Eleven chassis were sold to the United States through their New York agents, Wyckoff Church and Partridge, who were so

A 1913 CC Colonial-type chassis was one of the first Commer Cars to be sold to New Zealand. It was used by Searle's Motor Garage of Oamaru, and was fitted with power hauling gear.

enthusiastic about the new Commer Cars that they claimed it was 'the world's most efficient and economical high duty motor truck'.

In the summer of 1911 the Chicago Motor Club hired a Commer Car to carry its baggage from Chicago to Indianapolis. The vehicle returned to New York via Indiana, Michigan, Ohio, Pennsylvania and New York states, covering 2,535 miles (4,079km) in all. During the trip, many miles of soft clay roads were encountered, where wheels often sank to the axles, as well as 28 miles (45km) of deep sand between Cleveland and Akron. The durability of the Commer Car was proven conclusively when the little truck completed the trip with an average fuel consumption of 7mpg (40.4ltr/100km) and at an average speed of 16mph (26km/h). This was considered quite an achievement for 1911.

As well as the USA, Canada, New Zealand and Africa, Commer Cars would be sold to some of the most remote parts of the world like Patagonia and Siberia. Their sales literature claimed that Commer Cars ruled 'from China to Peru'. By 1912 the company had forty-one agents and distributors in twenty-three different countries around the world.

1911: Consolidation of a New Model Range

In 1911 the company offered a range of seven standard models with payload capabilities of 1–6½ton and three passenger models, as well as a new 'Torpedo' style charabanc body. These formed the basis of Commer Car products until the twenties. Such was the demand for the basic 'no-frills' RC-type chassis that it stayed in production until 1928.

Technical improvements, however, were constantly being made. The previous year had seen the introduction of the first worm-drive 'live' axle, eliminating the need for drive chains. The 30cwt BC chassis was the only model in the range to feature this arrangement. It was described as 'a fast, silent and economical vehicle, easier to drive than the average touring car and a distinct advance upon any machine of equal capacity on the market.' The chassis price was £355 and a set of tyres including steel rims was £55.

All models now had names as well as letter designations: the BC was known as the 'Brackley'; the 2ton MC – 'Braintree'; 3ton YC – 'Barnet'; 3½ton RC – 'Bridgewater'; 4½ton CC – 'Leeds'; 5½ton KC – 'Luton' and 6ton PC – 'Manchester'. All models featured the Linley patent 3-speed gearbox except for the PC, which had a new 5-speed gearbox for trailing and hauling purposes. For export markets, the PC Colonial chassis could be fitted with hauling gear. With this it was, for example, capable of winching a 4ton load of logs up a 1 in 3 grass bank, or was able to haul itself out of and up otherwise insurmountable places.

In 1912, the CC and RC models could be ordered with the 5-speed gearbox at an extra cost

This 1913 PC Manchester chassis is seen having its mechanical hauling gear tried out in the mud in what looks like a building site, but is more likely to be the ground at the rear of the factory at Biscot Road. The vehicle is also fitted with the patent oil-tight aluminium chain cases.

Passengers and drivers pose by a WP-1 Torpedo-type charabanc, of around 1912 vintage, operated by the Dorset-based Empire Coach Co.

of £15. Another new feature available on models of 3½ton and upward was the option of dust-proof, oil-tight, aluminium chain cases at £25 extra. Price rises of between 5 per cent and 11 per cent were implemented on the basic chassis, the most expensive 40hp PC Manchester chassis costing £665. Tyres and rims cost £115 a set. Since 1907, all models had been fitted with 'Lamplough' type radiators which worked on the thermo-syphon cooling principle. All of the 4-cylinder engines now had covers on valve spindles and springs. The engines in their oil-tight cases utilized a splash lubrication system. A Claudel-Hobson carburettor supplied the air/fuel mixture, and ignition was provided by a gear-driven Bosch high tension magneto.

Pedal-operated drum brakes were mounted between the differential and the gearbox. Side handbrakes operating on the rear wheels were capable of holding a vehicle on any gradient, fully loaded. A gravity feed petrol tank was mounted under the driver's seat, with a screw down valve to turn off the petrol supply. A leather cone clutch separated engine and gearbox and some of the larger models were fitted with an interrupted buffer drive, which helped minimize shocks and jars during gear changes.

A standard range of bodies was also offered for all chassis: a flat platform body; a lorry body with swinging detachable sides and tailboard; and a tilt van or box van. Additionally, special bodies for various applications could be built on request. Municipal vehicles such as street-sweeping and watering machines, tower wagons for overhead tramway lines, fire engines and ambulances were particularly well suited to Commer Car chassis. Other examples were a specially insulated van for ammunition and explosives and a tank wagon for petroleum.

Passenger models at this time came in three standard versions: WP-1, capable of carrying up to thirty-six passengers in a single deck, double deck or Kerry-type Torpedo charabanc body; WP-2, with up to a twenty-four passenger capacity; and WP-3, for up to sixteen passengers but with only the option of single-deck omnibus or Torpedo charabanc body. These passenger vehicles were called 'WP' models after W.W. Perks, who was employed by the company to promote the sales of Commer Car passenger vehicles. He campaigned tirelessly to establish the range with vehicle operators, so after meeting with much success in the form of repeat orders, it seemed only fair that the vehicles should carry his initials.

The continued success of the Norfolk Country House and Estate Car meant that it too could be ordered in three different versions: on BC, MC or YC chassis, to carry six, ten, or fourteen passengers, respectively. Chassis prices, including tyres, were £415, £495 and £565.

Many purpose-built Wagonettes and Estate Cars were supplied to Britain's aristocracy, whose praise for their Commer Cars was high. Amongst some of the testimonials were such comments as:

> Nothing could possibly have been more useful and better adapted for the purpose ... than my Country House Car. Yours faithfully ... Earl Lonsdale, 14, Carlton House Terrace, Pall Mall, London, S.W.
>
> My Motor Bus is satisfactory in every way ... She has never had any mechanical breakdowns and carries heavy loads over very bad roads. Last Saturday she took 27 boy scouts and 3 scout masters 92 miles! Yours faithfully ... Col. R. Mirehouse, The Hall, Angle, Pembroke.

Commer-Simonis Fire Engines

The fire-fighting equipment manufacturer, Henry Simonis & Company, of Walthamstow, East London, struck up a partnership with Commercial Cars in 1907, to design and build fire engines to add to the growing range of specialist municipal vehicles available on Commer Car chassis. The first Commer-Simonis fire engine was sold to the London County Council Fire Brigade, a year ahead of the first fire engine chassis from arch-rival Dennis and two years before a Leyland offering. Lacre and Halley also had designs for new fire-fighting machines in the pipeline, as did Merryweather, who in 1903 had built the first self-propelled petrol-motor fire engine to be used by a public fire brigade.

The Commer-Simonis fire engine was the first of eleven to be supplied to the LCC Fire Brigade. It featured a combined power pump, escape cart and chemical first-aid equipment. It was fitted with a 6-cylinder 50hp engine that was sufficiently powerful to propel the vehicle at speeds of up to 40mph (64km/h) and drive the three-throw double-acting piston type pump, which was capable of delivering 450gal (2,000ltr) per minute at 110lb (50kg). One turn of the handle was sufficient to start the engine – the only problem being that in order to achieve this, the operator needed to possess a physique resembling that of Hercules! Apart from its 6-cylinder engine, the vehicle shared most of the standard features found on other Commer Car chassis. In order to maintain the stability of the vehicle the track width was increased to 6ft 3in (1.875m) and it was fitted with twin wheels on the rear and De Nevers non-skid tyre bands.

The first-aid chemical reservoir featured on the vehicle fitted neatly beneath the driver's seat. It was a 35gal (160ltr) copper tank, tested up to 250lb (113kg) pressure and fitted with a safety valve set to blow at 150lb (68kg). The tank could be coupled by a hose to a hydrant and mains water could be fed via the tank to the hose. Also, as part of the first-aid equipment, a 20ft (6m) air bottle, charged up to 1,800lb (815kg) pressure and two spare cylinders were carried. The 180ft (55m) four-ply hose for the chemical tank was carried on a reel at the back of the body. The vehicle could be supplied with or without an escape ladder, with accommodation for either four or eight firemen. The equipment was completed by the provision of portable 3gal

This Commer-Simonis fire tender is one of the types produced in conjunction with Henry Simonis & Co., a partnership that was dissolved at the outset of the Great War.

(13.5ltr) extinguishers and hose boxes to carry eight 100ft (30m) lengths of lined hose.

By 1909, three 6-cylinder fire engines had been delivered to the LCC with 60ft (18m) escape ladders. A new 4-cylinder 36hp (RAC) (56bhp) model was introduced in 1911 on a Barnet-type chassis and by 1913, three 6-cylinder models were available: 50hp; 75hp; and 100hp. As the result of an order from Vancouver, Canada, tests were already underway on an even bigger 6-cylinder engine. Capable of 120hp and driving an 850gal (3,900ltr) turbine pump, it was the biggest Commer Car engine yet to be produced. After being exhibited at the Commercial Motor Show at Olympia in July 1913, it was rigorously tested prior to despatch to its new owner.

As well as many British fire brigades, Commer-Simonis fire engines found enthusiastic buyers in export markets. During 1912, one fire appliance undertook a rather unorthodox survival course when it literally took a dip in the River Neva at St Petersburg in Northern Russia. The engine, belonging to the St Petersburg Fire Brigade, was called to a fire in which a saw mill and thirty-two other buildings were gutted. The fire had spread so quickly that the fourteen steamers and the Commer-Simonis fire engine were having great difficulty in containing the fire. The motor fire engine was then engulfed on three sides by fire and the only way that it could be saved from catching fire itself was for it to be pushed into the river. It lay in its temporary watery grave for two days before it could be retrieved, but upon inspection was none the worse for its submersion and it continued in service. The St Petersburg authorities were so impressed with the quality of the machine that they placed an order for another machine for the municipality.

The Commer-Simonis partnership continued up to the Great War in 1914, but production of fire engines ceased after the war and the company 're-grouped' with a much changed municipal vehicle line-up.

Diversification and Further Expansion: 1912

The energy and enthusiasm of managing director Harry Underdown ensured that Commercial Cars Ltd never rested on its laurels. Output was high and the company was prosperous but he was always encouraging any efforts to come up with new ideas for products. Unfortunately, many of the examples of diversification from the standard product range ended up as stillborn one-offs.

For example, narrow-gauge trucks with 4ft (1.2m) diameter wheels were designed to replace the rickshaws used on the narrow roadways of

One of the main erecting shops at Biscot Road (1912).

Workers in the bodyshop and paintshop at Biscot Road (1912).

the tea plantations of India. A Commer plough was designed and built using a Commer engine and gearbox, but although it was demonstrated far and wide by engineer Bill Seeley, none was sold and a worthy project perished ignominiously. Trams with an engine at each end were also built but they, too, ended up rusting away quietly in a corner of the factory.

One project that looked as if it could have been a serious contender for production was on the drawing board in May 1911 and in prototype form by 1912. It was to be known as the Commer Tri-Car, a 3-wheeled parcel carrier with a box-type body capable of carrying loads of up to 6cwt (300kg). Initially, it was designed with a single-cylinder 4hp JAP engine. The prototype was fitted with a 6hp engine and by the time it was officially unveiled in 1913 it featured a twin-cylinder 9hp air-cooled engine with a 3-speed gearbox and worm drive to the rear axle. Even though it was priced competitively at £95, demand was virtually nil and it too was destined for obscurity. Perhaps a case of the right vehicle at the wrong time!

Another more profitable project that attracted Underdown's attention was the Southey paraffin gas producer. In 1912, Commercial Cars had procured the rights to make the producer which, they claimed, was different from other producers in that it was not a carburettor or vaporizer, but was 'designed for the purpose of generating a fixed gas containing only a small percentage of vapour'. The disadvantages of using paraffin as a fuel had, so the inventors claimed, been eliminated, so that the obvious advantages of easier starting from cold and reduced fuel consumption with a cheaper fuel became apparent.

After testing and modifications a production version of the paraffin gas producer was shown at the Royal Show in Bristol, fitted to a Commer Car chassis. The producer was available not only to operators of Commer Cars, but to owners and manufacturers of most other commercial vehicles. It met with favourable reaction as it was priced at £35 and offered a quick payback period for vehicle operators.

The success that the company was enjoying during this period necessitated yet another expansion of the factory. Conditions had become intolerable due to the cramped surroundings as the various departments in the factory had started to overlap one another. Attempts had been made to 'get a quart into a pint pot and several of the pint departmental pots showed signs of overflowing badly'. So Underdown, with the assistance of his new works manager, Ernest L. Coxhead (who had

Dogs that Bite with a Click: The Early Years

replaced Linley), decided to extend and reorganize the factory in 1912 to almost twice its size. The new buildings included assembly shops, fitting shops and additional stores for bought-in parts, work in progress, tool stores and storage for finished units. Conditions in the new factory for workers were greatly improved and the company was now in a position to take on badly needed additional workers to cope with the ever increasing output. One of the 'new boys' in 1912 was Ted Burrell, who was a skilled fitter.

> I cycled over from Watford, hoping like so many at the time, to join the car industry. I met a prosperous looking fellow at the gate, who set me on immediately. I later discovered he was the works manager.
>
> My wage was 37s. 6d. a week, working from 7am to 8pm week days and 7am until 12 noon on Saturdays. Those hours were short though, compared to our work in the Great War. Rarely did we finish before 10pm and on Fridays we worked from 7am right through the night to finish at 12 noon on the Saturday. We used to go round waking up the poor chappies who had fallen asleep through sheer exhaustion.
>
> We were making about five chassis a week. Two chassis members were lain out on wooden trestles and the vehicle was built up piece by piece on the spot, using the very limited equipment of the time.

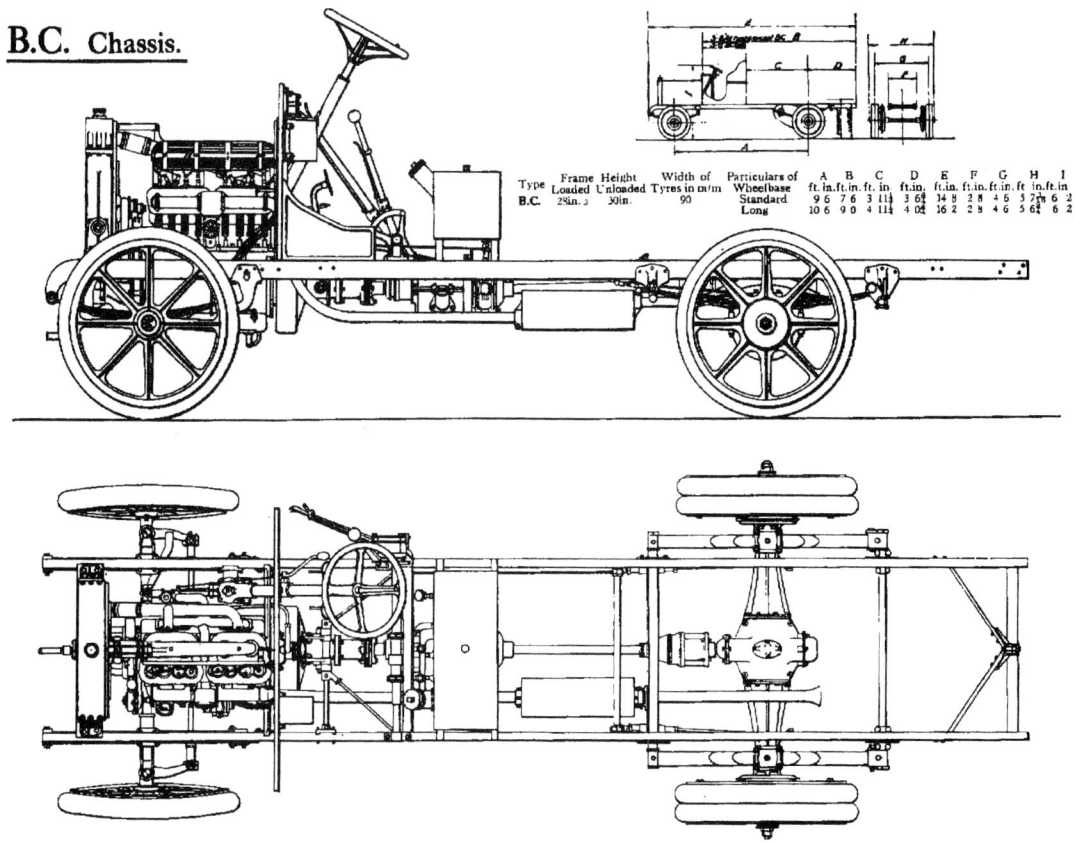

The line drawing of the 20hp BC 'Brackley' chassis shows the vehicle devoid of drive chains, this being the first Commer to feature a worm-drive back axle.

The War Office Subsidy Scheme

A subsidy scheme was announced by the War Office in 1911 as a means of enabling rapid commandeering of vehicles in the event of a war. Purchasers of vehicles that were accepted for subsidy by the Mechanical Transport Committee of the War Office would be paid for keeping the vehicle well maintained as well as receiving supplies of spare parts.

Germany already had nearly 700 subsidized vehicles and France had been carrying out military trials since 1909. By 1912, the Commission Centrale had received applications for seventy-six models to be considered for subsidy from eighteen manufacturers, with Peugeot, Delahaye, Lorraine-Dietrich, Bayard-Clement and Berliet among them.

In Britain, the War Office had decided that in view of the progress that had been made by other countries, procrastination was no longer a sensible option and duly commenced subsidy trials in 1912. Manufacturers were able to offer vehicles to a standard specification in two classes: (A) vehicles with a 3ton payload; and (B) vehicles with a 30cwt payload. One of the first fleets to be subsidized was that of Waring and Gillows' Commer Cars in 1911 and by 1914 Commercial Cars Ltd had been granted a subsidy certificate in Class A for the RC 4-tonner. Similar certificates went to Leyland, Dennis, Karrier, Thornycroft, Wolseley and Maudslay.

The Great War

The declaration of war in August 1914 saw the company in a position to make a considerable contribution to the war effort. During the war years production was concentrated on one model, the 'RC' 4ton lorry, of which some 3,000 were supplied to the War Office. A Red Cross Field Workshop on a 1ton BC chassis was a 'special' made in 1915. The commandeering of Commer Cars throughout the United Kingdom also led to a flood of orders. Peak production was reached in 1916 with 640 vehicles being completed. The

This view along Biscot Road in 1912 clearly shows the Commercial Cars factory as being one of the first buildings in the area. Visible also in this shot is the newly built extension to the factory.

Dogs that Bite with a Click: The Early Years

payroll topped 1,000 for the first time. Joe Lingar started as a boy in 1915, a few months after the outbreak of war:

> It was very hard to get in the 'Cars' in those days and essential to have someone to recommend you. I was lucky and was set on at 5s. 8d. per week, fetching tea at 1½d. a cup. We youngsters got ½d. an hour rise every six months until we were earning a man's rate.
>
> My foreman, Mr Harris, in the old running shop, helped me enormously and thanks to him I was put on the assembly, making strikers for the Linley gearbox. I ended up building gearboxes and many's the gearbox that went out with my initials on it. It took five days to build a gearbox and each box had the maker's initials stamped on it.

Ernie Dimmock started as bench boy in 1916 on the rear axle assembly doing odd jobs and machining. From there he went to the engine test shop. The engines used to be run-in using coal gas because of the petrol shortage during the war:

Outside the factory at Biscot Road, a mixture of Subsidy Type 'A' 4-tonners and wooden artillery wheeled 3-tonners await delivery to the British War Department in September 1914.

> We did a lot of experimental work with paraffin engines [Southey paraffin gas producer] under Mr Mongiardino, our chief tester at the time. It used to be quite exciting as the engines were always catching alight!
>
> Probably my biggest challenge was when I built my first engine. It was, so to speak, my passing out test. It took me the best part of a week to make it but it started up without any trouble. I glowed with pride.

Commer Cars figured prominently during the war as tough and reliable vehicles, not just for the British Army. The Canadians brought eight Commer Cars with them, the Indian contingent impressed ten and Russia impressed forty. One of the Commers supplied to Russia in 1912 was so popular that it was captured by the Germans in East Prussia, then later recaptured by the British in France. During the first three months of the war the British Government had over 500 in use. *The Commercial Motor* noted in its issue of 24 December 1914, that 'more Commer Cars were taken by the military authorities to accompany the Australian Expeditionary Force than vehicles of any other make'.

Towards the end of the war, Commers were still performing well, *The Commercial Motor* stating in March 1917:

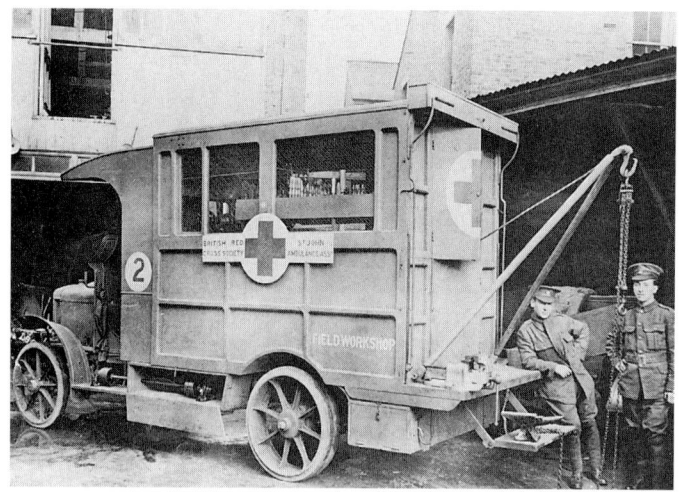

In 1915, a field workshop was built for the British Red Cross on a BC chassis fitted out with all the necessary tools and equipment to repair, or recover a military vehicle in the field.

(Above) Despite the onset of the Great War, the sales brochure for 1914–15 featured full-colour paintings of every model, plus technical drawings and full technical specifications in 138 pages. Shown is an RC 'Bridgewater' type 3½ton chassis which was one of a fleet of eight Commer Cars run by the brewers P. Phipps & Co. from their Bridge Street depot in Northampton.

A Subsidy Type 'A' WDS 4ton RC model, during the Great War.

Some of the first Divisions to come out here have whole columns of Commers. I hear there is no desire to exchange them for any other make, which fact speaks for itself.

The company also received recommendations from men on active service who felt it important to express their enthusiasm for their Commer Cars. One such letter from a demobilized man read:

I have had twelve months with a Commer Car, and I have never been in the workshops with it yet. I have travelled about five-thousand miles over some of the worst roads in France whilst loaded, and at one time carried 4½tons, four men, thirty gallons of petrol and a barrel of oil. I took this from Doullens to Amiens, twenty-eight kilometres away, and did not once drop down to first speed. I have done twenty-five miles per hour and maintained this for five hours. I can recommend a Commer Car for any sort of work or long distance ...

Employment in Luton

The well-deserved praise that had been lavished on the company's products during the Great War did much to add to the high-profile position the company was gaining in Luton. It is therefore important to view the position of Commercial Cars as a principal employer in Luton, in the years leading up to and during the Great War. Before the arrival of the new industries which were drawn to Luton in the early part of the century by the attractions of cheap land and electricity, the major companies in Luton were hat manufacturers and most of their employees were women. As well as unemployment in the slack seasons, it also meant that the large majority of the male population of Luton was unemployed.

In 1871, the population of Luton was about 20,700, of whom 12,912 were over thirteen years of age. In 1877, the Luton Chamber of Commerce was founded with a view to solving some of Luton's problems, with unemployment being high on the list. Within a few years the 'New Industries Committee' was established, comprising representatives of the Town Council and Chamber of Commerce. Its purpose was to attract new industries to Luton, which would absorb some of Luton's surplus labour. The pool of unemployed and under-employed male labour in itself became an incentive for companies to relocate to Luton.

It is no wonder that companies like Commercial Cars, the Davis Gas Stove Company Ltd, George Kent Ltd (an old established London firm which specialized in making meters for water, gas and oil) and the Skefko Ball Bearing Company (a Swedish subsidiary which opened a factory in 1910), were welcomed with open arms. By 1914,

The staff of the spare parts department at Biscot Road, with foreman Fred Hathaway (2 June 1916).

Commercial Cars was one of the biggest employers in the town. Luton had been transformed into a diverse manufacturing town, with engineering skills matching those of other industrial areas in the Midlands and the North. The committee had succeeded in attracting business and employment to Luton 'beyond its wildest dreams'.

Before the Great War, Luton had virtually no union presence, the hat industry being non-union. The new engineering firms to the town brought with them their own trade unions, but Luton enjoyed an enviable record of labour relations that was to continue after the war. Relatively minor problems did occur during the war, but the circumstances were more than extenuating. A one-day strike was staged by workers in Luton factories because of the badly organized system of food distribution in the town, which resulted in the re-organization of the Food Council. A ten-day Munitions Strike took place in 1917. This was the first big industrial dispute to hit the town and was over the issue of unskilled workers being allowed to do skilled work due to the dilution of labour.

By the end of the war, Luton's commercial profile had changed. Due to Luton's contribution to the war effort both by established companies such as Commercial Cars and also new firms such as Hewlett and Blondeau, which had opened an aircraft factory at Leagrave to deal with essential war contracts, the town had expanded and had sealed its future as a major manufacturing centre.

The Tramway and Railway World *magazine ran a series of advertisements for Commercial Cars featuring artwork like this Godbolt print from July 1918.*

2 The Twenties

The new passenger chassis ... should be much easier to drive ... and the driver should have as much comfort as his confrere of the touring car.

Commer Cars press release, 1928

The Post-War Slump

After the First World War virtually every British and Continental motor vehicle manufacturer faced the prospect of a collapsed market for new vehicles. For commercial vehicle manufacturers, this was compounded by a glut of well-maintained 'Subsidy' vehicles which came onto the second-hand market following the armistice in November 1918. Many companies faced bankruptcy. In France, for example, Berliet had been manufacturing trucks at around 1,000 per month until August 1918, when government contracts ceased. They were forced into an almost impossible situation

This evocative photograph sums up the atmosphere of the early twenties. Despite the rain, a sizeable crowd has gathered in Park Street, Luton, for this Peace Day parade through the town. The Commer Car 'RC' model taking part was operated by the Luton-based company, Davis Gas Stove Co. Ltd.

After the Great War, many ex-WDS vehicles were sold off, and continued to be used as serviceable, cheap to run vehicles for years after. This Commer Car 3-tonner was registered on 12 April 1920 to Henry Henly, a corn merchant of College Street, Swindon, although judging by its radiator grille, the design of which dates back to around 1915, it is likely that this vehicle was one of the many ex-WDS models that were refurbished and sold off after the war. The vehicle was bodied by William Bert Young of Marlborough Road, Swindon.

(Below) Another early-twenties RC type, but probably not an ex-Subsidy model. The only indication that this vehicle is a post-Great War model are the six-spoked cast-steel wheels. Is the gentleman standing by the vehicle actually Mr Robinson of Ramsbottom?

after the first French post-war government had imposed a tax on wartime industrial earnings. Berliet survived, but many other companies did not.

In America, at the turn of the decade even the mighty General Motors was feeling the effects of a worldwide slump, and in September 1920 the bottom dropped out of the automobile market. By November of that year all the major car producing divisions, with the exception of Buick and Cadillac, had shut down their plants.

During 1919, General Motors had negotiated to buy Austin, but Herbert Austin instead sought the assistance of Henry Ford as a possible saviour of the ailing Austin Motor Company. On 9 July 1920, Austin sent a detailed letter to Ford outlining his proposal for a merger. Mr Ford did not even reply in person; his General Secretary replied instead saying: 'I wish to inform you ... that Mr Ford does not feel inclined to entertain any proposition such as your letter sets forth.'

Many other British car and truck manufacturers were also fighting for survival, and for Commercial Cars Ltd the situation was equally desperate. After the war, many ex-soldier employees were welcomed back by the company, but sales had toppled, the order book was empty and there was little for the workforce to do. Some workers played football or cricket in the factory yard to while away their time when they ran out of work. Many would wait every morning for the mail to be delivered to see if any orders came in for them to build. Morale was low and the future looked bleak for the company and it was decided by the management that the situation could no longer continue. In August 1919, the company was put into voluntary liquidation. A month later, the Stock Exchange Committee had approved a refinancing package with a nominal capital of £250,000. A new company was registered with the same name with no changes in the management structure. Harry Underdown and Horatio Hutchinson, together with a new shareholder, Lt Col The Hon. Wilfred C.W. Egerton, were to be the principal shareholders and directors.

With the restructuring of the company complete, and the threat of imminent closure removed, Underdown and his new team (works manager Ernest Coxhead, chief engineer Mr Thomas and sales manager Robert Stafford) could now concentrate on putting together a new vehicle range to meet the decade ahead.

This vehicle, an RC chassis fitted with a 'Brewers Body with Tilt', was featured in the 1920 sales brochure. Green's Brewery was another Luton-based company that used Commer Cars.

Something Old, Something New, Something Borrowed ...

The line-up for 1920 was essentially a carry-over of the vehicles that had been produced before the Great War, in fact since 1912. The RC 3½-tonner had outsold all other Commer Car models tenfold, and it was still popular, due no doubt to its competitive purchase price (chassis £1,090 in 1920), its reliability and its uncomplicated and rugged construction. Along with the MC 2-tonner and CC 5ton chassis, the RC still had another seven production years left in it. The YC 3ton chassis and the WP1 36-seater passenger chassis filled in the gaps until the new models could be put into production.

New model designations were created for 1920, but the vehicles themselves, a passenger model that would take a 30-seater charabanc body and a 2½-tonner, were not actually that new. The passenger model, known as the 3P, had been around since 1915 when the original prototype had been built, and probably would have seen its way into the Commer line-up much earlier had the war and subsequent financial problems not got in the way. However, the time had not been wasted, as the prototype chassis had been used as a daily fetch-and-carry wagon by the works clocking up over 30,000 miles (48,270km). Sometimes it was driven on quite long journeys to and from iron and steel suppliers in the Black Country. The company had carefully monitored its running costs during the five-year period and calculated that the costs for repairs during the period, considering the vehicle had been subjected to some quite rough usage, came to an amazingly low total of less than £10!

The principal advantage of the 3P was a chassis frame made of pressed channel steel which offered strength and a degree of 'whip' and therefore improved shock absorbency on rough roads compared to the rolled steel section chassis frames of previous models. Its 4-speed gearbox was a development of the Linley gearbox that Thomas had succeeded in making more compact by reducing the shaft lengths. It was operated by a side lever through a gate change quadrant. The updated design was subsequently patented by Thomas. A worm-drive back axle and an enclosed propeller shaft made for a more practical final drive. The engine was the same 4-cylinder 36hp unit as used in the WP1 passenger chassis, but with a splash-pressure lubrication system and a 'tell-tale' dashboard light indicating the pump operation. The cooling system was still based on the thermo-syphon principle, the radiator being the gilled-tube type with cast aluminium top and bottom tanks. This was not as efficient as other methods of radiator construction at the time (honeycomb tube or corrugated strip), but it was cheaper, and cost reduction was a vital element in the company's battle for survival.

The other new model was a goods chassis, the 2G (2½ton payload chassis with a 25hp 4-cylinder engine and a 3-speed version of the Thomas Patent type gearbox). As with the 3P, a worm-type final drive was used, with ball bearings fitted on the differential as well as the engine crankshaft. Timken tapered-roller bearings were used for the cast-steel spoked wheels. Braking was effected by a hand lever which expanded internally on cast-steel drums on the rear wheels, or a foot brake acting externally on the rear end of the main gear shaft. A 16gal (73ltr) petrol tank mounted under the driver's seat fed the Claudel-Hobson carburettor. With a wheelbase of 11ft (3.35m), a platform length of 9ft (2.75m), and a chassis weighing in at 1ton 14cwt (1.7tonne), it offered the potential buyer a comprehensive specification, competitively priced at £955.

The product range would remain virtually the same until 1923 when the KC model was re-introduced as a 6ton chassis, featuring most of the attributes of its smaller new sisters but with the final drive through sprockets and roller chains to the rear road wheels. In 1922, a French style semi-limousine coach body was made on the 3P chassis and in 1924 a 3P 'Goods' chassis was offered, with a 2P 20-seater bus and a 3P 30- or 46-seater bus being added in 1925.

1923: A Receiver and Manager Appointed

Despite Commercial Cars' progress in obtaining new business in export markets like America and

South Africa and especially in the passenger chassis market, the business growth was not enough to ensure shareholders' complete confidence in the long-term future of the company. The restructuring of the company had turned out to be only a stay of execution, and in October 1923 at the first meeting of the creditors of The Hon. W.C.W. Egerton, it was announced that Commercial Cars Ltd (Luton), was going into receivership. H. Tansley Witt was appointed as receiver and manager.

Putting the company's situation into perspective it was hardly surprising that it had failed at this particular point in time. The previous month had also seen Commercial Car Hirers Ltd go into liquidation, after some fifteen years of trading. The market for commercial vehicles had still not recovered from the effects of the First World War. Manufacturing over-capacity and a collapsed market in France and Germany had done little to help the British manufacturing situation. Germany was also beset by rampant inflation and was experiencing chaos and suffering almost as bad as during the war itself. In 1923, the German mark fell to a one hundred thousandth part of its pre-war value. Meanwhile, Britain responded to its problems by electing its first ever, albeit short-lived, Labour government. Electoral 'musical chairs' would be played by the Conservative and Labour party throughout the turbulent twenties until the formation of a coalition government in 1931.

During this period, Commercial Cars limped on under the management of Tansley Witt, trying everything to encourage sales by making drastic price reductions, while still trying to assure any potential customers that although the company was in receivership it had not gone into liquidation and was still manufacturing. Unfortunately, all this effort was to no avail and the company soon found itself back in 'Carey Street' again. On 26 May 1925, a compulsory winding-up order was issued and Commercial Cars Ltd was put into liquidation.

1926: New Owners and New Beginnings

Although a decade of Commercial Cars manufacture under the auspices of Underdown had come to an end, new owners were found in the form of Humber Ltd. During November 1925, discussions were held with Tansley Witt and the management of Humber and by December a subsidiary company of Humber, Centaur Company Ltd, had purchased the assets and goodwill of Commercial Cars Ltd. The Centaur name was subsequently changed to Commer Cars Ltd. A new managing director was appointed by Humber: Col Thomas B. Keep. His new works foreman in charge of Erecting, Assembly, Blacksmiths and Sheetmetal Departments was Fred Faller, an experienced and capable man who had been with the company since the start in 1906.

A 1927 6ton RC.

He had replaced Laddie Williams who ran the factory during the latter part of the twenties.

The Humber acquisition had given the company a new lease of life and by the new year the reconstruction of the company had been completed. New models were put on the drawing board utilizing the engineering knowledge of Humber and the experience gained by Commer in the construction of lorries and passenger vehicles. This resulted in a new range of vehicles and a departure in some ways from the products the company had previously produced.

However, before the company could even think of building a new product range, their first priority was to dispose of vast stocks of unsold vehicles that were still on the books. This job was given to a new sales manager, Gerald Bragg, who was appointed from Bean Industries in 1928.

1928: The New Commers

On stand number 26 at the Commercial Vehicle Motor Show at Olympia in November 1927, the new Commers were unveiled. Seven new models were exhibited: four passenger models and three goods chassis.

The '30GP' model was a small, lightweight chassis designed to carry light loads where speed was necessary. It was also Commer's response to yet another revision of the motor taxation system. As from January 1928, petrol tax was reintroduced, replacing the old 'unladen weight' tax

How many men in trilby hats can you get into a Commer Car bus? This shiny new, loaded to the gunnels, 3PG double-deck bus, is seen at the top of Tennyson Road in Luton in 1928.

The 40LG featured a low-loading chassis with a hydraulic tipping body for refuse collection with a 2ton payload. It was fitted with small 20in steel wheels with 24in solid rubber tyres. A tight turning circle made this little vehicle highly manoeuvrable in cramped town or inner city environs.

that had been in force since 1920. A rebate of 20 per cent was also offered for commercial vehicles fitted with pneumatic tyres. The new 30cwt model was economical and was shod with Dunlop pneumatic tyres. It was powered by a 4-cylinder 15.9hp Humber engine with plain bearings and pressure lubrication, and was fitted with a 4-speed gearbox with a cone clutch and spiral bevel final drive.

A low-loading chassis with a 2ton payload was shown with a hydraulic tipping body for refuse

A 4GN 4-tonner from 1929–30.

A late twenties N4 'low-loading' 26-seater bus.

collection. The '40LG' was fitted with small 20in steel wheels with 24in solid rubber tyres. A tight turning circle made this little vehicle highly manoeuvrable and ideal for short runs in cramped town or inner city environs.

The other two chassis on show were a 2½-tonner (2½GA) and a 4ton model (4G) with an open-type brewers wagon body, but the stars of the show and certainly the ones that caught the attention of the press were the new 4 and 6-wheeled passenger chassis. Both were made available in forward control (F4 and F6) and normal control (N4 and N6) versions, to carry either twenty-six passengers or thirty-two passengers respectively. In their announcement to the press, the company stated of their new passenger chassis that they should 'be much easier to drive ... and that the driver should have as much comfort as his confrere of the touring car'. Lighter and easier steering was achieved with the Marles type patent steering gear. The front and rear drum brakes were servo-assisted, larger drums and wider shoes being fitted on all wheels, as well as a transmission brake. As it was anticipated that much larger saloon-type bus bodies would be fitted to these chassis, massive cross-bracing was fitted to prevent frame racking. A degree of standardization was also achieved, with the 4- and 6-wheeled chassis frames and main units being interchangeable.

To power these considerably heavier passenger chassis, a new engine was designed, a 4-cylinder monobloc type with detachable heads, aluminium pistons and an aluminium crankcase, the maximum output being 84hp at 2,500rpm. Power was transmitted through to the 4-speed gearbox by a cone clutch, and an undertype worm gearing transmitted the drive to the rear axle(s). An up-to-date 12volt electrical system featured 'an electric horn, C.A.V. electric starter and five lamp lighting set'. A gear-driven speedometer and mechanical tyre inflator completed the equipment list.

Behind a splendid polished aluminium radiator, the new Commer passenger models would befit any style of coachwork well. Although initial sales were slow, these new designs were important milestones for the company and would prove to be fundamental to the company's efforts to establish a permanent and credible position in the passenger vehicle market.

A 4GN chassis in the works (top), and a close-up of the radiator grille of the same vehicle.

Enter the Rootes Brothers

The twenties and thirties saw a period of rationalization in the number of motor manufacturers in Britain, partly through acquisition by other companies and also through business failure in these tough economic times. In 1925, Vauxhall was acquired by General Motors, and in 1928 Hillman and Humber (who had adjacent factories in Coventry) merged. The necessary investment in the new Commer models had financially stretched Humber to such an extent that by 1929 Hillman, Humber, and Commer yet again, were in financial trouble.

Their saviour came in the form of one of the most successful motor vehicle distributors in Britain, Rootes Limited. The Rootes brothers, William (Billy), and younger brother Reginald (Reggie), had created their company in Maidstone,

Sir William Rootes.

Sir Reginald Rootes.

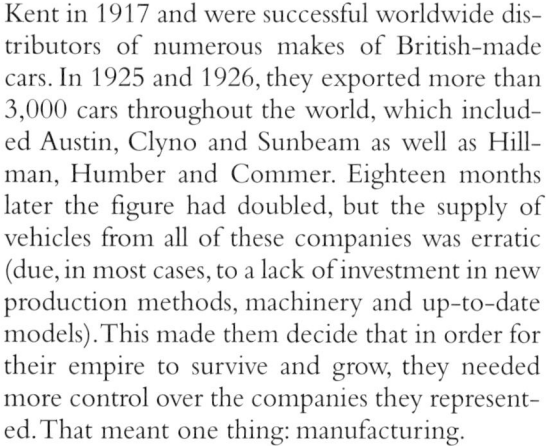

Kent in 1917 and were successful worldwide distributors of numerous makes of British-made cars. In 1925 and 1926, they exported more than 3,000 cars throughout the world, which included Austin, Clyno and Sunbeam as well as Hillman, Humber and Commer. Eighteen months later the figure had doubled, but the supply of vehicles from all of these companies was erratic (due, in most cases, to a lack of investment in new production methods, machinery and up-to-date models). This made them decide that in order for their empire to survive and grow, they needed more control over the companies they represented. That meant one thing: manufacturing.

The brothers had earlier tried to buy Clyno, but its management refused to sell and it subsequently went into liquidation. They then turned their attentions to Humber. A long association had existed between the Rootes family and Humber since the 1890s when William Rootes Senior had sold Humber bicycles. He later also sold Humber cars when he added motor sales to his successful general engineering business in Goudhurst, Kent, in 1897. Colonel Cole, the Humber chairman, had been a friend of the Rootes family for many years and was very keen for a closer business relationship with Rootes Limited.

However, if an offer was to be made by Billy and Reggie for Humber, they would not be buying one company, but three. Their major hurdle at this point in the race was therefore a lack of finance. The brothers turned for help to Sir George Hay, chairman of the Prudential Assurance Company, and 'The Man from the Pru' agreed to finance the two entrepreneurs. By 1929 Humber, along with Hillman and Commer, had become part of Rootes Limited.

For Commer and the Luton workforce, this acquisition was perhaps the most important point in the company's turbulent history to date, especially in terms of long-term survival. For the Rootes brothers, it was the beginning of one of Britain's most significant motor manufacturing groups.

3 Karrier Joins Commer: The Thirties

For Big Loads and Bad Roads – Karrier
Advertising slogan for Karrier, 1918

On 29 October 1929, the New York Stock Exchange crashed, devastating American business and manufacturing. Not only had the US economy plunged into a calamity that would take nearly a decade to shake off, but it also sent shock waves across the world.

Britain was affected greatly by the crash, but not in the same way as the USA. The British economy had not experienced the same meteoric rise as the US economy during the twenties. Some British companies were actually thriving, but in many cases British motor vehicle manufacturers, component suppliers, coachbuilders and the many other trades and services allied to the motor trade were struggling. The early thirties was, indeed, a volatile economic period.

Drivers stand by a row of Commer Invader buses at Braemar in Aberdeenshire, Scotland.

For the Rootes brothers however, Britain's economic situation offered an opportunity to turn a disaster to their advantage. As motor manufacturing firms became weak in their struggle to survive during 'The Depression', so the enigmatic brothers turned predators. In April 1933 the name of Rootes Limited was changed to Rootes Securities Limited. Within two years they had acquired the Sunbeam Motor Car Company of Wolverhampton and the Huddersfield-based bus and lorry manufacturer Karrier Motors, both of which were unable to carry on manufacturing without substantial financial investment.

The Invader with 'Silent Third'

Meanwhile back at Biscot Road, the Commer team was working hard on a new passenger chassis with some innovative features. The '6TK Invader' was launched in late 1929. With a chassis to carry a 20-seater bus body, it was a development of the '5P' model light bus chassis that had been offered earlier in 1929, but with some notable technical differences. The Invader featured a novel design 4-speed gearbox, which not only enabled rapid and easy gearchanges, but also featured a 'silent' indirect third gear and direct fourth. In its road test, *The Commercial Motor* magazine lavished praise on the new vehicle, in particular the gearbox.

> That the gears are truly silent was soon obvious. On top gear, which is direct, the engine note and the swish of the rear tyres were separately distinguishable when driving the chassis. This point was duly noted before testing the silence of the third speed. A change down

was then made at 30mph. Naturally, the engine note altered, but by turning one's head to the right the engine note was audible on one side and the hum of the tyres from the rear was still the dominant sound from that portion of the chassis; the gearbox, which was almost below the driver's seat, made no sound at all. The claim for the silent third speed was proved to the hilt.

The Invader was powered by the Humber 3,498cc 6-cylinder engine and featured vacuum servo-assisted front drum brakes, which:

> were found to give very sweet braking without wheel lock ... On the descent of Sharpenhoe Hill we took the opportunity of testing the brakes with a dead engine and the gear lever in neutral, thus putting out of action the vacuum-servo motor. We were able to hold the chassis on the 1-in-6 portion by the foot brake alone.

The Commercial Motor also noted that the Invader had another new innovation: 'Cowls to cover the wheel retaining nuts' – in other words, hub caps!

1930: A New Commer Engine

Designations of normal and forward control bus chassis were changed in 1929 but were essentially updated versions of the 'F' and 'N' series. The 'NF6 Avenger' passenger chassis announced in 1930 was powered by a new Commer-designed 6-cylinder engine which was rated at 100bhp and remained in production until 1933. The goods chassis that were on offer also had changed designations, but the models available effectively catered for payloads of between 2 and 5ton in normal and forward control versions, with only minor changes made in specifications until 1933. In 1930, a new 'long-normal control' 6/7-tonner was offered, which cleverly met the needs of transport managers who needed to carry a full 6½ton payload on a 4-wheeled lorry, without exceeding the legal back axle load limit, which was 8ton at the time. This was done by placing the engine forward of the front axle, therefore putting more of the engine, transmission and cab weight over the front axle, allowing more payload weight to be placed over the rear axle. It was also possible to utilize the largest size of twin rear tyres without the maximum legal width of 7ft 6in (2.3m) being exceeded. The G6 was also powered by the same new Commer 6-cylinder engine as that fitted to the Avenger passenger chassis, and remained in production until 1934.

The first Commer Avenger passenger chassis was built in 1929, for introduction in 1930. It was powered by a new Commer-designed 6-cylinder petrol engine. This NF6 Avenger is a 32-seater single-deck version operated by Wright Brothers of Ealing, West London. The Avenger name would remain synonymous with Commer passenger chassis for the next thirty years.

An NF6 Avenger chassis.

Raider and Centaur

Another example of the new Commer sales team meeting the needs of a rapidly changing commercial vehicle market in the early thirties was the 'B30 Raider' and 'B40 Centaur'.

Introduced in 1931, the Raider would prove to be a commercial success: a versatile, tough, but lightweight 1½-tonner. It was powered by a 3ltr 6-cylinder side-valve petrol engine with a four-bearing crankshaft and forced-feed lubrication. The Raider had been designed with driver comfort and

An early thirties photograph of a G6 tipper, showing the 'long normal control' design of placing the engine forward of the front axle, thereby allowing more useable payload weight over the rear axle.

B30 Raider 1½ton van. One of the many photographs taken for Commer by Charles K. Bowers.

convenience in mind, as well as practicability, low running costs, and a very full specification for its price class.

Easy accessibility to the engine compartment and reduced service and lubrication requirements were important considerations for buyers as were creature comforts such as 'a steering column mounted headlamp dip-switch, an instrument panel with concealed lighting, all in a roomy and comfortable cab'. What also made the Raider attractive to buyers was the range of inexpensive standard body styles that were available. A new Raider with a flat platform lorry body could be purchased for £262, or with drop or fixed sides for an additional £5, a hand tipping lorry, a box van or 'Luton' type van, a lorry with full tilt, or even an agricultural wagon for £295. The chassis price was £225 ex-works, finished in lead colour.

Hot on the heels of the Raider in 1932 came the B40 Centaur 2-tonner, with the same 6-cylinder engine as the Raider, while facilitating a 'longer than average body length on a less than average wheelbase'. The Centaur was also available with the same standard body-style options as the Raider, but with an additional long-wheelbase version offered plenty of choice to suit potential customers' requirements. Both models would feature prominently in the Commer line-up until 1935.

In 1933, the first diesel engine option (Perkins Lynx) to be offered in any British vehicle was provided on the Raider and Centaur. In addition, Dorman 4HW and 4RBL diesels were offered as standard on the 4 and 6ton chassis respectively.

The Combined Convention and Car-Derived Vans

The first Combined Convention to show the new products of the Rootes Group to the trade and press was held at Coventry on 27 September 1932. New models from Hillman, Humber and Commer were displayed. The LMS Railway heralded the event by arranging for two special trains from Euston to set up new speed records, both on the outward and return journeys. This they achieved, with the best time being 83 minutes for the 94-mile (151km) journey.

(Above) 1932 B40 Centaur 2ton lorry.

The buying office at Biscot Road during the thirties.

The first effects of Commer being able to draw from other companies within the Rootes organization showed in the 1933 Commer model line-up. The number of models virtually doubled from the previous year to twenty-eight by utilizing the resources of Hillman and Humber. The introduction in October 1931 of the Hillman Minx car enabled Commer to offer the first of what would turn out to be a very successful line of 'car-derived' light vans in 1933. The 8cwt van was essentially a Minx with a van body, using the same 1,185cc side-valve engine and 3-speed gearbox. This 'smart, speedy and economical van' (as the sales literature put it) was competitively packaged at £125 for chassis only, or £150 for the complete van, ex-works. The chassis could also be used for other body styles such as an open lorry (pick-up), milk delivery vehicle or estate car.

The new 15cwt De Luxe Van utilized the 2,810cc 6-cylinder side-valve engine of the Hillman Wizard 75, as well as much of the chassis components, radiator and bonnet of the Wizard, but the transmission was the Commer 4-speed 'Silent Third' gearbox. The 15cwt in its initial form would only be available for one year, however, as it disappeared in 1934 along with its passenger car

One of the early examples of what would turn out to be a successful line of car-derived vans based on the Hillman Minx: the Commer 8cwt van.

It had possibly been a consideration that Rootes would market a Hillman van before deciding on Commer as the badge for car-derived vans. This is the version based on the Hillman Wizard 75.

counterpart, the Wizard. A revamped 15cwt van, based on the Hillman 20-70, continued for another year before it was finally dropped.

Other derivatives of existing Commer models followed: a goods version of the Invader, the 2½ton G2, a larger 24- or 26-seater passenger chassis version of the Invader, known as the Corinthian, a Police van and a De Luxe Ambulance based on the Raider. In 1933, a light 3-tonner, the 'B3' was introduced. It was a development of the Raider and Centaur and was offered in response to the demand for vehicles to operate with a maximum load at 30mph (50km/h), in the £30 per year tax class.

At Olympia in October 1933, Commer showed a new and unusual short wheelbase 2-tonner: the Pug. It was designed as a highly manoeuvrable and economical delivery van, but although some were sold to companies like Carter-Patterson for local

The forward-control 25cwt version of the B20 (20/25 cwt) model delivery van was only made in 1934 and 1935.

The 15cwt De Luxe Van continued to utilize Hillman componentry for a short period after the demise of the Wizard. This example is shown on the Hillman 20-70 chassis, which was used until around 1935.

(Below) The Commer G2, the goods version of the Invader, looks quite diminutive alongside its bigger G3 brother.

A Commer Pug chassis outside Ladbroke Hall, Rootes' premises in Barlby Road, London.

parcel delivery work, it was soon discontinued as all development efforts were being placed on an entirely new range of vehicles: the 'N' Series.

Commer Cars and Karrier Motors

In the autumn of 1934, Rootes acquired Karrier Motors (Successors) Ltd, through their manufacturing subsidiary, Humber Ltd. Due to the Depression and the subsequent drop in demand for new vehicles, Karrier, like so many other vehicle manufacturers, had become financially weak. Management at Karrier was determined to keep the company a Huddersfield-based manufacturer with a local workforce, but by the early thirties it had become apparent that Karrier was unlikely to survive without outside help.

Rootes was not the first company to view Karrier through predator's eyes. In July 1932, Tilling-Stevens Motors Ltd (or T.S. Motors, as they had become) in Maidstone had negotiated a takeover of Karrier to create TS-Karrier Motors Ltd. Production would have been moved to Maidstone but, although management and shareholders agreed in favour of the merger, in mid-September 1932 the Karrier directors withdrew from the agreement. The company continued production in Huddersfield, but despite having a full order book, a receiver had to be appointed in June 1934. A subsequent acceptance was made for the offer from Rootes to take-over the company.

By 1935, Karrier production had been moved to Luton alongside Commer, in a further extended and modernized Biscot Road factory. Some of the Huddersfield workforce moved as well, but many were reluctant to uproot to what was a very different environment away from their friends and family, and instead took their chances finding alternative employment closer to home.

The Rootes roster was now starting to look impressive: Humber, Hillman, Sunbeam, Commer and now Karrier. In Karrier, Rootes had not acquired merely a badge or a down-and-out company with no future. Instead, they had acquired the expertise of a company with over thirty years' valuable experience in building a diverse and unusual range of commercial vehicles that complemented the Commer line-up.

With the transferring of Karrier production complete, work on building a new assembly shop for the proposed 'N' Series was well under way. Provision had also been made for Karrier production in a separate adjacent assembly shop, housing much of the machinery that had been brought down from Huddersfield. By the end of 1935, Commer and Karrier production was all on one site, and wholly owned by Rootes.

Under the 1935 Finance Act the government imposed additional fuel duties that directly affected the use of diesel-engined vehicles. Despite this, there was an appreciable increase in the number of commercial vehicle registrations during 1936. Exports, too, were up, with over 15,500 vehicles exported in the twelve months up to the end of September. Rootes had already grabbed the tiger by the tail with its considerable investment in Commer, so this was encouraging news to Rootes and to the Commer management.

Clayton to Karrier

The family business of Clayton & Co. had been established in Huddersfield before the turn of the century. In 1904, Herbert Fitzroy Clayton and his son Reginald formed a new company to 'manufacture commercial vehicles and accessories'. On 16 December 1904, Clayton & Co. Huddersfield Ltd was registered.

In 1908, with a workforce of thirty-five, the company began producing Tylor petrol-engined Karrier Cars. Their advertising slogan was 'Karrier Cars – For Commerce'. The first Karrier Car to be produced at the firm's Union Works was the 'A' Type, which was designed specifically to cope with hilly districts of Yorkshire. The driver was positioned over the engine in order to obtain as large a payload space as possible on a short wheelbase. Also known as the 'overtype', this practical, if unconventional design was perhaps the forerunner of the 'forward control' format that would be used by many manufacturers in the future. In 1909, fifteen vehicles were produced by Karrier, and a year later the range included the first of many passenger-carrying vehicles, bringing the production total that year to forty-six vehicles.

In 1911, the bonneted 'B' Type was introduced, and by 1912 the company was in need of additional premises, and so occupied the former Hopkinson engine works in Huddersfield. In 1915, the Standard Works, as it was known, was enlarged to become the Karrier Works. During the Great War, over 2,000 3 to 4 ton lorries were built to the War Department subsidy specification, and even after the war WDS-based models continued to be produced in order to satisfy the demand for vehicles until new models could be built.

In the months that followed the end of the war, it was decided to create a new company to concentrate on the manufacture of Karrier vehicles. On 27 February 1920, Karrier Motors Ltd was formed. Herbert and Reginald Clayton were still at the helm as directors. H.W. Hattersley, the sales manager, was also appointed to the board. The Karrier works manager was J.H. Arton and the chief engineer was R. Dean-Averns.

The company was not confined to the manufacture of commercial vehicles, however. As well as lorries and buses, Karrier Motors also made fog-signalling machines at Huddersfield and detonators at the Westhorpe

'Karrier Cars – For Commerce': the slogan that was used by Clayton & Co. in the early days to advertise their vehicles. This advertisement, showing a Karrier 'A' type, is from The Commercial Motor *issue of 21 October 1909.*

The Karrier Works in Huddersfield. A long line of WDS models stands outside the factory.

continued overleaf

Clayton to Karrier *continued*

The naming of military hardware was not confined just to aircraft in the Great War; army lorries acquired their own characters as well. This 1916 Karrier WDS 3-tonner was named 'Sally Brass'. Others in the fleet were called 'Bill Sykes' and 'Mr Squeers'.

Detonator Works at Penistone near Bradford. By 1924, the Claytons had set up overseas subsidiaries: Karrier Motors (South Africa) Ltd in Cape Town and Karrier Motors (Eastern) Ltd in Bombay, India, as well as being directors of Yorkshire-based textile and dying businesses in Huddersfield, Milnsbridge and Brighouse.

The early twenties would establish Karrier with a reputation for building innovative and reliable vehicles for the municipal market. As well as a number of motorbus models that were available, they had succeeded in developing vehicles for less glamorous municipal applications: road sweepers and refuse collectors. There is a saying in Yorkshire 'Where there's muck, there's brass!'

Within four years of the formation of Karrier Motors, the company was able to offer a range of goods chassis to suit payloads from 25cwt up to 3ton. It also offered passenger models that could meet most municipal and private applications, as well as being more innovative in design than the competition. Proof of this came in the form of the 'KL'-type low load-line chassis that entered service in June 1925. Twelve months later, the lighter Leyland Lion PLSC appeared with many features that were copied from the KL.

Another 'first' from Karrier also appeared around this time: the 'W6' goods chassis. This vehicle was the first rigid-frame 6-wheeler to be built and featured a semi-bogie construction for the four rear wheels, which enabled it to cross incredibly rough and undulating ground with

(Middle right) A Karrier WDS chassis next door to the Karrier works in St Thomas Road, Huddersfield.

(Right) A Karrier WDS model, complete with concrete slabs as test load, being inspected whilst on test in Church Avenue, Linthwaite.

ease. A development of this design gave invaluable service as military transport during the Second World War. In 1928, two WO6 type 6-wheelers were used in the MacRobertson Expedition to encircle Australia, a total of 11,000 miles (17,700km) over the most arduous terrain. The two vehicles were named Burke and Wills, after the famous explorers who set out on a tragic crossing of Australia in 1861, but their Karrier namesakes successfully completed the trek in twenty-two weeks.

Experience gained with the 6-wheeler chassis was also used for passenger chassis designs. The 'WL6' featured an unusual form of chassis frame design that became known as the 'spectacle' frame. The frame was formed with two holes around the rear axles that enabled the axle bogies to be withdrawn easily, whilst giving added strength as well as a low platform height of only 2ft (60cm).

Subsequent 4- and 6-wheeled, single- and double-deck bus chassis were built by Karrier right into the thirties, serving municipal transport needs all around Britain, and in particular those of Huddersfield Corporation. At their peak in 1931, 7 per cent of municipal motorbuses built in Britain were Karrier. Four- and 6-cylinder diesel engines built by Dorman's of Stafford were widely used in Karrier vehicles, but Karrier also built their own engines and local opinion abounded that they were superior units to the Dorman engines.

Karrier was never a company to rest on its laurels, and the early thirties saw a number of collaborative ventures with railway companies. A 'Chaser 6' bus was specially produced for the London Midland Scottish Railway which could run on branch railway lines as well as on roads. Called the 'Road Railer', it was fitted with flanged rail wheels, and pneumatic-tyred wheels that were lowered when road operation was required. A goods version was also built on a 3-tonner but, sadly, neither version saw commercial production. The bus version ended up in the corner of Commer's Biscot Road yard. Other more successful collaborative efforts with railway companies were made – the Cob 'Mechanical Horse' tractor unit would form a major part of the first Luton-built Karrier product range.

As far as Karrier motorbuses are concerned, the last model to be produced was the 4-wheeled Monitor. Although ten were supplied to Johannesburg, South Africa, fitted with Gardner diesel engines, it was not able to compete in the marketplace with the likes of the Leyland Titan or the AEC Regent.

(Above) Capitalizing on the Karrier's war effort, this advertisement appeared in The Tramway and Railway World *in January 1918.*

An 18-seater Karrier PB60 charabanc from around 1912. In June 1914, a Karrier charabanc made news when it climbed Porlock Hill, fully loaded with twenty-two passengers, during a trip from Minehead in Somerset to Lynmouth in Devon. Porlock Hill, at this time, was thought to be one of the steepest and most dangerous hills in the country for motor vehicles to climb.

Karrier Trolleybuses

The introduction to trolleybus manufacture for Karrier came when Clough, Smith & Co. Ltd were no longer able to buy basic chassis from Straker-Squire Ltd. of Edmonton, London, in order to manufacture complete trolleybuses under the Clough-Smith name. In 1926, they turned to Karrier as a would-be supplier. An agreement was entered into for Karrier to make the Karrier-Clough trolley-omnibus which would be marketed by Clough-Smith. This arrangement continued until March 1933 when it was announced that Clough, Smith & Co. Ltd would cease to act as sole agents for the supply of the Karrier-Clough omnibus. It was then left to Karrier to manufacture and market trolleybuses, which they did quite effectively until 1934 when the financial rug was pulled.

Under the Rootes umbrella, trolleybuses continued to be made under the Karrier name. When Karrier production was moved to Luton in 1935, trolleybus production went to the Sunbeam factory at Wolverhampton until the outbreak of the Second World War. Sales and marketing was done at Biscot Road, overseen by the Karrier sales manager, Norman Akroyd, a talented ex-Huddersfield publicity man. In 1936, Huddersfield Corporation placed an order for eighty-five trolleybus chassis, which was the largest order ever placed with any trolleybus supplier. A total of 316 Karrier-designed trolleybuses were built, of which 212 were 'E6' models built on the spectacle frame. The electrical equipment for the majority of Karrier trolleybuses was supplied by Metropolitan-Vickers.

OPPOSITE PAGE:
When trolleybus production moved to Sunbeam at Wolverhampton in 1935, publicity was put in the hands of Norman Akroyd and Eric Courtney at Luton. This advertisement is from the 16 April 1936 issue of The Transport World.

(Left) An E6 trolleybus in St Georges Square, Huddersfield.

(Below) The E6A chassis. Designed for a 30ft (9.1m) body, it had conventional chassis frames with Kirkstall rear axles and bogie, in preference to a Karrier rear axle and spectacle frame. This particular chassis was built for Newcastle-on-Tyne.

**BLOEMFONTEIN · CHESTERFIELD · DERBY
DONCASTER · HUDDERSFIELD · NEWCASTLE · NOTTINGHAM · PORTSMOUTH**

AND NOW SOUTH SHIELDS DECIDES ON

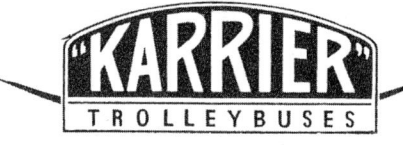

"KARRIER" TROLLEYBUSES

We have the honour to announce that the County Borough of South Shields has placed an order for a fleet of

56 SEATER FOUR-WHEEL
KARRIER TROLLEYBUSES

KARRIER MOTORS LTD., LUTON, BEDS.

KARRIER TROLLEYBUSES KEEP WELL IN THE RUNNING

The Mechanical Horse

The main disadvantage of a motor van compared with a horse and dray for local delivery work was that the van would effectively be out of action while being loaded and unloaded, and consequently not earning revenue for its operator. However the horse could continue in service on other delivery jobs while the dray was being unloaded and hence the idea of the 'mechanical horse' was born.

The LMS Railway was one of the pioneers of the 3-wheeled mechanical horse tractor unit. It was designed not so much as a replacement for its equine counterpart, but more as a practical alternative to the use of horses as the prime movers for local delivery work. The first mechanical horse prototype tests were carried out at the LMS Engineering workshops at Wolverton, using a Morris van chassis and a horse dray. The van was later substituted by a Roberts platform truck, as the van chassis was unable to manoeuvre in the tight confines of a goods yard. The third, and most successful prototype was built by Karrier: a 3-wheeled tug, powered by a Jowett flat-twin petrol engine, again with a horse dray trailer.

A prototype of the first Karrier 'mechanical horse', the 1G Cob, minus cab.

The first operational mechanical horse put into service was at Halifax in July 1931. Known as the '1G', it too had to be manually coupled and uncoupled. A similar version was also put into service by the London and North Eastern Railway.

Within a few months the LMS had produced another trailer which was still based on the horse dray principle, but could be coupled and uncoupled automatically. It also had two jockey wheels that supported it when uncoupled from the tug, instead of wooden cartwheels. In between the jockey wheels were two rollers which ran up two sloped channels on the rear of the tug. When the tug was reversed, these locked into position, ready to be driven away. This coupling was known as the 'Wolverton' coupling. A similar system was developed by Karrier, known as the 'BK' coupling, and this was widely accepted by many contractors and hauliers for local delivery operations.

continued overleaf

The 'BK' coupling system, which was originally known as the 'Wolverton' coupling, was the system developed by Karrier Motors. These two photographs are of a very early example of the Karrier Cob with the 'BK' system.

The Mechanical Horse *continued*

The Wolverton coupling was further developed by the engineering firm of Napier, which re designed the system by utilizing twin retractable jockey wheels that would sit inboard of the tractor unit wheels when coupled. Napier decided not to continue development of the coupling and sold it to Scammell & Nephew Ltd, whereupon it became known as the 'Scammell', or 'J type' coupling.

Both types of coupling were used by the railway companies, on both Karrier and Scammell tractor units, but by 1946 British Railways standardization procedures had favoured the Scammell coupling and the Karrier system was phased out.

(Top) A Karrier Cob with the later 'BK' type coupling.

A Karrier Cob 'mechanical horse' with a 'J' type, or 'Scammell' coupling, operated by the London & North Eastern Railways. Similar vehicles were used by the LMS and GWR during the thirties.

(Top) A Karrier Cob Senior with 'J' type coupling, being loaded at Shoreham, Sussex in October 1937.

The Karrier Colt was the truck version of the Cob tractor unit. Note the ditty on the side of the body of this Doncaster Rural District Council refuse collector: 'If the rates you would reduce – Reduce the refuse you produce'!

The Commer track at the top end of the machine shop in August 1935. The production lines are about to be reorganized, and new factory extensions built to take on Karrier production from Huddersfield.

1937: A Change at the Top

In the January of 1937, it was announced that Thomas Keep would be relinquishing his post as managing director of Commer Cars to rejoin the executive committee of Rootes Securities Ltd. In his new post, he would oversee the commercial vehicle operations policies of Rootes, which would include Sunbeam at Wolverhampton, as well as Commer-Karrier. His replacement was

By 1937, the 15cwt van was relying less on Hillman componentry, and became a true Commer in the 'N' Series style.

36-year-old Geoffrey Cozens, who had been the general manager at the Rootes owned Birmingham-based dealer, George Heath Ltd. D.P. Haydon moved from Commer-Karrier (Midlands) Ltd to take over from Cozens, and Harold Heath, general manager of Humber Ltd and the Hillman Motor Car Co. Ltd, was appointed to the board of Commer Cars Ltd.

Keep had been a competent and popular managing director during his ten-year stay at Commer. To show their gratitude, the workforce held a farewell ceremony for him at Biscot Road. A presentation was made by George Gibbs, who had been with the company since 1906, and was its oldest employee.

With Geoffrey Cozens in charge, one of the first changes implemented was an integration of the Commer and Karrier identities. Even the telephone receptionist was told to answer 'Commer-Karrier' as opposed to 'Commer Cars'. Keep had been a die-hard Commer man and kept both companies physically separate, even though they were on the same site. Eventually, both marques would be built on the same production lines, utilizing common parts.

Although Cozens was an entirely different character to Keep, he maintained the loyalty of the workforce and management and seemed to be a more 'accessible' character than Keep with a relaxed and more modern approach that was needed at this stage of the company's development. He also added new managers to deal with the new and enlarged product range: George R. Stratton, who had been the manager of Sunderland Tramways, became Karrier sales manager and Fred Longbottom was appointed as his assistant. Sid Cooper was taken on as assistant sales manager to Gerald Bragg. The new works director was F.G. Goddard. Fred Faller had been promoted to works superintendent in 1931.

By this time, some employees had already seen twenty-five and thirty years' service with the company, and in some cases several generations of the same family would come to work at 'the Cars'. Sid Lewis joined the company in 1914, and stayed until 1921 after an engineers' 'lockout'. He returned in 1925 and stayed until he retired, clocking up thirty-five years' service with the company. His son Harry went to work in the sales department in 1917, and in 1936 Harry's brother Fred, who wanted to 'get out of dirty overalls', joined the company from the Eastern National Omnibus Co. processing dealer orders. Many new employees started at Commer around this time and some would spend the rest of their working lives with the company.

Norman Smith started in 1932 at the age of fourteen, in the inspection department:

> One of my first jobs was to file a flat on axle shafts and Brinell test ... I then went on to the gear cutting section, checking concentricity of the gears, then milling,

A popular Commer passenger model was the full forward control PLNF5 included in the 'N' Series range introduced in 1935. This model was designed for operation as a 26-seater bus or coach, and powered by the Humber 80bhp 6-cylinder petrol engine. Among its features were 4-wheel 'Cowdrey' balanced safety brakes.

A new 8cwt van outside a dealer's premises in September 1937.

and a fairly comprehensive training throughout the machine shop during the next two years.

Fred Faller, our works manager, had a plan for me ... A vacancy came about for someone to work in the service department. I applied for it, and got it. Starting at the bottom, I was running to the stores getting replacement parts for the fitters ... and then working alongside the fitters. I then did bearing scraping ... main bearings, con-rods. You'd spend a week on a crankshaft! When I was 21 I was upgraded to 'skilled', and went on to build and recondition engines.

A fleet of Bantams operated by the London-based parcel carrier McNamara, which was a subcontractor to the Royal Mail in the City of London.

The kerbside view of a Karrier RSC sweeper-collector in 1937. Joe Borrett is the driver posing for Harry Harle's camera in Lansdowne Road, Luton, adjacent to Biscot Road.

Fred Faller was, without doubt, a disciplined and competent manager who demanded respect, and got it. His ability to motivate his workforce earned him the reputation as the man who could get 'So much out of so many for so little!' Fred Lewis remembered a comment of Faller's that stuck with him:

> Fred, if you ever get into the position where you're controlling people, go down the line and mow the whole bloody lot down, but make sure you stand them up on the way back!

In 1935 a new assembly shop was built for the 'N' Series, which incorporated new, faster, flow-line techniques. Prior to this, production and manufacture of vehicles had been virtually 'hand-built', with the chassis being moved by hand between the various work stations in the machine shop, then into the body shop for final fitting out. By 1936, all that had changed!

The First 'Commer-Karriers'

The following year, the first Luton-built forward control Karriers appeared. The 'CK-3' (3ton) was principally used for municipal chassis – in particular the gully emptiers that had been designed in conjunction with the Yorkshire Company. The

A Karrier-Yorkshire gully emptier on a CK-3 chassis, photographed for the front cover of the 1938 sales brochure.

'CK-5' was a heavy-duty 5½-tonner powered by an 80bhp, 6-cylinder petrol engine, and was marketed with alternative wheelbases. The longer 11ft 6in (3.5m) wheelbase was able to accommodate bodywork up to 17ft 3in (5.2m) in length, whilst the shorter 8ft 3in (2.5m) wheelbase was offered for tipper bodies. Although the CK-5 chassis was offered at a very reasonable price (£385) it did not prove popular and few were made, it possibly being overshadowed by its new 'N' Series stablemate.

The Bantam name, however, successfully re-emerged on the 2ton chassis used on a new range of refuse collectors.

'N' Series and Superpoise

The Commer 'N' Series represented an entirely new range of up-to-date goods and passenger

58 Karrier Joins Commer: The Thirties

(Left) Karrier CK-5 'Moving floor' lorry.

(Below left) The street washing system on a Karrier CK-3 ARP outfit being tested in the factory yard at Biscot Road (1938).

chassis. All goods models were available in normal and forward control versions, from a 20–25cwt 4-cylinder version to a 5-tonner fitted with the Humber 6-cylinder engine or, of course, a Perkins Leopard diesel unit.

In April 1937, a new 'light' 4/5ton model was added: the LN5, available in two wheelbase lengths and featuring the same 6-cylinder engine as the N5, also in forward and normal control. All LN models weighed in at 50cwt (2.5tonne), complete with standard bodywork, the choice of which was vast: short wheelbase tipper, complete with Bromilow and Edwards power-hydraulic tipping body; platform lorry, fixed or drop-sided; loose-tilt vehicle; and end or three-way tippers on the long wheelbase models. The build quality was excellent and, with other features such as three-point suspension and the fitting as standard of Bendix-Cowdrey brakes with self-energizing adjustment compensators, made these new Commers instant successes in the marketplace.

Towards the end of this decade, Commer unveiled their *pièce de resistance*, the Superpoise. With a payload range of 30cwt (1.5tonne) up to 6ton, these new trucks eclipsed all other previous models. The Superpoise was designed to compete with the 'semi-forward control' designs by Dodge, Austin and Bedford and to offer well-balanced loading characteristics, as had the Morris-Commercial 'Equiload' before it. The design of the innovative 'Diaflex' diamond-shaped chassis frame was a feature that made it a very rugged vehicle. The design allowed the chassis to 'flex' by enabling the superstructure to pivot on its front and rear mountings, isolating the drivers cab, wings, radiator and bonnet from the usual stresses to which a chassis frame would generally be subjected.

To coincide with the introduction of the Superpoise in 1939, the Luton plant saw yet another extension to the assembly shop, a re-equipped machine shop, and the addition of a new stove-enamelling plant. The Superpoise however, was Commer's war baby, and would have to wait another seven years to come of age.

(Above) Reginald Foort and his Gigantic Organ! Four Commer 'N' Series pantechnicons were needed to transport the biggest theatre organ in Britain. When the BBC theatre organ was destroyed by a bomb during the war, the BBC took over Reginald Foort's organ.

Two thirties 'N' Series Commers: an N5 normal control from 1936 (below) and a late thirties LN-5 forward control (bottom).

The interior of the despatch shop, with a line of brand new Superpoise models ready for delivery to dealerships.

COMMER Superpoise

Forty Fine Features!

1½ TON CHASSIS FROM **£214**
2 TON CHASSIS FROM **£220**
3 TON CHASSIS FROM **£237**
4-5 TON CHASSIS FROM **£275**
6 TON CHASSIS FROM **£333**

COMMER "SUPERPOISE" combines the advantages of FORWARD CONTROL—extra bodyspace, balanced load distribution and maximum visibility—with NORMAL CONTROL driver comfort and convenience.

MAGNIFICENT SPECIFICATION *including—*
- HYDRAULIC BRAKES
- ALL STEEL 'COMFORT' CAB
- IMPROVED 6 CYLINDER 'ECONOMY' ENGINE
- NEW 4 SPEED, SILENT 3RD., HEAVY-DUTY GEARBOX.

Superpoise publicity brochure (March 1939).

4 The War Effort

During the latter part of the thirties, the clouds of war had been looming over Britain. On 3 September 1939, Britain declared war on Germany.

The Commer-Karrier works was quickly put on essential munitions' work and plans were made by the War Office to decide which factories would make which products for the war effort. Many of the new Superpoise models lent themselves ideally to military applications with a minimal amount of modification. One of the first Superpoise models to be given a War Department registration was the 'Q4' 3-tonner; its rugged construction and 'Diaflex' chassis design made it an ideal 'General Service' load carrier. Powered by the excellent Humber 4ltr, 6-cylinder engine, the Commer Q4 was slightly ahead in terms of

Two N-Series Commers pose outside the vehicle despatch shop at Biscot Road, pre-war.

The main Commer-Karrier assembly track just before the outbreak of war. The Superpoise models on the track are Q4 Army 'General Service' truck chassis.

engine capabilities than the 3-tonners that were being supplied by Bedford and Austin (although it has to be said that Bedford's Chevrolet-derived 'Stovebolt-Six' was certainly no slouch, and neither was the Austin unit). One feature that possibly made the Bedford and Austin more popular with drivers was that, unlike the Commers, they were fitted with servo-assisted brakes!

A Commer Q4 'General Service' truck.

Humber Armoured Cars

By April 1940, the 'real' war had started and there became such a need for armoured fighting vehicles that Rootes were asked to produce scout cars and armoured cars in addition to those being made by Daimler. In 1938, the Mechanisation Board had laid down a standard specification for scout cars. Alvis, Daimler and BSA submitted prototype designs, but it was Daimler who eventually supplied their 'Dingo' and subsequent Scout Car Mk 1 in 1939. Hillman had produced a small, partially armoured scout car in 1934, based on the Minx, and would go on to make another fully armoured car in 1942, known as the 'Gnat'. Its engine was rear-mounted, had a full-length hull and turret-mounted Bren machine gun. However, only six were built.

The Humber Scout Car was similar in layout to the Daimler, although slightly heavier, and would be continued to be made by Humber at Coventry, and Bingley Hall in Birmingham, for the duration of the war. A total of 4,300 Humber scout cars were ordered by the War Office. The Humber Mk 1 Armoured Car was similar to the vehicle built by Guy in 1940, and was based on the pre-war Karrier KT4 artillery tractor chassis. Powered by a rear-mounted Humber 6-cylinder engine, it weighed 6.85ton and could carry its three-man crew 250 miles (400km), at a top speed of 45mph (70km/h). Its armament was one 15mm BESA machine gun and a 7.92mm BESA machine gun. An anti-aircraft version was also made, with four 7.92mm BESA machine guns. An initial production contract for 500 was placed for the Humber Mk 1 Armoured Car in 1940.

The production logistics for the Mk 1 were quite involved. The Humber petrol engines were collected from Coventry, and fitted into the chassis, which was made at Luton. The chassis was then shipped to Tipton to have the hull fitted at a temporary factory used by Rootes during the war. It was then sent to Bingley Hall, another temporary production site, for final assembly, armament fitting and testing. Prototype testing was done at Luton, and the factory had to make the best use of its local resources as far as 'test areas' were concerned. Armoured cars were sometimes seen being tested on the ramps and in the lake at Wardown Park, which was only a mile (1.5km) down from Biscot Road.

In 1941, a Mk 2 Armoured Car was produced. It had a redesigned hull, with the driver's visor built into the front plate and the radiator armour

Humber Mk 1 Armoured Car final assembly at Bingley Hall, Birmingham.

Humber Mk 1 Armoured Car chassis at Biscot Road.

altered at the rear, which increased its weight over the Mk 1. A still heavier Mk 3 appeared with a larger turret, which could take three men. The final Humber Armoured Car to see active service, the Mk 4, was fitted with an American supplied 37mm gun. This reduced the crew capacity back down to two.

Towards the end of the war, another armoured car project was put forward by the War Office: the 'Coventry Mk 1'. Due to ever-increasing demands from the armed forces for faster and heavier armaments, the Coventry heavy armoured car was built in 1944. The Coventry was a combined effort with Humber, Commer and Daimler and was designed as a replacement for both the Humber and Daimler armoured cars. Although substantial orders were placed for the Coventry, the war ended before it had a chance to prove itself.

Getting it to production gave Commer engineers a few sleepless nights. In January 1944, Arthur (A.J.) Smith was made Assistant Technical Engineer to Wally Limon, who was Technical Engineer during the war years, and it was Smith who was responsible for the Coventry project:

> It had an American engine [175hp Hercules RXLO] ... It was an engine chosen from one of three. They [Rootes] scoured America [for a suitable engine] and chose this one! I think there was a little bit of imagination on the part of the vice-president who sold us the engine, as to what it could do ... By the time we had finished building these 300 vehicles, we were re-boring the cylinders ... [to obtain the performance that was required] Daimler were responsible for the turret and for the independent suspension, Humber was responsible for the shell and Commer for the axle units and gearbox ... It caused me a lot of headaches!

Fred Lewis was transferred to the section covering workshop manuals and instruction books in

1939, and put in charge of the department in 1941. He wrote the workshop manual and parts list for the Coventry Mk 1, which took the best part of twelve months. Lewis was also on the Liaison Committee that used to attend meetings at the War Office in Duncannon Street, London. These were held once a month with officers from the field, to address any problems they might be having with vehicles supplied to the forces.

The War Effort at Biscot Road

For many of the workers at Commer-Karrier, the war meant that their lives would change inexorably. Those men who were not called up, even if they enlisted, were given 'reserved occupation' status, which meant that their particular skills were needed at home for the war effort. One such Commer employee was Norman Smith:

(Left) A Humber Scout Mk 3 armoured car in action. This was an official photograph issued by the Air Ministry in 1942 to show the importance of the RAF Transport Squadron's efforts to get supplies of petrol, water, rations and ammunition to the advancing 8th Army. The success of the operation enabled Montgomery's armoured divisions to carry on their pursuit across Libya without a break.

A prototype Coventry Mk 1 Armoured Car. Although the Coventry did not see action during the war, they were used after the war by the French in Indo-China.

During the war, municipal vehicles such as street washers and refuse collectors made ideal vehicles to convert to ARP, or 'Air Raid Precaution' outfits. This CK-3 ARP outfit is a refuse collector fitted with a water-throwing jet.

A young Eric Courtney driving an 8cwt Utility with a wooden pick-up body in August 1939, for a Commer-Karrier publicity department photo shoot.

> At the outbreak of war, I was accepted for the Tank Corps, and then sent back ... as I had had experience with armour plate. The armoured car had a welded hull ... there were certain stresses ... and in service it cracked.

These problems were addressed, and solved, by Norman and his team at Commer. What followed was a series of 'roving' assignments to sort out technical problems, but not always with Commer-Karrier vehicles.

> After I was sent back to Commer, I was then seconded to Leyland Motors at Kingston ... then to M.G. at Abingdon where they were overhauling Matilda tanks. From there, I went to Chilwell, Nottingham and then travelled around to units that had the Humber armoured car. I was at Newmarket ... and drivers were testing [the vehicles] going up banks and toppling over. You pulled them over back on four wheels again, but the oil had run out of the engine ... and we had engines blowing up left, right and centre! ... If it had a shortcoming, with a revolving turret it was a bit top-heavy.

Fun at the Factory

When the Publicity Department at Biscot Road was disbanded in 1939, Norman Akroyd was placed in charge of the Commer-Karrier War Fund. Sir William and Reginald Rootes were very keen on the Rootes Group being a major contributor to the War Fund, and Commer-Karrier was always in the 'top league' as far as contributions were concerned. Quite often, Commer-Karrier was second only to Ford at Dagenham, with over 84 per cent of Biscot Road employees contributing. Most of the funds raised were used to send food and supplies' parcels out to the forces. A typical parcel might contain items like cigarettes and tobacco, razor blade, pocket knife, toothpaste, brilliantine, shaving cream, boot laces, a Penguin novel, writing paper, envelopes, postage stamps, fruit cake and 'Ovaltine' tablets. Non-smokers were sent soap, HP Sauce and an additional novel in lieu of cigarettes!

As War Fund Secretary, Akroyd's promotional skills fitted the role ideally. His character and personality was said to resemble that of music hall and radio artiste 'Stainless Stephen'. According to Eric Courtney, who had been his 16-year-old assistant in the publicity department:

> He never stopped talking, grabbed listeners by their lapels and talked right into their faces! His appearance was somewhat eccentric as well – wearing a trilby hat with the dents pushed out, and the brim turned down all the way round.

One of Akroyd's ideas for raising funds for the forces parcels was to utilize the talents of Commer-Karrier's resident cartoonist, R.G. Shuff, an inspector in Machine Shop No. 1. When he was not actually inspecting vehicles, Shuff would be

Shuff's 'Fun At The Factory' cartoons. Regardless of rank or seniority, no-one escaped the pen of Shuff.

ESSENTIAL JOURNEY!
A. E. TOWNSEND
Transport Dept.

THE CULPRIT!
R. G. SHUFF,
Inspection Dept.

IT'S NOT ON THE LAYOUT!
J. R. LOWE,
Planning Engineer.

THE STYLIST!
E. G. M. WILKES,
Drawing Office.

YOU'RE TELLING ME!
N. AKROYD, Publicity Manager,
War Fund Secretary.

busy immortalizing the workforce of Commer-Karrier in one of his hilarious cartoons. No-one escaped the pen of Shuff, regardless of their position in the company. He was also something of an eccentric himself: a quiet, Meerschaum pipe-smoking bachelor who, although engaged for nine years, never married. When seen out walking with his fiancée, they would walk about three yards apart, not speaking. Akroyd had booklets of Shuff cartoons printed and entitled 'Fun At The Factory'. They sold for 2s. 6d. and added greatly to the War Fund effort.

Other employees at the factory also found themselves in different jobs to their peacetime roles, and some were moved to various jobs around the factory to suit circumstances. After working for Akroyd, Eric Courtney was put in the spares department, then sent to the chassis control office at the end of the production line:

With shortages of supplies during the war, many vehicles were coming off the production line with temporary out-of-specification fittings. These vehicles were road-tested, then left parked (through shortage of space) in the streets adjoining the factory – much to the annoyance of local residents, whose fear was that they would attract the attention of the Luftwaffe as targets for bombing. My duties at this time included a weekly Monday morning inspection of these vehicles ... to identify which parts were out of specification and in need of replacement. The gears for the speedometer might be, for example, for another model, or the wrong wheels or tyres were fitted ... This was a full-time job for three men in the rectification department.

Courtney spent twelve months on this job and was then transferred to the rate-fixing department:

Women workers completing the assembly of a Q4 truck at Biscot Road, July 1942.

Many of the women performed repetitive functions in the machine shop, on capstan or bar lathes. I met my wife-to-be, Mary, who worked on a bar lathe making bonnet buttons and wheel studs in Machine shop No. 1. The skilled setter who set up the bar lathe for these operations was Leslie 'Ginger' Barford. The setter ranked between foreman and operator in the machine shops, of which there were two. Charlie Curry's section was a turret lathe section ... and then there were the centre lathes, which were operated by skilled engineers, who read the drawings and performed their own setting-up.

Many new employees, both men and women, came to Commer-Karrier to work for the war effort. As with the First World War, employee numbers swelled. At its busiest, Commer-Karrier employed in excess of 2,000 people during the war, from just 700 during the late thirties. Norman Lawrence joined the company in October 1939, in the stores office:

> I'd had a bad leg injury in 1938, and had an iron on my leg, and as war had broken out I had to do war

Automatic lathes in the machine shop. 'Herbert' Auto juniors on the left and 'Herbert' No. 3 Autos on the right. The foreman in the white coat is Archie Hetherington.

Grinding machines in the machine shop. A group of 'Heald' Sizematic is on the left and a 'Precimax' grinder on the right.

(Right) Assembling transfer boxes for the Humber Armoured Car.

(Above) The club house, July 1942.

Entrance to the office block, or the 'old house' as it was known, at Biscot Road, September 1942. An ornate staircase with Commer Cars' 'wheel' emblems as banister rail supports led to the first-floor offices.

The Commer Cars' Home Guard, on parade on Harpenden Common. F.G. Goddard is the CO in charge.

work, I came to Commer's. My father [Fred Lawrence] was foreman in the work-in-progress stores ... I worked for two years in the stores, but [I] wanted to work on [the] trucks. I used to wander into the works ... and one day I was talking to one of the foremen, Reg Baker, who said that if I could walk without the iron, he would think about me coming into the 'shop. Eventually, I did walk without it and started in the running shop as a fitter in 1942.

Although Commer had always benefited from an excellent relationship between management and the workforce, there was a very brief period during 1943 when this relationship came under threat. Fred Lewis was unwittingly dragged into this situation:

During the war [the workers] got a war allowance which was merged with their salary, but [some] staff decided that it wasn't good enough, and they got various agitators – a tailors cutter from London, and a German film executive called Hamilberger ... and they wanted to call a strike. I was so incensed that they wanted to strike in wartime, when people from the factory were fighting, that I went to their meeting ... and stood up and asked them 'what the hell they were playing at' threatening to strike during wartime! Two days later, a letter was sent to Geoffrey Cozens by the local union organizer, to say that I had been made chairman of the union, and in future would be their spokesman. When Geoffrey called me up, I told him that I only went down there to say my party piece against the ruddy union!

The situation was quickly nipped in the bud. Lewis was a union member for just two days!

The Commer Cars Home Guard

As with other companies, towns or areas, Commer too, had its own 'Dad's Army'. F.G. Goddard, the works director, had been a Colonel in the British Army, so he was a logical choice to run the Commer Cars' Home Guard. Full uniform and Government Issue gun were the order of the day, but initially, the gun was a wooden replica, to be used for parade ground practice only. Later, proper .303 rifles were issued, together with

First Aid Group and Ambulance. Eighth from the left in the middle row is Fred Faller, works superintendent. On his left is managing director Geoffrey Cozens, and F.G. Goddard, works director. In the same row, Eric Courtney is second from right.

ammunition: two bullets when on duty. An unfortunate incident involving the firing of a round during the works night watch led to these rounds being confined in brown paper and sticky tape, the opening of which, on the order of a Sergeant or Officer, was not easy! Firearms instruction, of sorts, was given to the 'troops', as Eric Courtney recalled:

> A man who worked in the tool stores had experience of weaponry, and taught us how to dismantle and assemble a Bren gun ... All night manoeuvres took place on Harpenden Common, with breakfast at the White Rose Restaurant on Market Hill at 8am.
>
> Separate from the Home Guard and Fire Watchers, was the Observer Corps, who watched for enemy aircraft. The Government encouraged the continuance of work until the factory watchers gave the alarm for workers to stop, and go to their own air-raid shelter.

One night, Eric Courtney witnessed a bomb that had been loosed by a German pilot, which looked to be on target for the Commer-Karrier works. In the event, it landed on a hat factory in Old Bedford Road, Luton killing amongst others, a girl who had left Commer Cars for higher wages.

Before the war, a garage had been built underneath the despatch department, and as Norman Lawrence remembers:

> It acted as an air-raid shelter during the war, as well as a store for paperwork that could have otherwise been destroyed in fires. When we were in the Home Guard, we had our H.Q. down there. At night, when we was doing patrols, we used to take it in turns to sleep down there.

Mr Goddard guided the Commer Cars' Home Guard throughout the war years, only to have his life cut short through a motor accident shortly after the war. He was accompanying Wilf Foden, who worked in the planning department at Biscot Road. They were returning from the Hillman-Humber factory at Coventry when their Hillman Minx was in collision with a lorry at the Weedon crossroads on the A5. Foden survived the incident with a broken leg, but sadly Mr Goddard was killed.

6 November 1944: 'The Day That Changed Our Lives'

Although not heavily bombed, Luton got regular attention from the Luftwaffe, due partly to the Skefco bearing works being one of only two ball-bearing manufacturers in the country. Ironically, bombs often hit pubs instead of their intended targets. The railway station was hit, and so was the Vauxhall-Bedford works. On one occasion, a parachute mine fell on the bus depot and got

(Above) The complete factory personnel, First Aid Rescue, firemen and Home Guard.

The factory wartime First Aid Squad. The three gentlemen in the front row, flanked by the nurses are from left to right: F.G. Goddard, works director; Dr Garret, firm's doctor; and Bill Steven, in charge of first aid. The nurse behind Dr Garret (5th from right) is Madge Shorter, and second from right is Edna Burgoyne.

caught in the overhead steel girders. Brave drivers moved the buses out of the way of the unexploded mine, where it hung by its parachute webbing until a bomb disposal squad could remove it.

The Commer-Karrier works had escaped serious bomb damage, until a fateful day in 1944. On 6 November, at around 10.30am, a V2 bomb landed on the Commer-Karrier despatch department, killing 19 people and injuring 196. The death toll could, however, have been much worse. Had the bomb landed during the night, men could have been asleep in the air-raid shelter underneath the

The rebuilt despatch shop in 1945. Norman Lawrence and Roy Cooper are standing by the left wing of the Superpoise.

despatch department, and had it dropped five minutes later, the newly built canteen would have been full of workers taking their mid-morning break. Another saving grace was that the rocket fell on the town side of the despatch department. If it had hit the other side it would have gone right into the machine shop, which was full of people at the time.

This incident would forever be etched in the minds of Commer-Karrier personnel: Fred Lewis was in his office, on the telephone to his brother when the bomb exploded. He immediately got under his desk, still with earpiece to ear. Eric Courtney was across the road at number 42, a house on the corner of Lansdowne Road, which was used as temporary offices for the Karrier sales department. George Stratton and Fred Longbottom were on the first floor in a middle room of the house. They, along with other survivors, assisted in rescuing fellow employees from the rubble. The air-raid shelter below the despatch department was used for first-aid treatment, and then an army ambulance took casualties to hospital.

The following day, Courtney (in his capacity as National Savings Promotion Officer) became concerned over what was then a considerable sum of cash (£60 plus savings certificates), which was still in a cupboard in his ruined office. He returned to find Fire and Rescue Services attempting to clear the site. After finally allowing him to search the rubble, he came across the cupboard, complete with money and certificates, but with the door of the cupboard hanging from its hinges. The next morning presented a very different scene; the premises had been totally razed to the ground. Among those who died were Charlie Hancock, the security guard, company chauffeur Alf Squires and final inspector George Coop. For Norman Lawrence, the V2 bomb incident created unexpected promotion:

> A day or two after the rocket, Fred Faller and Bill Reeves [chief inspector] had me in the office ... and wanted me to take George Coop's job, and concentrate on getting the smashed up vehicles repaired. I did this temporarily and eventually permanently, so through the V2 I went on [to] inspection. From there I became chargehand on the assembly line and [in] the running shop.

Another temporary home for the Karrier sales department was found in the air-raid shelter, and where houses had been demolished in-between the factory and Curzon Road, temporary huts were erected as offices. The sports ground building at Wardown Hills was used as rough stores for items such as gearbox casings and castings for axles. Life at Biscot Road carried on.

Thirty Thousand Wartime Vehicles Produced

The quality and diversity of vehicles produced by British manufacturing organizations during the war had shown how versatile and flexible they could be when the gauntlet was thrown down. Commer-Karrier was no exception. Products made by the Rootes Group included weapons' components and aircraft spares: ammo boxes; mortar bombs; and stern frame spares for Blenhiem bombers (which were made at one of the Rootes' shadow factories at Coventry). Other aircraft spares included Griffon cowling sets, engine and radiator mountings, and various pressings for Spitfires. Many of these parts were manufactured by British Light Steel Pressings Ltd (BLSP) in Acton, a company that Rootes had acquired in 1937. Many of the body panels for Commer and Karrier vehicles were made by BLSP: cabs for the Karrier CK6 6-wheelers; Commer Q4 panel sets; Karrier gun tractors; and panels for the Karrier Bantams, production of which was transferred back to Biscot Road in April 1943.

From 1940, Sunbeam Commercial Vehicles Ltd was the only firm in Britain manufacturing trolley-bus chassis. By the end of 1944 Sunbeam had produced 236 trolleybuses, which included 147 of the 'W' type chassis made under the authorization of the Ministry of Supply. In all, Sunbeam had supplied chassis for twenty-three individual Municipalities and operating companies. As well as trolleybuses, they had also made an array of aircraft parts: pilot's dual seats and flying controls and various valves and switches for Stirling bombers, fuel jettison valves for Lancasters and undercarriage assemblies for Beaufighters.

According to Ministry of Supply, figures for the number of vehicles produced during the period 3 September 1939 to week ending 31 January 1944 at Biscot Road was 31,268, of which 8,179 were Karriers, including 3,366 Humber armoured cars. Commer and Karrier vehicles were supplied to many Government and War Office departments: Q2 and Q4 general utility vehicles, Q15 and Q25 vans for the Admiralty and the Air Ministry, as well as the Superpoise tractor units used for hauling the huge (60ft/18m) 'Queen Mary' aircraft trailers for the

Karrier CK6 chassis.

78 The War Effort

Air Ministry, and Karrier gun tractors for the India Store Department.

Due to AID (Armourments Inspection Department) requirements, all of the vehicles produced during the war were built to a very high standard, helping to build a reputation for quality in Commer and Karrier vehicles for decades to come.

In 1942, Billy Rootes became Sir William Rootes KBE. In addition, in the New Year's Honours List of 1943 was the name of Fred Faller. He was made a Member of the British Empire, in recognition of his thirty-six years' service to Commer-Karrier, King and country. He received his decoration from His Majesty King George VI on 9 March.

Commer Q25 forward control chassis (1941).

(Below) 'The last of the V.2 bombs arrives in London'. This was the headline in the Evening Standard *for 10 September 1945, as this peaceful exhibit was paraded on a Superpoise tractor unit and Queen Mary aircraft trailer at Trafalgar Square for Thanksgiving Week.*

5 The Export Drive

The few years I had at Luton were very happy ... a happy family
Norman Lawrence, Inspection Superintendent, Commer Cars Ltd

Britain emerged from the war a very different place. The country had used much of its wealth on the war, and by the autumn of 1945 was only able to pay back about 40 per cent of its overseas expenditure. In essence, Britain was virtually bankrupt. On 23 May 1945, the wartime government came to an end, and on 5 July voting took place to elect a new government. The result of the general election was not declared until 26 July, due to the delay in receiving postal votes from returning servicemen, but it was clear that the British people wanted a complete and radical change in the government of post-war Britain. A Labour government under Clement Attlee was elected with a majority of 146 and 47 per cent of the vote.

Sir Stafford Cripps, the Chancellor of the Exchequer was challenged with turning the economy around and creating recovery. In 1948, agreements between the USA and Britain resulted in a $1,263m 'Marshall Aid' package from the USA. In August 1949, Cripps devalued sterling and later implemented import restrictions and an export drive to help the recovery. For the first time since the turn of the century, financial institutions and government would be forced to invest in, and take seriously, British motor vehicle manufacturing capability. This sector of industry would play a key role in Britain's recovery plan.

Within months of the new government coming to power, a massive nationalization programme had been instigated. In 1947 the National Coal Board was formed. Transport was nationalized in 1948. The same year saw the creation of the National Heath Service, which would prove to be a popular and valuable jewel in the nation's crown. Unfortunately, only the opposite could be said of the nationalization of the road transport industry. By 1948, many privately-owned passenger and haulage operations had been taken under the wing of the government. The creation of a nationalized road haulage industry, in the form of British Road Services, was met with a highly-charged backlash from all sectors of the industry, not least the powerful road transport lobby. Road transport was one sector that won its argument to be operated by private enterprise. Subsequently, it was de-nationalized by the Conservatives, under Winston Churchill following their general election victory of October 1951. Although the Attlee government had been re-elected in 1950, in the words of Richard Crossman: 'In 1951, the Attlee government quietly expired in the arms of the Whitehall Establishment ...'.

Once back in power, Churchill did openly embrace the new 'mixed-economy' that had been created by his wartime deputy, Attlee, and it was now up to British manufacturing to help get some prosperity back into the nation.

Export or Die!

The Rootes Group actually came out of the war with a £1.5m profit, so they were ideally poised to take on, and meet, the government's target for steel allocation: that of producing 70 per cent of their production for export. The Group's assets were rapidly eaten into, however, in order to meet the challenge of export production while funding the changeover from military to a new civilian product range. The Hillman Minx was ideally suited for export markets, and would soon be seen in dealerships alongside Commer-Karrier products on the Continent, as well as in traditional Colonial export markets like India. Billy

British Motors a/s were Commer distributors in Denmark. This is a view of their stand at the 'All British Exhibition', which was held in Copenhagen from 18 September to 3 October 1948. On the left is a pre-war Superpoise, which looks decidedly 'old-fashioned' compared to the new QX cab forward-control model on the right of the picture. Within a few months, both the Superpoise and the little 8cwt Supervan in the centre would find their places in Danish dealerships taken by new post-war replacements.

Rootes set off to the USA immediately after the war to see how they were going to crack the North American market, whilst brother Reginald, who in 1946 was also knighted, held the fort back at Devonshire House.

One of the first major changes in the commercial vehicle activities of Rootes after the war was the selling of the trolleybus operations to Brockhouse & Co. Ltd in July 1946. In June 1948, Brockhouse changed their name to the Sunbeam Trolleybus Co. Ltd, which was then sold to Guy Motors in October 1948. The first vehicles produced at Biscot Road after the war were the pre-war 'N Series' and 'LN Series'. The first post-war Commer products were centred around the 'Superpoise Q Range'. Nine models covering 2/3ton to 6½ton payloads were offered until 1948, when a totally new 5/7ton forward control range was introduced.

Karrier models remained much the same as in the pre-war period. The RSC sweeper-collector however, had gone, and all municipal duties were being handled by either Bantam or the CK-3 9ft 3in (2.8m) chassis, which had a redesigned cab. A Dropsider body was also available on the longer 11ft 3in (3.4m) 4ton CK-3 chassis.

Immediately after the war, Arthur J. Smith became Technical Engineer. A.J. (as he was known) came to Commer in 1929 as a draughtsman, after serving his engineering apprenticeship at Thorneycroft. During the thirties, he was assistant technical engineer to Wally Limon before taking over the reins in 1946. This was a particularly significant move, as for the next three decades his name would be indelibly stamped on all Commer vehicles that would follow. The respect that A.J. gained was enormous, and his engineering skills cannot be overstated. He was a pedantic perfectionist, and his engineering genius would be responsible for many of the technical innovations seen on post-war Commer and Karrier designs.

Commandos in the Commonwealth

By 1947, the Rootes Export Department at Devonshire House was starting to obtain some

The Commando took on various guises depending on the type of coachwork used, as this 20-seater BOAC observation coach demonstrates.

(Below) Two 'x-ray' illustrations showing the 'Diaflex' chassis frames of the Mk I and Mk II Superpoise. Both illustrations were used in contemporary Rootes' sales literature when the vehicles were introduced in 1939 and 1948 respectively.

reasonable orders for Commer and Karrier vehicles. The 'Commando Q4' bus chassis was sold to the Indian government in CKD (completely knocked down) form for assembly by Dadajee Dhackjee & Co. Ltd of Bombay. The 30-seater bodywork was to be made by McKenzies & Co. Ltd, of Bombay. Norman Smith, Commer's export service representative, was charged with the difficult task of getting the factory up and running:

> I was asked about going to India ... I had a meeting with Geoffrey Cozens, and [it was] agreed that I had six weeks before going out to Bombay.

Upon arrival at the plant, Smith discovered that the Indians had already made a start, but unfortunately their expertise in vehicle assembly did not match their enthusiasm:

> The local dealer out there had undone some of the packing cases ... and got about thirty or forty Indian chappies [who had] started to assemble three vehicles ... [One chassis had] the radiator going one way, the scuttle the other ... we had to call a halt to that, but eventually we got some sort of assembly going. [The factory] was leased by the dealer, but it had been previously occupied by the British Army.

One of the first hurdles Smith met was that of trying to convince a representative of the newly formed Bombay State Transport Organization that the Commando, with its Perkins P6 oil engine, would give reliable service and good performance under the most adverse conditions. So he laid down a challenge:

> We got an order for 66 [Commando] Q4s from my meetings with the Bombay State Transport, but they didn't seem to have any faith in the Commer vehicle, so [with] the first completed vehicle with a body ... I suggested a test. I said, 'Name your route, have as many observers as you like, we'll load it up to the maximum gross weight and we'll take it on [your] route.'
>
> [For the test run a few days prior to the official run] ... our plan was to go up to the hill station, spend the night there and come back, but unfortunately the oil pump on the Perkins P6 engine gave trouble. So on the test run I got a red face because on the Western Ghats, near Poona, an expensive noise developed and we had to be towed back to Bombay. Fortunately, Reg Hancock, the Perkins representative was out there and it was all put right.

On the official run everything went according to plan. Starting out from Bombay on its 345 mile (555km) trek, the Commando was taken up the 1 in 6 gradient of the Bhor Ghat. Even with its payload of sandbag ballast weights giving a total running weight of 6ton 9cwt (6.56tonne), the climb was made in second gear. At the summit of Bhor Ghat, the radiator temperature registered 151°F (66°C), against 84°F (29°C) ambient. The engine oil temperature had risen to 180°F (82°C). In 6 miles (10km) the Commer had climbed from 170ft to 1,804ft (52–550m) above sea level. Katraj Ghat presented an 11 mile (18km) acclivity from Poona, rising from 1,887ft to 3,034ft (575–925m) above sea level.

The most difficult climb of the course was from Wai to Parsini Ghat, where the road rose from 2,467ft to 4,133ft (752–1,260m) in 8 miles (12.9km). It was here that problems with the engine were expected due to the high altitude, but there was no power loss, even on full throttle.

The braking efficiency was tested to its full on the descents, negotiating hairpin bends with top gear engaged! This deliberate misuse of the brakes was all part of the test, and there was no need for apprehension on the part of any of the crew, which consisted of Norman Smith, Major H. Walmsley, the deputy general manager of the state transport in Bombay, Mr Hoolihan, of McKenzies, Mr Forbes, a representative of the Commer distributors, and one other driver from the factory.

Because of its running weight, the Commando could not be driven across the bridge over the River Pen, which was constructed in 1850, so it had to ford the river up to its axles in muddy water. Apart from a temporary loss of braking due to wet linings, no apparent harm was done to the vehicle.

On the return circuit, the 80 miles (129km) of bad road surface between Poladpur and Chowk severely restricted the speed to about 20mph (32km/h), but of the trial as a whole, Major Walmsley was delighted with the way the Commer had performed. He concluded that the Commando had proved its 'ability to operate, with full satisfaction, in any part of the Bombay area'.

Nine months later, a repeat order was placed for 100 more Commandos to add to the initial quantity of 66 ... Game, set and match to Norman Smith of Commer Cars Ltd, Luton!

Rootes exploited the old Colonial territories to the full during the late forties. They eventually established a factory in Bombay to assemble the Hillman Minx: 'Automobile Products of India'. For the next few years, 'our man in the Colonies', Norman Smith, was involved in the development of export sales and service of Commer vehicles all over the Commonwealth. Occasionally Smith got to deal with Hillman and Humber cars, as most of the consuls had Humbers, as did many of the Iranian oil companies:

> [After Bombay] I returned to London, and they wanted me to go out to the Middle East and the Persian Gulf, so I had three weeks off ...
>
> In 1948, I went to Cairo and the Sudan. [We had] quite a business in Sudan – 2,000 trucks or more. A Colonel Grant-Richards was in charge of transport there ... I then went to Tehran, and the Rootes representative and I took a Q4 tipper round the oil companies in Persia, but the London office had laid down the

The Export Drive 83

(Above) The Commer 'N' Series re-emerged in the immediate post-war period and remained until the early fifties. This 25cwt forward-control van, photographed in April 1949, has a special 'travelling shop' body by Carbodies of Coventry.

(Left) This CK-3, photographed in December 1949, is fitted with a tower wagon body by Eagle Engineering of Warwick.

specification, and hadn't specified export cooling (bigger five row, instead of four row radiators and a cowled fan), but we had it changed, and it wasn't a major problem. In Aberdan, there were Chevys, Bedfords, as well as Commers. We modified a bus chassis for them to use as a tractor unit, but before they could order it they threw us [the British] out of Iran! That was 1949.

Then I went to Bombay, Madras and Karachi. Vehicles were ordered via the Rootes representative in Calcutta – the gin and tonic man. Whilst in Calcutta I visited the tea gardens in Assam, and there were about a hundred vehicles collectively, and it was a jolly good excuse [for them] to entertain an Englishman from the old country. We had a fair proportion of the business ... but some business was done by the 'greasing of the palm', and there were the long drawer desks for your donation!

84 The Export Drive

The pre-war Commer Commando formed the basis of the passenger chassis requirements until the introduction of the new forward-control chassis in 1948, as well as the CKD chassis kits supplied to export territories like India.

In Karachi, a London Commer dealer, Manton Motors of Croydon, had bought some ex-WD extended wheelbase Q45s with P6 engines, and sold them to Karachi Tramways. Then they had some problems, and Commer refused to acknowledge them when there were warranty claims. The trams in Karachi were converted after the war and had a 4-cylinder Perkins diesel engine. The driver changed gear on the 2-speed gearbox with a huge signal box type lever.

I then went to Lahore. I had a cable from Devonshire House to say that a CKD Commer had been dispatched to the Northwest Frontier, and that they

Karrier was successful for a number of years in selling vehicles to colonial territories, particularly to South Africa. Twenty years separate the late forties' CK-3 on the left from its well-worn but still serviceable counterpart.

Shiny and new, but not for long! A Karrier Bantam 7 cubic yard refuse collector, just prior to its delivery to Hayes & Harlington Urban District Council in 1946.

were [going to be] assembling them [CKD Commer Army trucks] at Fort Sandiman, and that I should meet Colonel Peter Garrett. I got up to Peshawar and reported to the British Consulate who told me, 'You can't go up there without an Army escort.' So, I hired an old Buick Straight 8 and had an Army escort up to Fort Sandiman. Garrett was off on leave and his stand-in was there. They had built one vehicle ... and had one or two problems with assembly, which were resolved. When I had finished, I asked for an escort back, but the Officer [in charge] said, 'No need, you're one of us ... but when you get to each village the head man will be waiting with a cup of tea and something to eat.' ... And sure enough, there he was with a greasy mug of tea and a hard-boiled egg ... at every village! They were interesting times.

By the fifties, Britain's exports were booming. In 1950, exports rose to a staggering £2,254m, compared to £920m in 1946. The commercial vehicle manufacturing sector alone was responsible for contributing over £66m during the first half of the year. The impact of these figures was

The Karrier CK-3, with its redesigned cab, continued to fill a multitude of municipal functions. This is a 10 cubic yard refuse collector.

86 The Export Drive

lessened slightly by a balance of payments crisis that arose in the summer of 1951, which was not anticipated. Britain was on target for recovery however, and Rootes were playing a crucial role. Sir William's influence as chairman of the Dollar Export Council made it all the more important for Rootes' products to be star players in the export game. Rootes' vehicles were now sold all over the world, including North America and Canada. Commer and Karrier vehicles had some well-established markets. Holland and the Scandinavian countries were particularly enthusiastic about Rootes commercials, as were Australia and New Zealand. In November 1951, the Rootes Group claimed an export record for the biggest single shipment of vehicles ever to be sent to Australia. A specially chartered ship, the 11,000ton vessel 'Hoperidge', was dispatched with Rootes vehicles, which included Commer and Karrier trucks, worth over £400,000, and spares valued at over £150,000, but as Fred Lewis remembers, some rather strange conditions were attached to the sale of some export vehicles:

> With CKD vehicles for Australia ... they would not accept wood-built vehicles unless all the wood had been fumigated, and a certificate provided, due to the wood wasp. On another occasion, we supplied a number of vehicles to the Indonesian government, and I negotiated a £2m parts deal for them, but [as part of the deal] they also wanted about a hundred suit lengths and various tools. We had a meeting at the Export Guarantee Department in London and I said that I couldn't enter into anything other than to supply parts!

1948: the New Forward-Control Commers ... with Chrome Bores!

The most exciting news to come out of Biscot Road after the war was the introduction of a completely new range of forward control 5- and

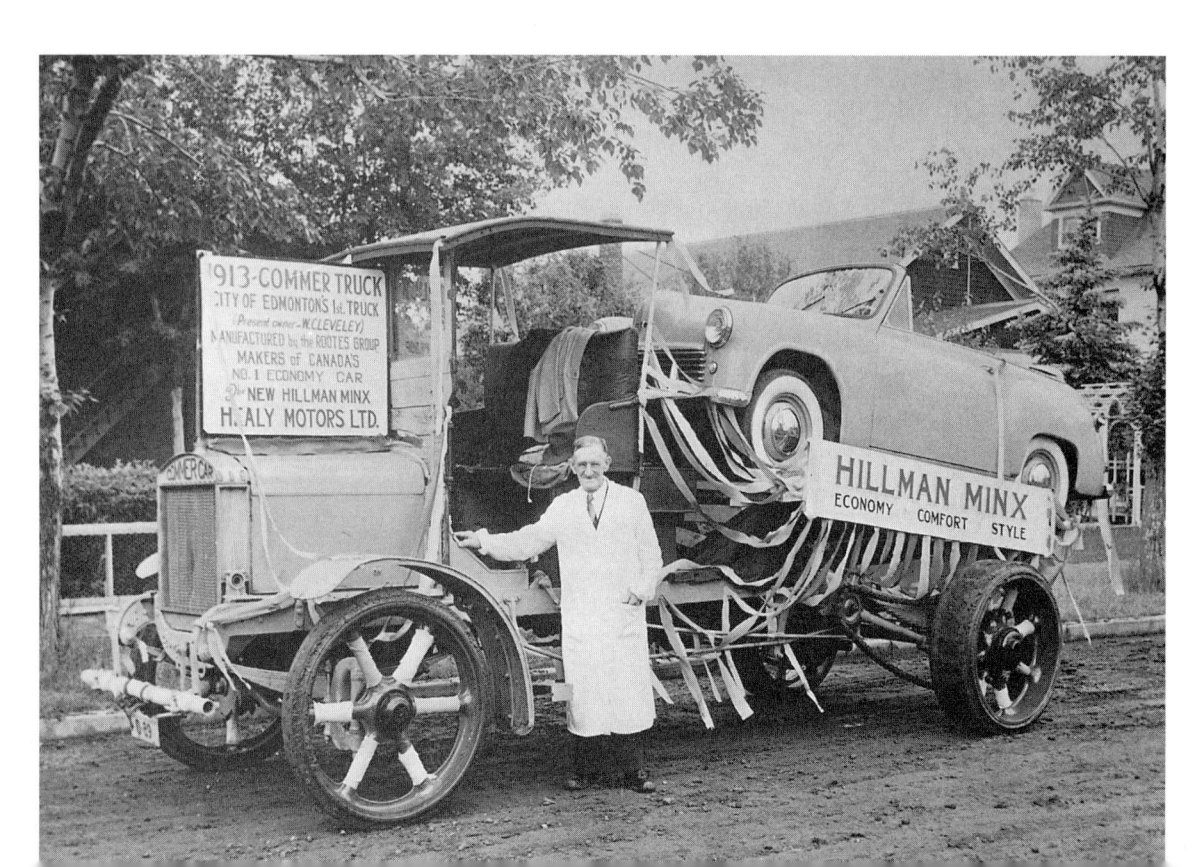

One way of publicizing a new vehicle is with an old vehicle from the same stable. Healy Motors Ltd, a Rootes dealer in Edmonton, Canada did exactly this, using an old Commer Car truck to show off an early 1950s Hillman Minx Convertible.

(Above) The Commer stand at the Commercial Vehicle Show, 1948. Note the Sunbeam trolleybus stand behind Commer.

The Commer QX, with its underfloor engine and chrome cylinder bores, rapidly gained a reputation for incredibly long mileage before de-coking became necessary. In testimonials, operators were claiming 100,000, and even 200,000 miles with little or no evidence of cylinder bore wear. Pictured is a 7ton, 9ft 7in (2.9m) wheelbase R715 dump truck.

7-tonners from Commer. Known as the 'QX' range, which was the cab style designation, it was a radical departure from other Commer designs. Although its general stance was not unlike other forward control trucks of the period, it offered operators and drivers alike advantages that were found in few other British-built trucks. The clean and uncluttered lines of the stylish new QX cab were created by the Stoke Aldermoor design team of Ted Buckle and Bill Oliver, under George Payne, chief body engineer, who was also responsible for Rootes car design at Coventry. The cab was built by the Rootes subsidiary British Light Steel Pressings (BLSP) at Acton.

At the heart of the QX was a new 6-cylinder, 109bhp overhead-valve petrol engine which was mounted under the cab floor. By laying the engine on its side (at 66 degrees to the vertical) it was possible to build a roomy cab with a flat floor, bereft of any obstructions, which enabled a crew of three to sit in relative comfort. The under-floor design also offered easy access to the engine as well as allowing the cab to be mounted well forward in order to improve load distribution. One feature that enhanced the longevity and increased the reliability of the new engine was the use of chromium-plated cylinder bores. This method of finish, known as the 'Listard

The Export Drive

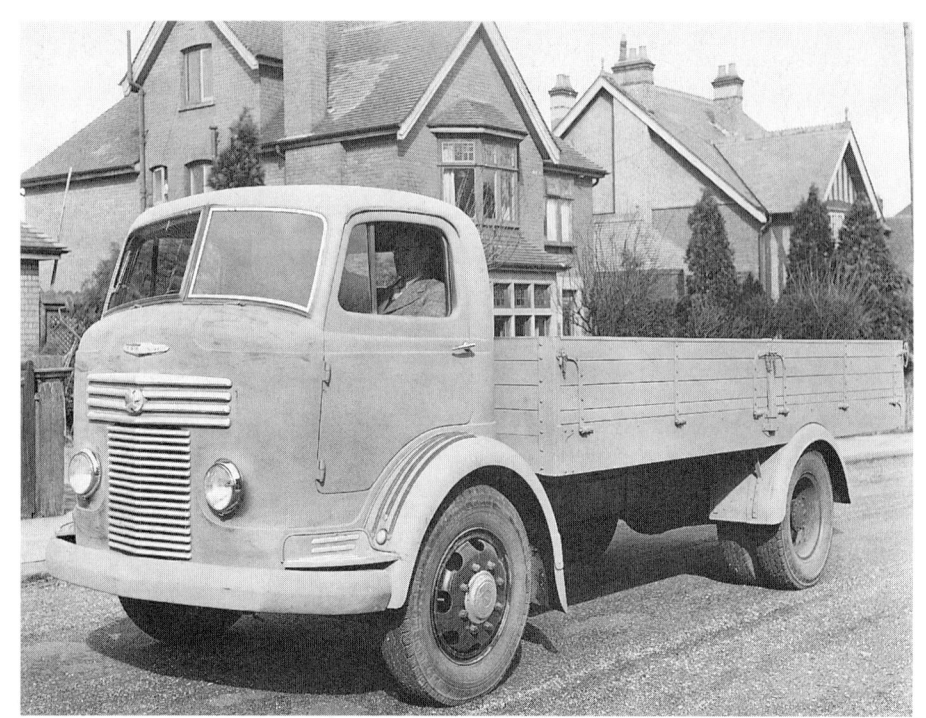

September 1947, a prototype QX with a mock-up cab outside the factory.

(Below) As well as enduring thousands of road miles during development, the QX underwent extensive testing that was ongoing through production. Here, a 7ton C762 model is being driven over the corrugated or 'washboard' track at the Motor Industry Research Association test facilities at Nuneaton.

The announcement of the new QX cab 5- and 7-tonners on 4 March 1948 at Rootes, Maidstone. Present are (left to right) Ald. T. Armstrong; Councillor H. Fletcher; G.D. Ashby, sales manager, Rootes Maidstone; Geoffrey Cozens, managing director, Commer-Karrier; and William Day, Mayor of Maidstone.

Sir William Rootes tries out the new QX cab at the Commercial Motor Show, Earls Court.

process', enabled engines to virtually double their mileage before de-coking became necessary.

After the initial development period in 1946, testing of the new models was carried out in the winter of 1947, under severe conditions in Mexico and Scandinavia, as well as in Britain. One prototype was driven continuously for 100,000 miles (161,000km) until the development engineers working for A.J. Smith were happy that the QX would meet their exacting standards.

In February of 1948, the new Commers were launched. A 'briefing meeting' was held at Ryton, and was attended by about eighty Rootes' personnel from London, Coventry, Manchester, Birmingham, Canterbury, Rochester, Maidstone and Luton. Managing director Geoffrey Cozens gave an address and sales manager Gerald Bragg gave an in-depth talk about the new trucks, followed by a close inspection for all present, of the QX and its engine.

On 28 February came 'Announcement Day'. The new models were officially unveiled to the press and dealers at Ladbroke Hall, North Kensington. A speech was made by Sir William Rootes. In part of his speech, Sir William emphasized Rootes' achievements, especially with regard to exports:

> We, in the Rootes Group, take what I hope is a just pride in the new vehicle we are introducing today. It joins a family of vehicles which have given outstanding

Coachbuilders quickly caught on to the advantages of the full-forward control Avenger chassis. This example is fitted with a 33-seater All-Weathers body.

(Below) The Karrier stand at the Commercial Vehicle Show, 1950.

and renowned service to users for close on half a century ...The fact that we have recently exported to over fifty countries is, I submit, a test of suitability for overseas conditions, particularly when one bears in mind that we have many large fleet users in various parts of the world ... In the opinion of several commercial experts who have seen the new model we are announcing today, it is one of the greatest advances in commercial vehicle design for many years.'

At the same time as the official announcement was being made, a 'National Commer Week' was inaugurated, with forty major towns in Britain having the new models on display in main dealers' premises. Along with the 5 and 7ton truck chassis came a passenger chassis, the 'Avenger'. Bodybuilders such as Plaxtons, Harrington and Beadles of Dartford, quickly saw the advantages of this new chassis for coaches. Beadles, the

(Above) An aerial view of the Luton factory in 1950.

The main assembly track at Biscot Road in 1950. Behind the Q15 Superpoise is a Karrier Bantam being inspected by Norman Lawrence.

Due to lack of space at Biscot Road, long-wheelbase QX models were assembled at Stoke Aldermoor, Coventry. Here, they are shown on the production line in 1950.

company with which Reginald Rootes' wife's family was connected, also became part of the growing Rootes Empire in 1954.

Commer had always maintained a close co-operation with outside suppliers to guarantee the quality and supply of components. Before the war, chassis frames (except for the Karrier Bantam) were supplied by Sankey's in Birmingham, Rubery Owen of Darlaston, or Projectile of London. Briggs of Dagenham designed and produced bodies for the Superpoise, as well as Commer CKD cabs. Ford took them over in 1948, preventing them from making bodies for Jowett. This was partly responsible for sending Jowett under. Sankey made wheels (and then cabs) for Commer. BLSP built cabs and panels for Commer and Karrier vehicles. Electrics came from either Lucas or Smiths of London.

In 1949, with the QX to add to the list of other Rootes' successes (Hillman Minx, Humber Hawk, Sunbeam-Talbot and so on), Rootes went public. Rootes Securities Ltd changed its name to Rootes Motors Ltd, and was converted into a public company.

By 1950, the success of the QX was keeping production at Biscot Road very busy, producing up to thirty-five vehicles a day. New models were being introduced all the time: a 15cwt pick-up truck, based on the Superpoise chassis was now offered, initially for export only, together with a fire engine chassis for the QX, followed by a long-wheelbase QX 7-tonner, which would be made at the Stoke Aldermoor plant in Coventry. A.J. Smith and his team had not been complacent either, with constant improvements being made to the QX. The new long-wheelbase QX was available with a light-alloy platform body, enabling the vehicle weight to remain within the 3ton limit for vehicles entitled to travel at 30mph (50km/h). Other changes across the QX range included larger brake linings and larger fuel tank.

Karrierings on at Commer!

Even through the difficult times of the Depression during the thirties, or the two world wars, a great social and supportive atmosphere had always been

Luton – Number 1 Machine Shop during the fifties.

in evidence at Biscot Road. Management, right from the early days, had established sports and social club activities, as well as regular dinners and works outings, which no doubt went a long way to maintaining a happy and co-operative workforce. A typical example of the humorous efforts of Commer-Karrier staff could be witnessed at a dinner and social evening, held on Friday 30 November 1951. *The Luton News* reported that 'an enjoyable and different evening was held at The Three Horseshoes, Leagrave, for foreman and senior staff of Commer Cars Ltd.' Its headline was 'Karriering On By Commer'.

The opening speech by the genial Master of Ceremonies, Fred Lawrence, was in rhyme and it is highly likely that 'guest appearances' were made by characters such as Neddie Seagoon and Bluebottle during the course of the evening. In 1951, Michael Bentine's *Crazy People* started. Shortly after, it became the legendary *Goon Show*, under the guidance of Spike Milligan. Radio comedy was at its most influential during this period. The menus took the form of a planning sheet. 'Operations' were the various courses, while 'Jigs, fittings etc.' were cutlery and condiments. Various grades of 'Oil' became light ale or hock. The chairman, Harry Lewis, Supply Manager, referred in his speech to Commer Cars as being: 'a happy ship, in which each member of the crew carried out his duties in harmony with the rest'.

The highspot of the evening was the 'Comm(er)unity Singing'. All took the advice given on the programme to 'Let your voice Karrier thro' to the tune, and with apologies to 'Widdecombe Fair':

Supply, Supply, oh where are the parts,
Production's falling lamentably,
Can't you see you're breaking our hearts,
George Swallow, Lawrence Hurdley, Dennis Leach, George Brown,
Old Harry Lewis and all,
Old Harry Lewis and all.

Design, Design it's really quite time,
All your mods were brought into line,
It seems to us you make too much fuss,
Alec Single, Beau Brandon, Bert Edwards, Hector White,
With A.J. the pride of them all,
A.J. the pride of them all.

And now for you, production crew,
Dream no more of that distant shore,
The outlook's black, fill up that track,
Fred Bugress, Bert Crabtree, Tom Pritchard, Percy Marsh,
Old Freddie Faller and all,
Old Freddie Faller and all.

Alec Single was chief body engineer, and Arthur (Beau) Brandon was chief chassis engineer during the forties and part of the fifties. Bertie Edwards and Hector White were both engineers under A.J. Smith. Norman Lawrence, Inspection Superintendent, affirms the sentiments in Harry Lewis's speech:

Biscot Road was a happy workforce. We all knew one another and one anothers' jobs ... If, for instance, we had a problem with exhaust pipes, say, if the bend was

94 The Export Drive

Two views of a C5FT fire tender with body by Alfred Miles Ltd of Cheltenham. The vehicle featured a 6-seater cab, a 400gal (1,500ltr) water tank and enough storage capacity to carry a full complement of fire-fighting equipment. The second photo shows the array of first-aid hose reels.

slightly wrong, I'd go up and see Fred Wright, the blacksmith, in his shed at the top by the railway line ... he'd take it away, heat it up and bring it back. If there were forty or fifty, he'd rectify those pipes so you got the job finished. It was the same if you had any problems in the machine shop, you'd go and see Percy Marsh ... and he'd rectify whatever was wrong and before you knew it ... you'd be back on the job again ... The few years I had at Luton were very happy ... a happy family.

The upbeat mood at Biscot Road was generally reflected in the rest of the nation. In 1951, the Festival of Britain was on at London's South Bank. This massive exhibition was seen as Britain's opportunity to shake off the grey, drab days of the war, with a colourful celebration of design, architecture and technology. It represented the dawn of the 'modern' age. Motor vehicles played their part in the demonstrations of modern technology, and on the commercial vehicle display, Commer showed off a new forward-control fire engine chassis with bodywork by Alfred Miles of Cheltenham.

Other opportunities to display the new Commers, away from dealer's premises, presented themselves during 1951. Comprehensive displays of Commer and Karrier vehicles were shown at the four main Royal Agricultural Shows round Britain from May to July, following an important export display in March, at the International Motor Show in Geneva. The Swiss authorities had placed restrictions on the number of heavy commercials exhibiting from Britain, although the same restrictions did not seem to apply to Switzerland's truck-producing neighbours from France, Italy and Germany. Commer had a representative display, however. The biggest vehicle exhibited by Commer was a QX 5-tonner with a Swiss-built drop-sided body. Other vehicles included: a Superpoise 4/5ton chassis and cab; two Superpoise 25cwt; a van and a chassis cab, with their newly re-styled front ends; and a left-hand-drive Express 8cwt van. Other British exhibits were from Austin, Dodge, Bedford, Seddon, AEC, Bedford and Morris-Commercial.

1951 was a pivotal year for Commer. With the success of the QX, it was becoming clear that the Biscot Road plant was too small to cope with the projected output for Commer and Karrier vehicles. With production of the long-wheelbase (over 12ft 9in/3.8m) QX-style forward-control range and development of the new TS-3 opposed-piston 2-stroke diesel engine at Stoke Aldermoor, that too was outgrowing itself.

Rootes Acquires Tilling-Stevens

At the 1952 Commercial Vehicle Motor Show held at Earls Court in London between 26 September and 4 October, some familiar names were missing: Panhard, Reo, Studebaker ... and Tilling-Stevens and Vulcan. In 1951, the Rootes brothers had been shopping again, and in addition to buying 100 acres (40.5ha) of land at Dunstable in Bedfordshire, they had acquired the old-established Kent-based truck manufacturers Tilling-Stevens and Vulcan.

The site at Dunstable was to enable Rootes to build a new truck assembly plant, but the Maidstone premises of Tilling-Stevens and Vulcan would eventually become the headquarters of the Rootes Diesel Engine Division, concentrating on the development and subsequent manufacture of the new TS-3 engine.

Some of the management who eventually relocated from Tilling-Stevens to Commer thought that much of the Vulcan/Tilling-Stevens product range was being needlessly scrapped, and disagreed with members of the senior management at Maidstone who wanted to throw in the towel. Freddie Best and Cyril Corke were two managers who were reluctant to give up the fight, as Corke explained:

> When Rootes bought Vulcan-Tilling-Stevens in the fifties, we were producing a range of vehicles – 7ton rigids; 12ton articulated, diesel-engined vehicles with Gardner or Perkins engines. Commer, up until 1952–53, did not have a diesel-engined 7ton vehicle, and yet we had an order book of four years at the time, and they shut our production down. We were also the first to have a tilting cab, and yet the Rootes family decided it was best to shut us down and throw away all that.

Best and Corke had considered trying to continue to manufacture Vulcan vehicles if they could

Tilling-Stevens and Vulcan

The origin of Tilling-Stevens goes back to 1897, when a company was formed to manufacture electric motors, dynamos and generators under the name of Messrs Stevens and Barker. When Mr Barker retired in 1902, the business was carried on by Stevens. In May 1906, a private limited company was formed under the name of W.A. Stevens Ltd. It was then that experiments with petrol-electric transmission began. A dynamo was fitted to a 20hp motor car, and very soon Thomas Tilling Ltd of Peckham became interested in the vehicle. Stevens and the chief engineer of Tilling's, Percy Frost-Smith, collaborated to build a petrol-electric omnibus for Tilling's to operate on their busy London bus routes. Successful trials of the petrol-electric transmission resulted in the formation of Tilling-Stevens Ltd in 1913. In 1919, when production of a range of petrol-electric chassis was under way, the name of the company was changed to Tilling-Stevens Motors Ltd.

The twenties were the heyday of the petrol-electric chassis, with which they had become well-known, as well as their earlier association with Tilling's, the omnibus company. In 1924, they had also made an arrangement with Skoda in Czechoslovakia to market their vehicles throughout Eastern Europe under the name of Skoda-Tilling-Stevens. A similar agreement was made the following year with the Gray Motor Corporation in the USA. This also gave Gray manufacturing rights of the electrical equipment.

By the thirties the company had already started moving to more conventional chassis manufacture, and so decided on another name change in August 1930. In a letter to *The Commercial Motor*, the managing director W.R. Shephard stated the reasons for the change to 'T.S. Motors Ltd':

> To remove the lingering impression that our products are confined to the manufacture of petrol-electric vehicles. To emphasize ... that the operating company bearing a similar name has no financial or other interest in our company.

In 1937, T.S. Motors Ltd reverted to its original name: Tilling-Stevens Ltd. The following year, the company obtained the manufacturing rights to another well-known and respected chassis builder, Vulcan, having failed to buy Karrier in 1932. Following the announcement, production was transferred from the Vulcan factory at Crossens, near Southport in Lancashire to Maidstone.

The Vulcan Motor and Engineering Co. (1906) Ltd had enjoyed a reputation for tough, well-built trucks for over thirty years. A sister company had also manufactured a range of motor cars since 1902 until the late twenties. Experiments carried out between 1897 and 1899 by the brothers Thomas and Joseph Harapson resulted in the first Vulcan car in 1902: a belt-driven single-cylinder voiturette. By 1905, Vulcan were offering cars with 4-cylinder engines of 3.1 and 5.2ltr capacities and although they continued to make cars right up to the late twenties, after the First World War the company concentrated on

A Tillings-Stevens petrol-electric bus, model TTA1, from around 1911.

Two illustrations from the 1915 sales brochure. Each colour page featured 'Well known Commer Cars'. Shown is a 1ton BC Brackley type chassis (above), which the brochure claimed 'fills a long-term want. Its design includes all the latest improvements and is a distinct advance on any 1 ton chassis on the market'. The WP-2 chassis shown (below) is a 24-seat omnibus.

This dramatic rendering of a Commer Superpoise by well-known artist Terence Cuneo was for a Rootes Export Division showroom poster.

THE COMMER "AVENGER" WITH 'PLAXTON' BODYWORK

COMMER 1¼ TON FORWARD CONTROL VAN

A PRODUCT OF THE ROOTES GROUP

(Top) This front cover of the 1952 Commer Avenger brochure showing Plaxton bodywork was as colourful and dramatic as any of the imaginative illustrations used for Humber, Hillman or Sunbeam-Talbot.

(Above) The BF was known in public as the '1¼ ton forward control van'. This brochure cover is from November 1955.

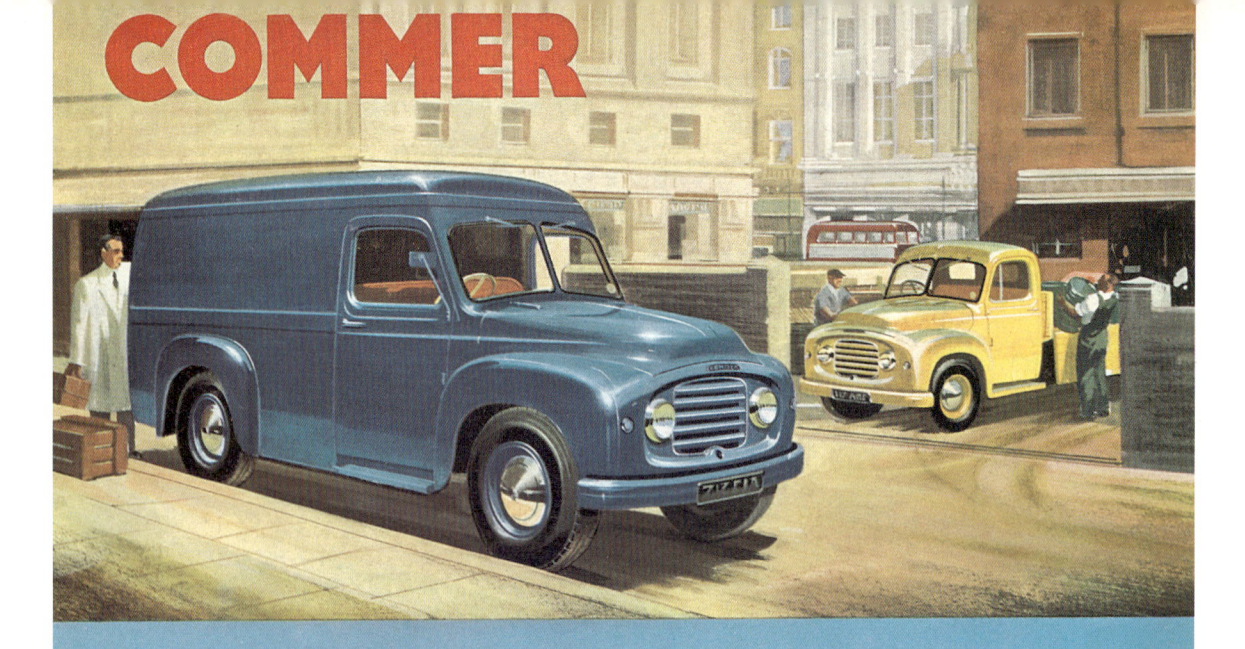

(Top) A 1955 brochure issue for the B Series Superpoise.

(Above) The 1957 brochure for the big forward-control range, or QX as it was known 'in-house'.

COMMER

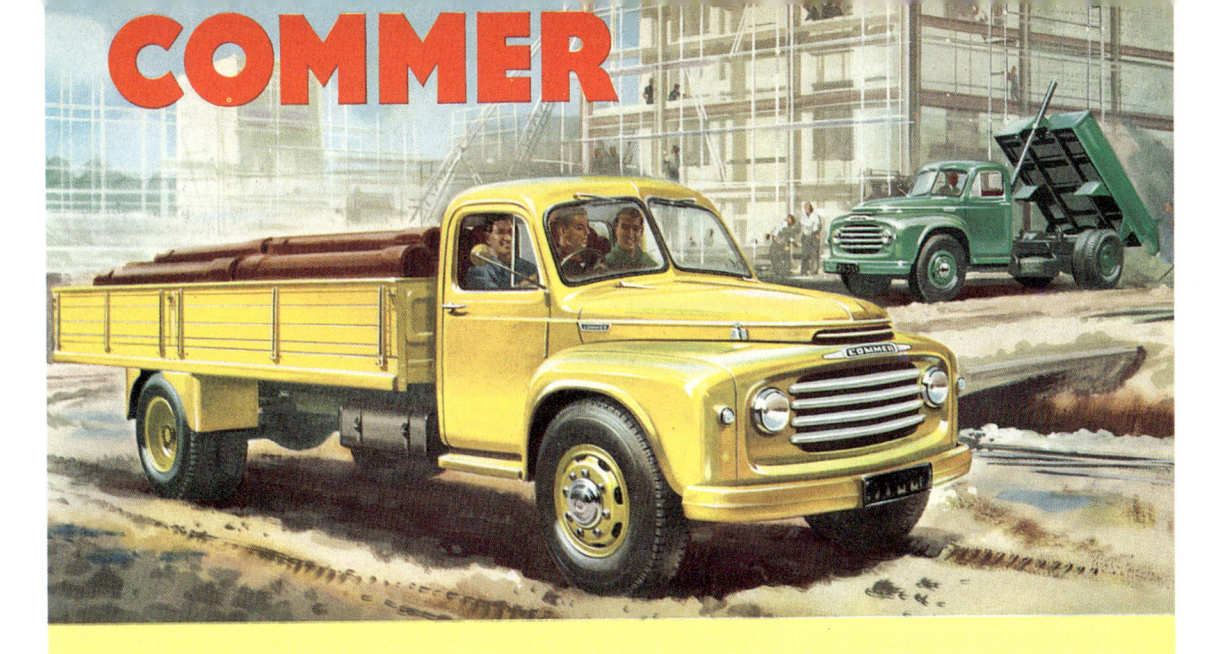

'SUPERPOISE' 5 TON TRUCK and 5 TON TIPPER

ROOTES PRODUCTS

KARRIER

'BANTAM' 4-5 TON TRACTOR
PETROL OR DIESEL   A ROOTES PRODUCT

(Top) This 1958 brochure depicts the last version of the Superpoise, the Mk4.

(Above) A September 1958 brochure for the Bantam showing a tractor unit with a BK-type coupling gear. When the Bantam gained a one-piece windscreen in the sixties, the same illustration was used on brochures with the screen split airbrushed out. This was a typical Rootes' cost-cutting exercise.

(Top) The infamous Commer ¾ton van, or PB as it eventually became known. Here it is shown in its 1960 Series 1 form.

(Above) The 1961 'Municipal' brochure for the Karrier Gamecock.

COMMER

'COB' LIGHT VAN

A ROOTES PRODUCT

COMMER 'WALK-THRU'

1½, 2 and 3 TON MODELS

PETROL OR DIESEL ROOTES PRODUCTS

(Top) The Cob van in its early sixties' guise. This brochure was for the 1963 model year.

(Above) Commer Walk-Thru brochure from April 1964.

COMMER 'V' RANGE
G.V.W. 145-250 cwt. G.T.W. 350 cwt.

with all-steel luxury cab affording built-in safety and comfort

- Extra-wide cab with controlled ventilation and effective heat insulation
- Wide choice of engines— petrol and diesel
- Power assisted brakes
- Nylon Ply tyres for long life
- Complete and easy engine accessibility

Backed by Rootes world-wide Parts and Service Organisation

(Top) This October 1965 brochure shows the first evidence of factory designations being used as model designations. The 'V' Range was the single-headlight little brother to the 'C' Range.

(Below) Rootes produced a series of stylish brochures with which to re-launch the Dodge 500 Series. This is the September 1968 issue.

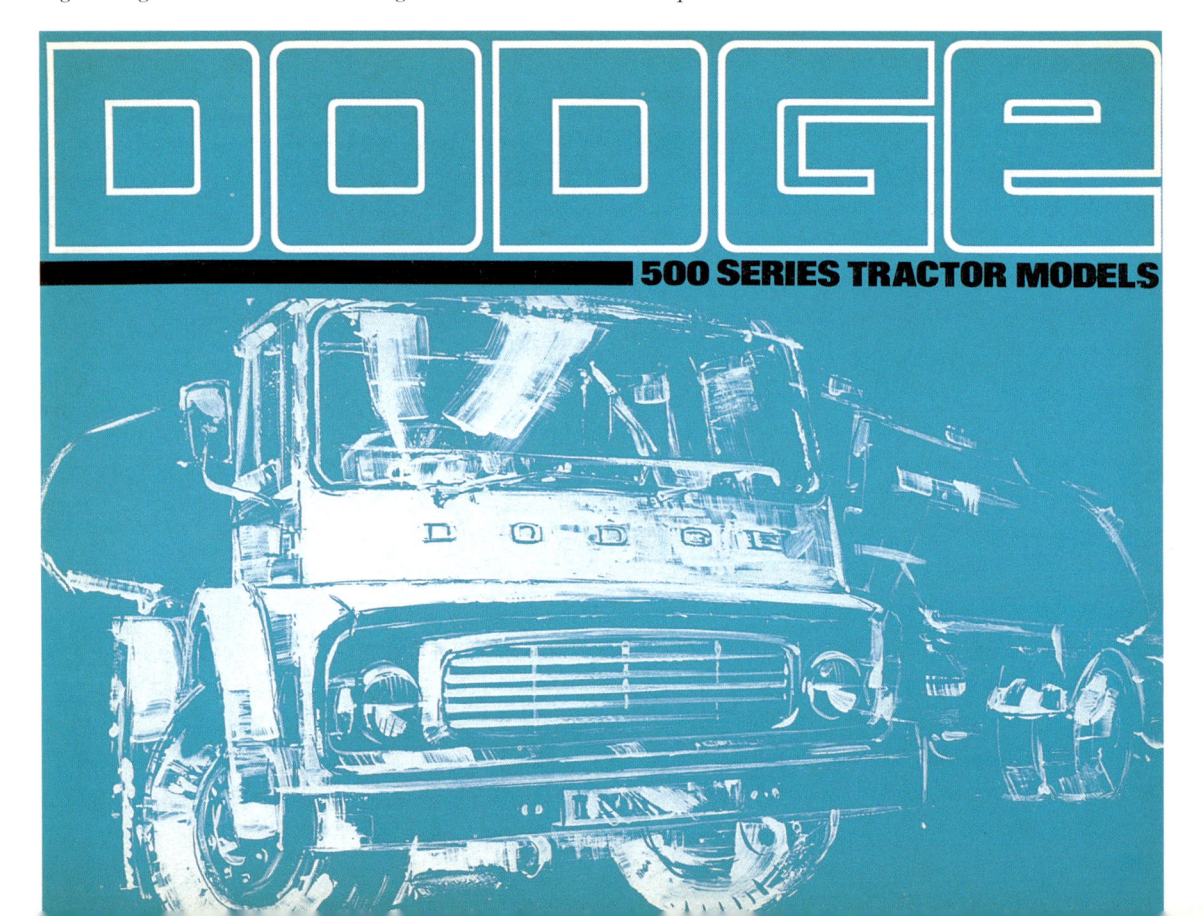

DODGE
500 SERIES TRACTOR MODELS

The front cover for a late forties Vulcan sales brochure.

trucks. Notable models during the thirties were the 'Retriever' 2-tonner and the 'Jubilee' forward control 2-tonner. Introduced in 1935, the Jubilee was followed by a normal control version a year later. Diesel engines were not offered in Vulcan trucks at this time, most being fitted with a 3.3ltr, 4-cylinder petrol unit developing 20bhp.

Vulcan trucks continued to be produced at Maidstone, alongside TSM passenger and lorry chassis, until the fifties. During the Second World War, the Tilling-Stevens petrol-electrics came into their own again as searchlight/generator trucks. However, during the post-war period of change, Tilling-Stevens and Vulcan found it difficult to keep up with the times, even though they had a comprehensive range on offer, including rigids, tippers, artics, and a bus chassis. In August 1950, an announcement was made by the chairman of Tilling-Stevens Ltd, V.C. Ponsonby, regarding the possibility of a merger with Commer:

> ... For the company's future success, a policy of expansion will be necessary. Under existing conditions, financial and otherwise, the problem is extremely difficult.

continued overleaf

Tilling-Stevens and Vulcan *continued*

By September 1950, Tilling-Stevens Ltd and its subsidiary, Vulcan Motors Ltd, had become part of the Rootes Group. Sir Reginald Rootes was elected chairman and Geoffrey Rootes, deputy chairman. Sir William Rootes and Geoffrey Cozens also joined the Board of Directors.

A Vulcan 7GF tipper truck.

(Bottom) The Tilling-Stevens stand at the 'Commercial Vehicle Exhibition' of 1950.

persuade Sir Reginald and Sir William to sell them the brand name 'Vulcan', but the Rootes brothers already had their plans laid out for Vulcan, and shortly after the acquisition, both the 'Vulcan' and 'TSM' brands disappeared.

By 1954, Rootes would have a diesel engine available to complement the proprietary engines that were being bought in from Perkins. The revolutionary TS-3 would be produced at Maidstone, eventually replacing the 109bhp under-floor engine in the QX. Initially though, the Maidstone plant was used to produce axles and gearboxes for a new Commer 4×4 Superpoise army truck, and the Humber 1ton 4×4.

Freddie Best moved up to Biscot Road in 1951 as Works Manager, to replace Manny Sherwin, and was then sent to Canada in 1952 as managing director of Rootes Canada. For a while he also ran the Rootes New York office as well as Rootes Canada after Brian Rootes (Sir William's son) had suffered a heart attack. Best came back to England in 1959 as sales manager for Commer after Gerald Bragg retired.

Cyril Corke moved to Commer in July 1952 as assistant to the assistant sales manager, and in 1961 was out on the road as a sales representative for about eighteen months before becoming municipal sales manager for Karrier. For Corke, the move to Commer-Karrier turned out to be a fortuitous one, as it was there he met his wife, Veronica.

The Hallmark of Quality

Development of new and updating of existing models continued to move at a pace at Biscot Road during this period. Commer-Karrier was on a roll! The Commer range in 1951 boasted a range of vehicles from the 8cwt Express to the QX 10/12ton tractor unit, all being marketed with the slogan, 'The Hallmark Of Quality'. An updated Mark III Superpoise was available with an 85bhp overhead-valve, 6-cylinder petrol engine (an upright version of the under-floor unit) as well as a Perkins Diesel. The Superpoise range consisted of: a 25cwt van; a ¾ton or ⅘tonner up to the 'Commer-Hands' 8ton articulated 6-wheeler unit designed in conjunction with Hands Ltd of Letchworth. A QX 6½ton hydraulic end tipper utilizing 'Telehoist' under-body tipping gear was a new offering in the mid-payload

The Superpoise continued to be a very popular vehicle with the British Army in the post-war period. They ordered a number of 3ton 4 × 4 General Service and tipper trucks in the early fifties, many of which were assembled at Tilling-Stevens at Maidstone. Here an Army 3 tonner fords the muddy waters of the War Department testing grounds at Farnborough.

A ¾ton tipper version of the post-war Superpoise, introduced in 1948. In 1951 the Mark III received the 85bhp overhead-valve 6-cylinder Humber petrol engine, and servo-assisted hydraulic brakes. The Mark IIIA was updated with a synchromesh gearbox in 1954, but cab styling remained the same on the big Superpoise models from 1948 until the Mark IV Superpoise was announced in 1955.

(Below) The 'new' Karrier Bantam. Shown is a 10 cubic yard refuse collector with a seven-seater cab.

Glover, Webb & Liversidge built the body for the Karrier-Transport Loadmaster compressing refuse collector. Later versions were fitted with crew cabs by Carbodies of Coventry. A similar sized moving floor refuse collector body was also made for the Gamecock chassis.

(Below) The reintroduced Karrier-Yorkshire RSC (Road Sweeper Collector) featured servo-assisted brush lifting gear, a body that could be end-tipped hydraulically and an all-steel cab mounted in a position that enabled the driver to easily view all operations.

A TS-3 engined Karrier Gamecock, of the soft drinks firm Allens of Leicester, delivering to a Northamptonshire pub.

QX range. Eaton 2-speed rear axles were available on all QX and Superpoise models.

Karrier were also using the new BLSP cab on Bantam municipal and industrial models, but with a different radiator grille, behind which a 4-cylinder 45 or 48bhp petrol engine hid. It was essentially a low-compression version of the Humber Hawk engine. A redesigned and strengthened chassis frame of a riveted construction complemented the new face-lift. The big news for Karrier was a new compressing refuse collector: the Karrier-Transport Loadmaster. Karrier had built up an excellent reputation for meeting the needs of municipal operators, proven by the fact that over

Examples of the Commer Avenger with Plaxton bodywork. There were plenty of other examples as well ... Avengers with bodywork by Duple, Harrington, Myers and Bowman and of course Beadle.

SOME EXAMPLES OF THE
COMMER "AVENGER"
WITH 'PLAXTON' BODYWORK

COMMER CARS LIMITED, LUTON, BEDS.
EXPORT DIVISION: ROOTES LTD., DEVONSHIRE HOUSE, PICCADILLY, LONDON W.1

750 public authorities used Karrier municipal vehicles, and the new vehicle would ensure Karrier would stay on top of the pile – so to speak! The Loadmaster, with a body built by Glover, Webb and Liversidge Ltd of London, was capable of accepting 25cu yd (19.1cu m) of refuse when compressed. It was destined to become the standard for rear-loading refuse collectors for years to come.

Along with the Loadmaster came the re-introduction of the RSC (Road Sweeper Collector), a name that had not been seen in the Karrier range since before the war. Powered by the same 85bhp 6-cylinder unit that was in the Superpoise, the Sweeper-Collector had been brought back by popular demand, but this time in a completely redesigned form. Although older features such as the road sprinkling equipment and reversible gutter brush were retained, new innovations included servo-assisted brush lifting gear, a body which could be end-tipped hydraulically and an all-steel cab mounted so that the driver could easily observe all sweeping operations.

At the 1952 Earls Court Show, it was announced that Karrier too was going 'under-floor' with its engines. The trusty old CK-3 was to be replaced by the Gamecock 3/4-tonner. The Gamecock

The 'art-deco' styling of this chrome-laden Avenger with closed-in wheel arches is by Plaxtons and was one of the standard body styles offered by Commer in 1953. Standard powerplant was the 109bhp 'under-floor' engine.

(Below) An Avenger coach, with under-floor petrol engine, in service with Greyhound Coaches in Australia. The photograph is dated April 1954.

A Karrier 14 (14-seater) bus with bodywork by Reading of Portsmouth. The 50bhp 4-cylinder petrol engine was capable of propelling the vehicle from 0–50mph in under a week!

was powered by the 6-cylinder 85bhp overhead-valve engine (the Humber 'light 6'), which was ideal for placing below decks, as in the QX. At the same time, a 14-seater coach chassis version of the Gamecock was announced, but with the vertical 50bhp 2.26ltr 4-cylinder unit from the Bantam. Standard bodywork was by Reading, although Churchill Constructors Ltd of Norwich showed a 14-seater on the bodybuilder's stand. Both new models featured the 'corporate' new front-end treatment.

By 1953, output at Biscot Road was an astounding 215 per cent up on its pre-war 1938–39 period, but the production facilities were outdated and so the decision was made to transfer production and assembly of all Commer and Karrier vehicles to a new purpose-built plant on the recently acquired land at Dunstable.

Fred Lawrence presides over a social-club game with fellow employees, 1954.

6 Dunstable: A New Era

Built Stronger to Last Longer!
Commer publicity slogan

In July 1953, work commenced on the building of the new assembly plant at Dunstable.

To finance the construction, Rootes sold nearly 70 acres (28ha) of their newly acquired land to Vauxhall, for a proposed new plant for Bedford truck assembly. In August 1954, the Board of Trade agreed to a five-year expansion plan for Vauxhall-Bedford, costing £36m. The Bedford plant at Dunstable was to have the lion's share, with an extension to the factory of 1,150,000sq ft (106,800sq m) Within two years, the biggest competitors to Commer would be manufactured right next door.

The building of the 250,000sq ft (23,200sq m) Commer-Karrier assembly plant was completed in September 1954. However, it was not operational until the early part of the following year, as much of the plant from Biscot Road and Stoke Aldermoor had to be moved to Dunstable.

Although Biscot Road was no longer to be used as an assembly plant, the site was retained for gearbox and back axle manufacture as well as design and development. The closing of the Luton production line on 21 October coincided neatly with Commer's fiftieth anniversary. On 27 September 1955, the last vehicle off the Biscot Road production line was a Karrier Bantam bound for Sweden.

Although the new plant would solve some of the complicated logistical problems caused by producing vehicles on two sites that were 40 miles (64km) apart, it also created a whole range of new problems. Much of the Luton workforce was reluctant to move to Dunstable, and combined with a general shortage of labour in the area, this created a nightmare for those responsible for personnel recruitment. To exacerbate the situation, many skilled and semi-skilled workers were

The new Dunstable plant.

'The Class of '55'. A group shot of the factory personnel in 1955 at the new Dunstable plant.

(TOP ROW): 1–4 unidentified 5 Jack Hoare 6–8 unidentified 9 Maurice Sharman 10 David Witton 11 Bert Whinnett 12 unidentified 13 Harry Kirton 14 unidentified 15 George Burton 16 Mervyn Kemp 17–19 unidentified
(SECOND ROW): 20–24 unidentified 25 Veronica Bailey 26 unidentified 27 Liz Taylor 28–38 unidentified
(THIRD ROW): 39 unidentified 40 Clarence Norman 41 Sammy Adams 42 Bill Wills 43 & 44 unidentified 45 Dick Sealey 46 unidentified 47 Bill Holmes 48–50 unidentified 51 Norman Lawrence 52–55 unidentified 56 Bert Fensome
(FOURTH ROW): 57 Norman Tipping 58 Mervyn Base 59 Ross Williams 60 Sid Pedder 61 'Curly' Grinter 62 George Parrott 63 Tom Greenwood 64 Mr Markham 65 Jack Best 66 Jim Martin 67 unidentified 68 Ken Harrison 69–71 unidentified 72 Bill Mansfield 73 Vic French 74 unidentified

employed at Vauxhall and Bedford, who generally paid higher wages than Commer. They too had an expanding workforce, and in 1955 the combined number employed at the Vauxhall plant at Luton and Bedford's Dunstable plant rose to nearly 17,000.

After being moved to Coventry for four months to supervise the run-out of the Stoke Aldermoor plant, Norman Lawrence returned to Dunstable as foreman inspector, during the second week of February 1955. He remembers the problems that were encountered getting Dunstable up and running:

> We had a hell of a time trying to get this place going. I got a Commer Cars stomach ulcer, working long hours for very little money ... I remember my father [Fred Lawrence, welfare officer who was responsible for recruitment] going all round the country to get labour, which was nearly all 'green' labour. He used to go to different labour exchanges – [as far as] Yarmouth, Lowestoft to get people to work at Dunstable.

The population of Luton after the war had virtually doubled since the late twenties to over 100,000. With the influx of new people to the area to work in the motor industry, both Luton and Dunstable had a shortage of housing. The first post-war slum clearance had started in Luton in June 1954, to make way for new blocks of flats and both Luton and Dunstable were starting to extend their boundaries with new housing estates. Commer had made certain provisions for employees to relocate nearer the new plant by renting some properties along Dunstable Road. Norman Lawrence took the opportunity to move:

> We were living in a small terraced house in Luton, and one day Vic French said to me, 'I'm moving to Dunstable to a firm's bungalow ...' so I wrote to Mr Singer [R.T.A. Singer, company secretary] to ask for one for me and my family. Vic said that number 36, a big house, was available ... Mr Singer offered me a bungalow, but I wanted No. 36 ... so he said [that] I could have it for two years only as they were going to build

(Above) The twin assembly lines at Dunstable. The Bantam line is on the left and the QX cab line on the right.

Lowering the cab on to a Superpoise chassis at Dunstable.

a new showroom there. [Norman moved into No. 36, and to this day, he and his family are still there!]

After a difficult transition period, production at Dunstable did get under way, in an environment that was a culture shock compared with the old carefree days at Biscot Road. Commer-Karrier was now in the big league.

The mid-fifties saw many motor manufacturers starting to concentrate, once again, on the home market. It was possibly as a result of pressure from Commer's sales manager Gerald Bragg that Geoffrey Cozens decided that they too should start to look at home-market sales as well as exports. In 1954, output of British-made vehicles touched the one million mark for the first time;

commercial vehicle production being 270,025, of which 48 per cent was for export. The first three-quarters of 1955 showed commercial vehicle production figures leaping ahead of previous years to over 320,000. Exports showed no signs of slowing down either, although the 1950 and 1951 figures of 62 per cent of commercial vehicle production going overseas was unlikely to be repeated if the demand from the home market was to be satisfied. Ministry of Transport figures issued in 1954 reported that the volume of traffic on Britain's roads was 38 per cent higher than before the war, with double the amount of lorries!

Built Stronger to Last Longer

The TS-3 opposed-piston 2-stroke diesel engine was introduced in 1954, and by 1956 it was beginning to find its way into more and more Commer QX forward control and Avenger coach chassis that previously would have had a petrol 'under-floor' unit. The Commer line-up was also beginning to show a 'family' resemblance in terms of styling. The appearance and design of a van or truck was in the late fifties becoming as important as the styling of cars. The influence of Detroit was starting to appear in Rootes' commercial vehicles as well as cars. Rootes were not shy to use 'Detroit-ese' in their catchy new sales slogan: 'Built Stronger To Last Longer'.

The design departments of Hillman, Humber and Sunbeam-Talbot cars, had always been separate from trucks: the twain shall not meet! The attitude of the 'car boys' was a bit like an over-protective mother who did not want her daughter to mix with those rough lads who worked in the factory down the road.

All that changed after the war, when the design of cars and trucks was centralized at Coventry. During the forties, Ernie Wilkes looked after the drawing office responsibilities at Luton, which moved to Stoke Aldermoor after the war. Under George Payne, who had overall responsibility of all Rootes, styling, the Aldermoor design department was able to give a 'corporate' look to all Rootes' products, and this influence started to show in late fifties' examples of Commer and Karrier vehicles. The Minx-inspired 'chrome grin' look of the Express van soon permeated into the BF 25cwt and the Superpoise range.

A 1954 TS-3-powered Avenger with a 33-seater Harrington body, which was provided with a courier seat!

During the fifties, the drawing office at Biscot Road continued to be a busy place, with more new designs being created, as well as constant facelifts of existing models. The man in charge of the body shop at Luton in the fifties was Alec Single, with A.J. Smith running the whole design and development shooting match. Under Single were some competent draughtsmen who were responsible for many of the fifties' Commer and Karrier styling cues: Stan Ives; Derek Scrivener; David Streeton; and Gerald Broadbent, who came to Luton for a few years from Jennings of Sandbach, the company that made the cabs for ERF.

Dave Streeton, who started with Commer as an apprentice in January 1947, had ambitions of being a coachbuilder. His apprenticeship took him from sawmill to eventual chief engineer of body design:

> At the age of 15½, I wasn't allowed to work in the machine shop [so] I was put with the jig making bench which was at the edge of the sawmill ... the wood came in as logs, and we planed it down to the thickness we wanted.
>
> Exactly on my birthday I was put into the sawmill to work ... [I was there] for about three years ... then [put] into the machine shop, short-term, on a gearcutting machine.
>
> The cabs were wooden framed ... made out of ash, with steel or aluminium panels. All wood was dipped into an anti-insect compound – for the export market. At that time [early fifties] we were still making the metal-clad wooden-framed vans [Commer 25cwt] with 'hockey sticks' over the roofs.
>
> When I was in the drawing office of the body section [as a draughtsman], we used to do full-size drawings ... on cartridge paper. [It was hung] by a batten across the top, the paper would be soaked with water, stretched and battened all the way round. Then we'd wait for it to dry! [To work on the drawing] we used to have to climb up and down a step ladder.

Both the QX and Superpoise went through several facelifts during the latter part of the fifties. In 1955, the bonneted Superpoise was also given a full-width smiling grin, and a flatter, squarer frontal appearance for its Mark IV version. This had been its first facelift since 1948, and was to last until 1962. The QX received an interim makeover in 1956, which consisted primarily of a band of additional chrome flashes that extended around the front end, together with a larger 'Commer' badge.

To visitors of the 1956 Earls Court Commercial Motor Show, it might have seemed that Commers and Karriers were in evidence almost everywhere. Exhibits on the Commer stand were bristling with new features. The smaller Superpoise range was now available with the 2.26ltr 4-cylinder Rootes 'light diesel' engine, as well as the overhead-valve Humber petrol unit. A TS-3-engined QX 7-tonner with a drop-sided body, and a 10ton tractor unit showed off the heavy end of the range. The tractor unit was a new addition to the QX series featuring Scammell automatic coupling gear, and an option of air pressure hydraulic brakes, which were also optional on the 5 and 7ton forward control models. The new 12ton tractor units were also available with air brakes as well as power steering. Cob and Express vans, and a new Mark IV Superpoise completed the display.

Commer-engined coaches were well represented. An Avenger, also with optional air-brakes, was on the Duple stand, while Beadle showed off two TS-3-engined Commers outside at the Warwick Road entrance to Earls Court, as well as the new 'chassisless' coach which was on show at the Beadle stand.

The Karrier stand had four Bantams and a Gamecock. If that was not enough, British Light Steel Pressings displayed a Karrier Bantam refuse collector, which would be off to its new owners, Colombo Municipal Council, as soon as the show was over.

The 1956 show was evidence of how the British commercial vehicle manufacturing sector had grown. With more than 440 stands covering 275,000sq ft (25,550sq m), this show was the largest ever held since it began at Olympia in 1907.

During this period, specialist bodybuilders other than municipal vehicle builders began to recognize the versatility of the Karrier range. With the Gamecock now on an 11ft 9in (3.5m) wheelbase, and with the option of the TS-3 engine, the options for bodybuilders were widened.

(Above) Two Beadle-bodied TS-3-engined Commer coaches at the Warwick Road entrance of the 1956 Earls Court Commercial Show.

The 'Commercial Motor Transport Exhibition', to give the show its full and proper title, of September 1956. An export Karrier Bantam is on the British Light Steel Pressings stand. In the frame on the wall are pressings of a QX radiator grille and dash panel.

One of the BBC Television outside broadcast 'roving eye' camera vans built by Mickelover Transport on a Karrier Bantam chassis in 1956.

British Railways had been a loyal Karrier operator for years, and in 1957 it ordered specially built Gamecocks which were designed to carry a crew of eleven men and equipment, for the signal engineer's department of the Western Region of British Railways.

The BBC ran a variety of very specialized television broadcast vehicles, amongst them were Commers and Karriers. In 1956 'the Beeb' ordered nine Bantam outside broadcast vehicles with bodywork built by Mickleover Transport, of north-west London. Four of the vehicles were used as 'roving-eye' camera vans, with provision for a camera and zoom lens to be fitted on a ring mounting on a slot in the roof, so that the operator could film and pan through a full 360 degrees. Another camera was mounted to the left of the driver, which could be used to film through the front screen or side window. Saturday afternoon 'Grandstand' was never complete without one of these Bantams haring alongside the rails, filming the winner of the 2.30 at Kempton Park! The other five outside broadcast units were used as static ancillary outfits, linking the moving units with main transmitters.

The late fifties saw British lifestyles starting to change. According to the 1957 Distribution Census, the turnover of food shops and off-licences was £3.6m, representing goods that would have been delivered by vans or lorries of some kind. Small independent grocers and general stores gave way to larger grocery and food chains like 'Home and Colonial' and 'Macfisheries'.

With fewer small grocers' shops, butchers and fishmongers to cater for the needs of people who were unable to get into towns, a new market was created: home delivery and the mobile shop. The Karrier Bantam was the perfect vehicle for specialist bodybuilders to use. Smith's Delivery Vehicles Ltd of Gateshead-on-Tyne was one company that built hundreds of their mobile butchers', grocers' and fishmongers' vans on the Bantam chassis.

Although the immediate post-war period saw the demise of the Karrier Cob 'Mechanical Horse' there had been an attempt to bring in a new and up-to-date mechanical horse. David Streeton worked on designs for it, but the project was shelved and it was not until the early fifties with the introduction of the new Bantam that a suitable compromise was found. The Bantam 4/5ton

A familiar sight in towns and villages around the country during the fifties and sixties were Smiths Mobile Shops on Karrier Bantam or Gamecock chassis. This Smiths Gamecock was used by Crewe Co-operative Friendly Society.

tractor-trailer unit with either BK- or J-type coupling gear had been available only with a petrol engine, but in September 1956 it too became available with the 2.26ltr 'light diesel' engine: the ubiquitous 'gutless wonder'! The engine, although reliable, had an apt nickname. It was originally a Massey-Ferguson tractor engine, and may have been fine as an alternative power unit for the Standard Vanguard, in which it was used for a time, but it was not the liveliest of engines for a commercial vehicle. However, a diesel power plant was what operators wanted, and it sold very well.

In 1956, Commer-Karrier had a record year for sales, although certain members of the sales force felt that some ground had been lost in the home market. Brian Rootes, managing director of Rootes' export division announced to the trade press in May 1956:

> Production of commercial vehicles last month was an all-time record and during the first quarter of this year was 49 per cent higher than during the first quarter of 1955. This is the direct result of the commencement of our expansion programme.
>
> During the past twelve months, despite new import regulations and restrictions abroad, vehicles have been sold and delivered to nearly every market in the world, with the exception of those behind the iron curtain.
>
> The introduction of the TS-3 engine has enabled the organization to open up a number of markets which were previously biased in favour of foreign petrol-engined vehicles. Sales to dollar countries during the first quarter of 1956 were 28 per cent higher than last, and exports in Europe were doubled.

1956: Rootes Acquires Singer

In 1956 Rootes acquired Singer Motors Ltd, which wiped out any residual profit, leaving the group in the red in 1957 with a loss of over £600,000. To compound the problem, due to a

The Commer-Karrier stand at the 1956 Geneva Motor Show.

recession in the UK and the USA in 1957, all motor manufacturers were having a tough time. A general credit squeeze and the knock-on effect of the Suez Canal crisis the previous year, saw a reduction in sales of Rootes' products generally, but especially cars. By the end of the decade the books looked a little healthier, with a profit of £3.9m just beating their previous best year of 1955 by £300,000.

The acquisition of Singer caused yet another change for Commer. Production of Singer cars was phased out at their Birmingham factory during 1956. It was moved to their premises at Canterbury Street in Coventry and the Rootes' factory at Ryton-on-Dunsmore, where the new Singer Gazelle, an up-market, badge-engineered version of the Hillman Minx, was to be produced. The Birmingham factory was converted to house a new centralized parts operation for cars and trucks.

Since 1951, Fred Lewis had been assistant parts manager under Joe (J.J.) Newsome, an ex-Karrier man, and was one of the first Biscot Road managers to be involved in the integration of the car and truck parts operation at the old Singer factory:

> In August 1956, Rex Watson Lee [Parts Director] took us up to Singer one Sunday to see the place ... I used to go up three times a week prior to moving up to Birmingham ... a more run-down place you could never come across. [In] the management canteen you had to shield your soup for fear of the plaster falling off the ceiling ... On the whole of the front of the place [outside] were Singer Hunter cars, which Rootes sold off cheap. My brother had one – it was built like Leeds Town Hall – too much weight for a little engine, but a nice car all the same.

Fred Lewis became home sales executive, and following that the assistant sales manager, and covered home and export sales for the parts operation.

Express and Cob Light Vans

The car-derived light van series based on the Hillman Minx, introduced in the thirties, continued to play an important part in the Commer line-up. They had always helped Commer to widen their payload capabilities from 8cwt to 8tons, but more importantly in the fifties, to keep the competition out by enabling Commer to offer delivery vans to 'C' licence fleet operators. In 1953, Commer closed the door to the competition even tighter by introducing an all-new, all-steel 25cwt panel van (the 'BF') to complement the B-series Superpoise. A light-duty Minx-derived pick-up was also introduced, along with the Hillman Husky-based Cob light van making an appearance in 1956. With its slightly larger brother, the Express Delivery Van (or 'EDV') still available, the competition had a tough job on their hands if they were serious about selling vans in an area where Commer had set out to be market leaders.

Although most of the Rootes car-derived light commercials mirrored the Hillman Minx in one form or another, there were also some weird and wonderful vehicles produced on Humber chassis. An ambulance version of the Humber Pullman appeared in 1951, and van versions of the Humber Super Snipe, operated by United Service Transport, were for many years a common sight whizzing around London as *Evening Standard* newspaper delivery vehicles.

The first post-war Commer light vans were based on the pre-war 'Phase I and II' versions of the Minx, and known as the 8cwt 'Supervan'. In 1949, an all-new version of the Supervan appeared, based on the new Raymond Loewy designed 'Phase III' Minx. It was quickly renamed the Express and remained unchanged, except for

The Phase I Hillman Minx provided the basis for the 8cwt Supervan until 1948 when the first post-war Minx design, the Phase III, appeared in the form of the Express 8cwt van.

Dunstable: A New Era 115

This is the first version of the 7cwt Commer Cob van in 1956, which like its estate car brother the Hillman Husky, was based on the Hillman Minx. The Cob was available in addition to the larger Express 8cwt van.

(Below) A new Commer Express 8cwt Mark IV Delivery Van, supplied by the Rootes dealer Cripps & Co. of Nottingham in November 1950. This van version shared styling and componentry from the Hillman Minx Phase IV.

This 1957 BD1512 ¼ton Superpoise van, with its 9ft 4in (2.8m) wheelbase, was fitted with the 54bhp Commer 'light-diesel' engine as an alternative to the 56bhp petrol unit. A ¼ton pick-up and a 1½ton van version were also available.

Brew Brothers Ltd were one of the Rootes Group's main London dealers during the late fifties and sixties. The Superpoise ¼ton pick-up made an ideal service tow-truck.

detail and trim changes, until 1953 when, in Mk VII form, a new wide-grinned chrome radiator grille of horizontal bars adorned both van and pick-up. Its side-mounted synchromesh gearbox remained, as did the side-valve 1,265cc 4-cylinder engine, although with redesigned combustion chambers and a Solex downdraught carburettor, to improve power and economy.

When the Cob 7cwt van appeared in 1956, it was as a van version of the Hillman Husky (or maybe the Husky was an estate car version of the Cob?). Both were short-wheelbase versions of the Minx Mk VIII. By 1957, the Cob and Express were utilizing the new Hillman 1,390cc overhead-valve engine as well as a floor-mounted gearchange for the 4-speed synchromesh gearbox. The Express 8cwt van carried on well into the 1962 model year. The Cob, with its single, side-opening rear door and neat push-button door handles, continued on to 1965, when it was replaced by the Imp van.

Many British manufacturers offered excellent light commercials during the fifties, but some also had inconsistencies in their ranges that weakened their market penetration. Standard, for example, offered a 12cwt pick-up and a van version of the Vanguard until 1953, but did not have another 'light-commercial' model available until the mid-fifties when their little 6cwt van and pick-ups based on the Standard 'Ten' saloon cars became available. Morris, to whom Commer generally came second in the light-commercial stakes, did have a ¼ton van and pick-up, as well as the bigger J2 van and pick-up. These were serious competitors to Commer in the medium-duty area, but Morris did not become a real threat to Commer's light-duty range until the late fifties when the Morris Minor-based 6cwt van and pick-up was introduced. This new 948cc overhead-valve version of Alec Issigonis' successful saloon car competed directly with the Commer Cob.

The Commer Cob (left) and Express (below) vans in 1958 benefited from the 1,390cc overhead-valve Hillman engine.

(Above) All Karrier models, like this ¾ton Gamecock dropsider, had by 1958 gained a full width, single-piece windscreen.

(Left) The 'saloon car comfort' of the 1958 Express van.

Cheap, well-built, reliable offerings from Standard, Austin, Morris and Ford were available during the late fifties. Some of these light-duty vans and pick-ups offered slightly lower running costs than the equivalent Commer, but few were able to offer the genuine saloon car comfort and features of the Cob or the Express. The Hillman Minx, after all, was aimed at buyers of the more luxurious mid-range family saloon cars, such as the Morris Oxford, Ford Consul and Vauxhall Wyvern. This did not mean that the prices of the car-derived van range reflected the comfort and high standard of finish that they offered. A 1957 Cob van finished in Seacrest Green would cost £452.18s.8d, including purchase tax. Compared with a Standard Ten van at £442, or a Morris 5cwt van, Ford Thames or Austin A35 van sold at similar prices, the Commer offered very good value for money.

An illustration from the 1957 brochure featuring the Commer 5-tonner that was, in effect, a stripped-down Karrier Gamecock. It was badge engineering for trucks!

Bridging the Gaps

Towards the end of the decade the competition in the home market was hotting up. Both Bedford and Austin offered petrol-engined 5-tonners for under £1,200 in 1957, and so, in order to remain competitive, Commer responded with price cuts in 1957 and 1958. Manufacturing costs were cut where possible, which resulted in a stripped-down version of the 5ton Karrier Gamecock, with a Commer badge – one of the first examples of Rootes' badge-engineering on trucks.

Chrome plating as ornamentation was kept to a minimum, and the famous chrome cylinder bores were plain, with only the top piston rings being chrome-plated. Instead of a synchromesh gearbox, a constant mesh 4-speed box was now fitted. This Commer 5-tonner was a very basic, cheap, no-frills truck. A de-rated version (70bhp) of the TS-3 engine was offered which, complete with a standard dropside body, could be bought

KNM 239
FWO
449

ROOTES GROUP
176
R.G. LEAF,
Secretary,
HUMBER LTD
COVENTR

OPPOSITE PAGE:
(Top) Biscot Road – 1957.

(Bottom) Henry, the Rootes Group's 'Seal of Perfection', who amused thousands of people at the 1956 London Motor Show by twirling a rotating Hillman Minx engine on the tip of his nose, says farewell before leaving London for the Geneva Motor Show. Seen here on 5 March 1957 is the Commer QX 7-tonner with a 16ft (4.9m) crate containing the supports, electric motor, plinth, water tanks, the Minx engine and guard rails to keep out over-enthusiastic admirers. The 3ton trailer also had several tons of exhibits for other Rootes Group stands

THIS PAGE:
After production was moved to Dunstable, more space became available for new administrative buildings at Biscot Road. This is the Planning Department in August 1957.

Luton – Number 2 Machine Shop in the late fifties. The front and rear hub line showing 'Ryder' multi-spindle drilling machines making bearing bores and facing wheel stud flanges. These machines were also used for multi-spindle drilling and tapping wheel stud holes and drilling and tapping of rear axle flange drive holes.

Luton – 'Drummond' gear shapers in No. 1 Machine Shop – late fifties.

for £1,265 plus £303.2s 4d. purchase tax. This represented a saving of £32 over the previous year's model. The Superpoise also received the constant-mesh gearbox on the 2 to 5ton range. The synchromesh gearbox continued to be available as an option, but was standard on all other TS-3-engined QX models.

The 1958 Commer-Karrier range boasted a twenty-model line-up. This included the new Unipower 10ton forward control (QX) 6-wheeler, produced in collaboration with Universal Power Drives. Price reductions of up to £46 were implemented: not exactly a king's ransom, but still quite a lot of money in 1958! The QX received its last makeover, with a new rectangular grille and one-piece windscreen, and along with the rest of the line-up this would last, virtually unchanged, until 1962. Karriers also got the one-piece windscreen treatment.

The Superpoise 6-tonners were offered with Perkins P6 or R6 diesel engines. A proprietary diesel engine, the Perkins C.305 horizontal engine, was initially the only diesel option on the 4, 5 and 6ton QX series. An 85bhp TS-3 was offered on the 5-tonner the following year. The TS-3 was also still available on the QX range of 7ton and upward, along with the Commer petrol engine, which was available right across the range.

Evidence of how well the BF 1½ton van was stacking up against competition from Britain and the continent was shown in 1958 when the Dutch National Railways sanctioned orders for 525 vans. Worth £350,000, the vans were to be operated on behalf of the railways by Van Gend en Loos, making it the largest single-make fleet in Holland. In 1959, Commer bridged the gap between the 15cwt Superpoise and the 1½ton van by introducing the BF 1ton van. Outwardly similar in appearance to its bigger brother, the smaller 1ton model was easily created by the fitting of lighter springs at the rear and shortening the wheelbase by about 1ft (0.3m). With a diesel engine the standard model went out at £843 and a petrol version at £723.

Racing driver Peter Collins and his new wife Louise, in 1957, chose what must have been one of the most unusual vehicles in which to go on honeymoon: a TS-3 powered QX 5ton truck. Sadly, Collins' racing career was cut short when he crashed and was killed at the 1958 German Grand Prix at the Nürburgring.

Optimism for the Future

In October 1959, Britain's first motorway, the M1, was opened to traffic. Figures released at the same time revealed that the British commercial vehicle manufacturing sector was booming, and showed that output was up on the previous year by 38 per cent. A total of 84,478 goods vehicles were manufactured in 1959. The same year, Ernest Marples became the new Minister of Transport, replacing Harold Watkinson.

Much of the entrepreneurial skill and vision of Sir William Rootes was starting to pay off, and in the New Year's Honours List for 1959, Sir William was made a Baron, to become Lord Rootes of Ramsbury.

Commer-Karrier ended the decade in a very strong position, and with Rootes' profits starting to increase, due much, it has to be said, to the unsung heroes at Luton and Dunstable.

A Commer Superpoise 1½ton truck in 1958, owned by English China Clays Ltd., of Cornwall, showing that it can cope with all kinds of slippery situations. The clay roadways it had to drive around on proved that it was no stick-in-the-mud truck!

124 *Dunstable: A New Era*

(Above) The final makeover for the QX cab came in 1958. This is a 12ton tractor unit (factory code designation HDY1294).

Special refrigerator bodies on BF 1½ton and Gamecock chassis, built for Fropax Frozen Foods in 1959.

7 The TS-3 Engine

I had one of those Commer 2-strokes ... It was like driving a racing car compared to any of the other wagons I'd had!

Doug Tipler, lorry driver

Many people, upon mention of the vehicles made by Commer during the late fifties and throughout the sixties, immediately recall the TS-3-engined lorries and passenger vehicles, if only for the distinctive sound they made! The 3-cylinder, opposed-piston 2-stroke engine was not like any other petrol or diesel engine available at the time, and TS-3-powered Commers would sound their approach with a characteristic exhaust note and blower whine.

The engine was a most unlikely product for an organization like Rootes. Their approach to engineering generally was much more conservative, leaning more towards tried and tested conventional engines rather than the radical approach of an opposed-piston engine, but embrace it they did, and for nearly two decades the TS-3 remained the central product of the Rootes Diesel Engineering Division.

Concept

The Rootes TS-3 diesel engine was the brainchild of Eric Coy, chief engineer of Rootes Power Units. The idea behind it was to produce a compact, lightweight, under-floor engine, that would give excellent fuel economy and low maintenance costs, as well as equivalent, or improved performance over conventional petrol engines.

A 2-stroke engine with opposed pistons was certainly compact, and as the design dispensed with valve gear, pushrods, camshaft and cylinder head, it offered a considerable weight-saving over conventional engines. This design of the engine was also conducive to a high thermal efficiency which, combined with its light weight, made it very fuel efficient. A well-designed 3-cylinder 2-stroke engine would also be able to offer the same power output as a conventional 4-stroke, 6-cylinder in-line engine. Therefore, it was felt that much of the criteria for a new engine could be fulfilled with this design.

Design and Operation

The basic design was a high-speed, direct injection 2-stroke, water-cooled unit with opposed pistons to actuate a single crankshaft through rocker arms. The porting of the cylinders was based on the Kadenacy design principles, with scavenging assisted by a Wade 'Roots' type blower. Armstrong-Whitworth held the patent for the porting methods developed by Michel Kadenacy:

> The design of the exhaust ports ... ensures that as a result of the rapid opening of ample port area, exhaust gases escape at such a speed that they leave behind a partial vacuum which helps to charge the cylinder by a sucking action. This constitutes the first stage in cleaning the cylinder and it takes place while the inlet ports are still sealed.

The description overleaf of the full operational cycle is taken from the contemporary Rootes' TS-3 literature.

Development and History

Although the opposed-piston engine was a new concept in commercial vehicles, it was not new as far as other applications were concerned. The following is an extract from a paper written by

Cycle of operation of the TS-3 engine.

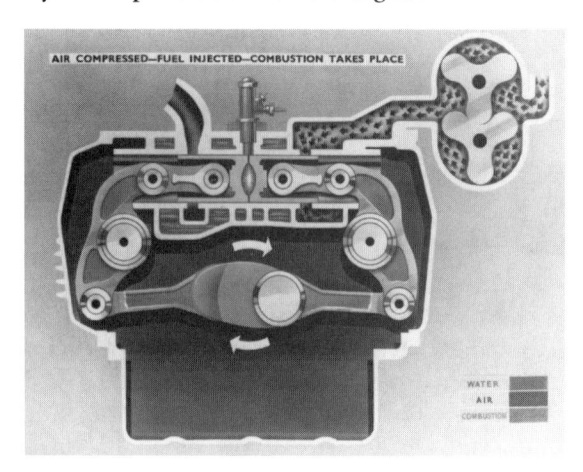

Fig. 1: Exhaust and inlet ports are sealed by pistons as they approach mean inner dead centre. Fuel is then injected into the cylinder and combustion takes place.

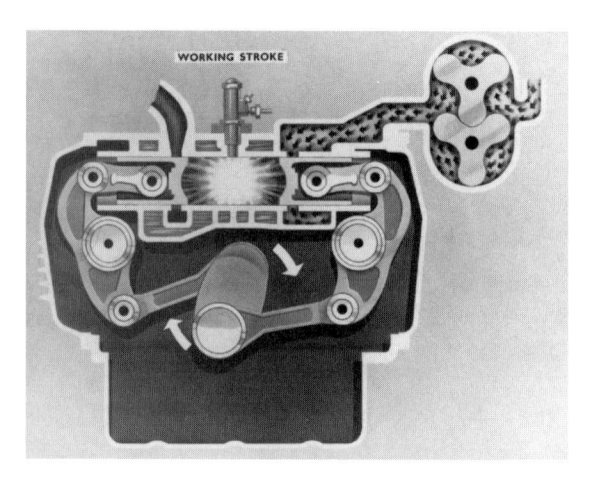

Fig. 2: The high pressures generated by combustion force the pistons outwards on their working stroke, so actuating the linkage to turn the crankshaft.

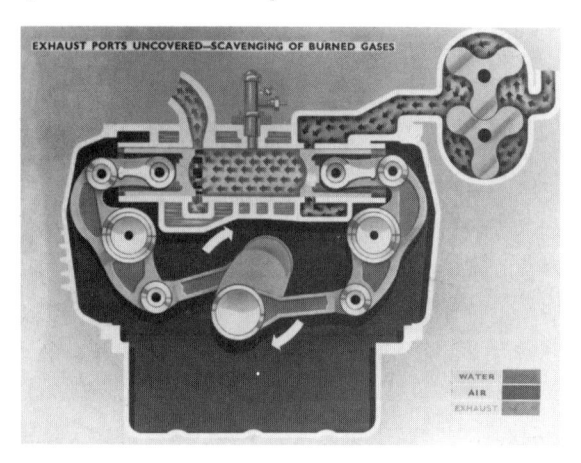

Fig. 3: Towards the end of the working stroke the phasing of the pistons and location of ports enable the exhaust ports to open before the inlet ports. Exhaust ports are so designed that burnt gases are rapidly expelled from the cylinder into the exhaust system.

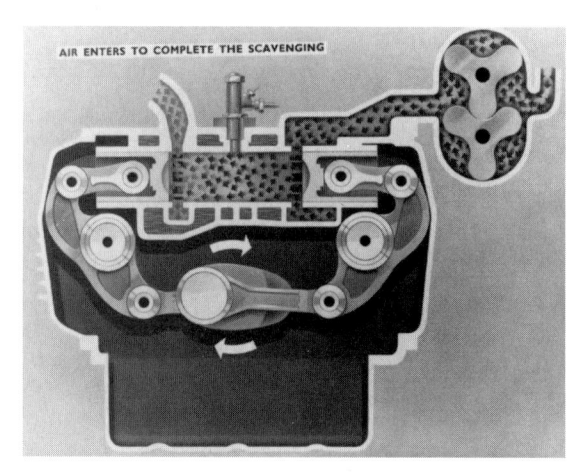

Fig. 4: Shortly afterwards the inlet ports are uncovered and air, supplied to the air chest from the low pressure blower, rushes into the cylinder and sweeps remaining exhaust gases out through the exhaust ports.

Eric Coy in 1959, concerning the history of the opposed-piston engine.

The opposed piston construction was first evolved in the 1870s and examples are Wittig and Linford of 1878–79. In the form in which we now know it, however, the type first made its appearance in 1892 as the Oechelhauser/Junkers gas engine.

Development of the type as a compression ignition unit did not make much headway until during and immediately after the 1914/18 war when Doxford in Sunderland started to build large marine oil engines which have been successful for forty years. In Germany, Junkers, after some misfortune with heavier engines, introduced in the early thirties a lightweight high speed engine known as the Jumo. Others have

The TS-3 Engine

followed suit but it would be fair to say that, up to the 1939/45 war, Doxford and Junkers were the two chief exponents of the opposed piston engine with Sulzer coming third. A common feature of both Doxford and Junkers was their high performance and good fuel consumption.

Development of the TS-3 was started in 1948 by Eric Coy and his design team at the Humber plant at Stoke Aldermoor. Two of the original members of the team who played an important part in its development were Alec Brown and Roland Golby. As well as the 3-cylinder engine, a single-cylinder engine was also produced to enable piston, ring and liner combinations to be developed. A study was made and a prototype built of a 2-cylinder version. Roland Golby, Senior Design Draughtsman, remembers some of the problems that were encountered early on:

> The first prototypes were based on an aluminium crankcase. The first aluminium crankcase engine ran without trouble for 56,000 miles ... until there was a severe failure, which led to a complete re-think of the linkage system. The rocker lever had a forked end at the bottom and a simple, straight con-rod. The later design had a forked con-rod and a straight rocker lever. The failures occurred in the forks of the early rocker lever.

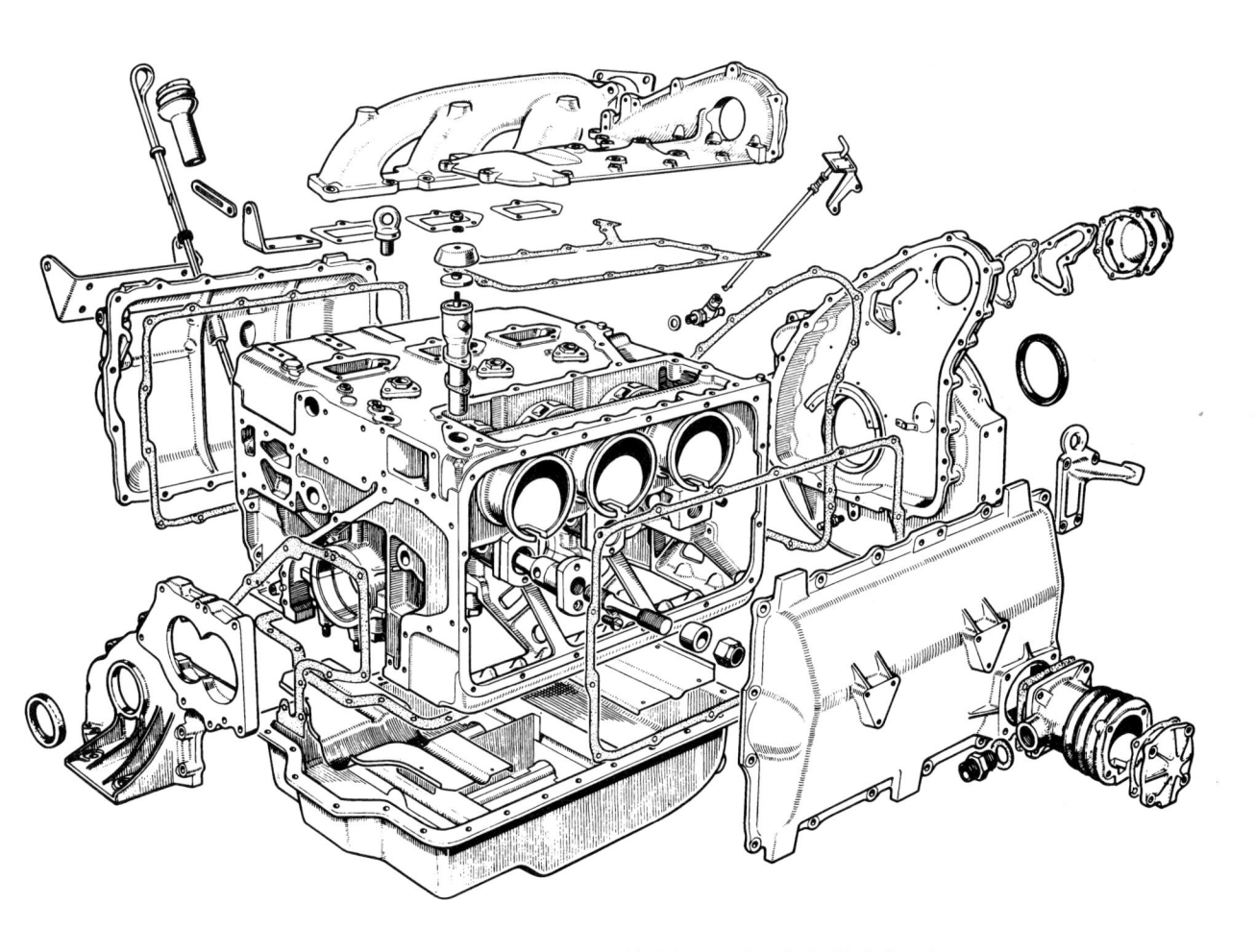

An exploded view of the first TS-3 production engine (3D.199 – 105bhp) showing the cylinder block, liners in position, side covers, sump and manifolding arrangement.

The TS-3 Engine

The engine had a relatively long development and prototype period, and many changes were made including the decision to use a cast-iron crankcase instead of aluminium, but changes and improvements were being made even after production had commenced ...

[The early production version] was originally introduced in a downrated form, at 90 bhp, [in May 1954] principally because the early transmissions could not take the full torque [of the engine]. When the uprated version [105bhp] came into production, further changes became necessary. The original thinking on the linkage system was that the con-rod would never be stressed in tension to any degree because the loading was always of a compressive nature, but failures did occur when, for example, if a driver missed a gear, the engine speed would rise dramatically, and that was sufficient to put a great load on the con-rod bolts, so they were increased initially from ⅜in diameter to ⁷⁄₁₆in and finally to ½in [on the 215cu in version]. An increase to the con-rod ends was also made at the same time.

Rig testing was also undertaken at Ryton-on-Dunsmore, until the vibrating beam in the rig fractured! As well as continuing test-bed development, the TS-3 underwent rigorous testing in vehicles over thousands of miles, under some of the most arduous conditions, including altitude tests in the Alps and in Mexico, and cross-country journeys in Africa. Norman Smith was responsible for carrying out tests with TS-3 engined vehicles in Mexico:

> It was an ideal test area as there were many conditions and terrains ... sea-level, high altitude, frost at night, tropical heat. On altitude tests the TS-3 went fine ... I did the self same run with a Perkins P6, but the TS-3 was superior, it was less affected by altitude.

Here they were tested to destruction, and some of the early rocker lever failures occurred on the fast

A sectional drawing of the 3D-199 engine.

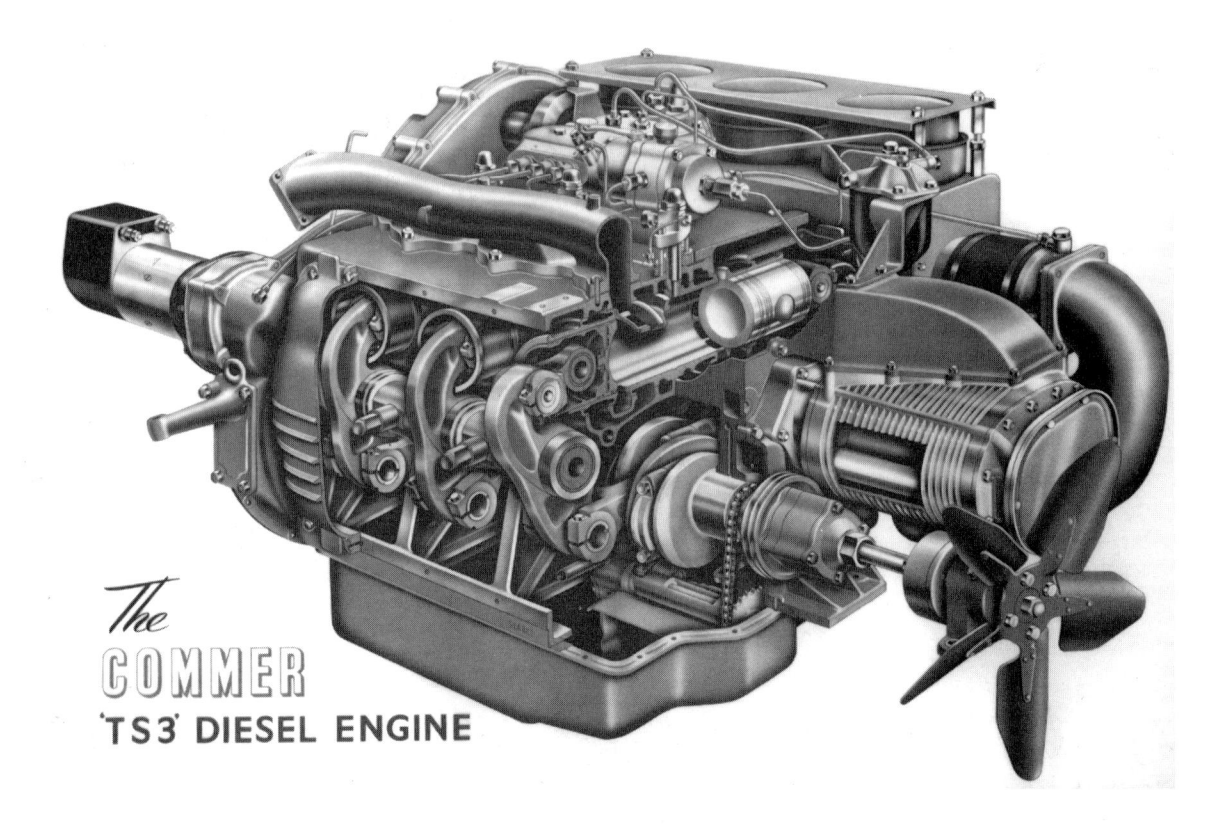

A three-quarter front view of the engine showing the Roots-type blower and triple oil bath cleaners and silencers.

The TS-3 front end.

(Below) The TS-3 with cover removed, showing rockers and rocker shaft.

A TS-3 mounted in a 7ton forward-control chassis.

downhill overspeed tests. Rootes were not the only company to use this part of Mexico to test vehicles. General Motors used the same mountain roads to test their 2-stroke V-8 engines for Greyhound buses, but with the TS-3 the Commer test drivers could 'put two fingers up at the GMC 2 strokes on the climbs', much to the embarrassment of the General Motors' engineers.

During the test period in the UK, Norman Smith had first-hand experience of the 'de-coking' abilities of the TS-3:

> We installed a pre-production engine in an 'India Tyres' 12ton tractor unit running between London and Glasgow. The design of the ports was very clever ... as they became self-clearing. Sometimes during the night, if it felt like clearing its throat, you got a firework display, as carbon was literally blown out of the exhaust pipe!

Although initial development and production design of the TS-3 was done at Stoke Aldermoor, as Rootes had acquired Tilling-Stevens at Maidstone in the autumn of 1950, it was decided that production of the engine should be moved to Maidstone. In 1953, the test beds were moved to the Romney works, where most of the development and testing was done and a team of Humber manufacturing engineers, lead by Tommy Clay, planned and installed the manufacturing facility at the adjacent St Peters Street works.

Bill Garner was made general manager of the Rootes Diesel Engineering Division in July 1952 and Bill Seaman was taken on as chief development engineer, under Eric Coy, in 1953.

Another early foible of the TS-3 was brought to the attention of the design team in the pre-production period at Maidstone. The first version of the engine had an in-line fuel pump fitted with a pneumatic governor, which was a very good system. The only problem was that the in-line pump was a direct-drive type and as there was no valve gear or timing, if a vehicle stalled it was possible for the engine to kick back in reverse rotation. This sent the vehicle backwards instead of forwards, much to the alarm of the driver and any poor unsuspecting motorist who suddenly found a Commer lorry sitting on his bonnet!

Don Kitchen was also a Senior Design Draughtsman at the time and remembers the modification that was made:

> One day our development driver was at traffic lights in Maidstone, and he stalled his engine. When he started it up again it kicked back and ran backwards

Allenways operated this elegant TS-3-powered Avenger with bodywork by Burlingham.

... so we developed a ratchet ... [a sprung-loaded dog drive] so that when it stalled and went out of phase, the ratchet locked and re-phased the engine, then it could be restarted without the possibility of crankshaft contra-rotation.

The TS-3 was officially unveiled at the 1954 Commercial Motor Show in an Avenger coach chassis. It was greeted very favourably by the press and potential buyers. The 7ton truck chassis was also TS-3 powered and benefited from a new, larger gearbox and rear axle to cope with a higher payload and the increase in torque of the uprated production engine. It remained in production until the early sixties, when the new C Series 7 to 12ton range replaced the old QX range.

For a brief period in 1958 the vertical version of the Perkins 6.305 (the C.305) was fitted into the QX medium range. In 1962, the Perkins 6.354 was fitted in the popular QX 7ton chassis, although the TS-3 did find its way into the new CA 8-tonner when it made its debut in March 1962. However, in order for Commer to meet the growing demand for an improved power to weight ratio for the new generation 'C' Series, clearly something had to be done to update the TS-3 to keep it ahead of the competition.

In 1963 the engineers and design staff at Tilling-Stevens responded to the plight of the Product Planning Department at Dunstable by raising the output of the TS-3 from 105 to 117bhp. This was achieved solely from increased thermal efficiency. Various internal modifications were made: for example, the steel-crowned cast-iron pistons of the earlier engine were replaced by one-piece cast-iron pistons, and to cope with the greater heat being generated, an oil cooler was fitted in the filtering circuit. One significant improvement was for the rear auxiliaries (in other words the blower, fuel injection pump and power-steering pump) to be gear driven, replacing the chain-drive rear end of the old engine.

All of these improvements came at a cost, however, and as the company had advertised the new version of the engine with no increase in price, this cost had to be taken out of the production of

(Above) Dealers were given opportunities to show off the new TS-3 engine alongside the new QX truck. This display is at the Rootes dealership of Galway Smith Ltd in Leeds.

A mechanic's-eye view, showing easy access to the fuel pump, blower and injection equipment.

(Above) The CAV in-line pump used on the early versions of the engine.

the engine. This was done by replacing the in-line fuel pump with a lower cost CAV DPA distributor-type fuel injection pump with a mechanical governor. On the face of it, this was an acceptable compromise, but the reality was quite different, as Norman Smith explained:

> With the in-line pump its point of injection is the same, regardless of the speed, whereas on the distributor type pump it's late on light running and it advances as the speed goes up. As a result you could get a smoking of the exhaust at low speeds. The only cure was to over advance it, but that meant [that] the bearings were being overloaded at low speeds ... almost getting a bearing lock.

Despite these problems, the design engineers were eventually able to make the rotary pump work efficiently in the TS-3, but there were also quality problems, particularly with porosity, in the crankcase castings. Consequently Tilling-Stevens changed from their British supplier, Dartmouth Auto Castings Ltd, to a French casting manufacturer, Usine Metallurgique, who were able to provide consistent high quality in their casting manufacture.

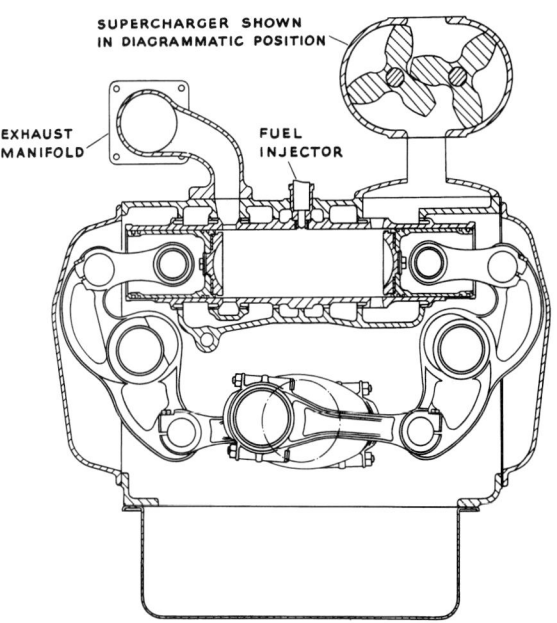

Cross-sectional diagram of the engine.

For the 1963 model run, the TS-3 was fitted into the 7½-tonner, as well as the rest of the

(Above) The Beadle TS-3 'chassisless' coach at the 1954 Commercial Motor Show.

A glass-covered panel in the floor of the coach on the Beadle stand at the 1954 Show allowed visitors to view the new TS-3 opposed piston diesel, and see how well it suited being mounted under the floor amidships.

Commer heavyweights. The Avenger coach chassis, however, retained the old version of the engine, complete with in-line fuel pump and chain-driven rear auxiliaries. Instead of a 5-speed constant mesh gearbox, a new 5-speed synchromesh box was now available in the C Series. A.J. Smith had the gearbox modified: 'This was the old Tillings' box that was re-drawn for manufacture at Luton, by an excellent gearbox man – Eric Gill.'

The last specification change for the TS-3 came in 1965. The pressure was still on for even bigger engines, to power the even heavier vehicles that were coming into the market. At the Earls Court Commercial Motor Show in 1964,

Geoffrey Rootes, Sir Reginald Rootes and Commer sales manager Freddie Best discuss the merits of the TS-3 engine on the Commer stand, during a pre-opening tour of the 1962 Commercial Motor Show.

(Below) The 'Rootes Diesel' badge under the grille on the CA Series denoted a TS-3 powered Commer.

TS-3 in a 7ton CA8 chassis (1963).

Commer had taken the bold step of entering the maximum-gross vehicle market with the 16ton Maxiload. In October 1965, at the Glasgow Commercial Motor Show, an even bigger Commer model was announced, a 24ton tractive unit.

For the new Maxiloads, it was decided, in order to obtain the necessary extra power that was required, to increase the cylinder bore size from 3¼in to 3⅜in, resulting in a cylinder displacement of 215cu in, which effectively boosted gross output to 135bhp. For the lighter C Series models, Commer engineers decided not to push their luck with the big engine, and so offered a de-rated version of the new 215cu in engine at the familiar 117bhp output. These versions were made available on big Commers until 1972, although production officially ended in 1968.

The Multi-Fuel Option

A common misconception about the TS-3 was that it had been built as a multi-fuel engine. This was not the case. The engine did, however, lend itself very well to easy conversion to multi-fuel operation, due to its unique design. In comparison with other types of engines, virtually no changes were required, except to the fuel injection equipment. When using alternative fuels like petrol, for example, which tends to cause vapour lock, an electric booster pump was fitted in order to supply petrol under pressure to the fuel lift pump. When diesel was being used the booster pump could be switched off. A positive pump lubrication system was also installed for use on 'non-oily' fuels.

Although it was the intention of the company to market the multi-fuel ability of the TS-3 as an option, it was never really taken seriously as a viable commercial proposition, either by the company or, one must assume, by the marketplace. It was, however, a serious consideration for the Army.

For five years, since 1954, the Fighting Vehicles Research and Development Establishment at Chobham in Surrey had been researching the practicalities of multi-fuel operation for military use. In the latter part of 1959 it organized a 'Symposium On Multi-fuel Engines'. Present were various senior engineers and designers from some of Britain's most experienced commercial vehicle engine manufacturers. Eric Coy represented the Rootes Diesel Engineering Division.

As well as the TS-3, five other 'omnivorous' engines, for various applications, were under scrutiny. The Leyland L60 (a 6-cylinder opposed-piston unit, designed to develop 700bhp at 2,400rpm), was for use in the Chieftain tank. Rolls-Royce offered their 'K' range of opposed-piston 2-stroke engines as an option to their medium-power B40 and B60 petrol engines. A Coventry Climax vertically opposed piston engine with twin crankshafts was discussed, principally as an auxiliary engine in fighting vehicles. Weslake and Co. reported on their research with two engines: the BMC 5.1ltr diesel engine and the AEC AV 690 11.3ltr, 6-cylinder diesel used in the 10ton 6×6 chassis.

In 1966, Commer built twenty-six 3/5ton split-cab 4 × 4 trucks for the Army. Based on the 'C' Series, they were fitted with TS-3 multi-fuel engines.

(Below) One of the few multi-fuel TS-3s to be built was used in this QX 7-tonner as a demonstrator at a late fifties' British Trade Fair in Moscow.

The criteria for multi-fuel requirements for military applications was that vehicles should be able to run on any fuel ranging from: diesel; Aviation Gas Turbine fuel; a 50/50 mix of petrol and diesel; as well as various grades of petrol including 'civilian' premium grade petrol. This was quite a tall order for most of the companies present and certainly the BMC 5.1ltr engine made the grade for use in the Austin 3/5ton chassis. However, it was the Commer TS-3 that made most impact, not only with the FVRDE, but with other manufacturers all acknowledging the merits of the 2-stroke opposed-piston engine as 'a natural choice for multi-fuel operation'. The impact of the TS-3 was such that a request was made to Rolls-Royce by the FVRDE, that there should be:

> a cessation of the development of the 4-stroke engine for multi-fuel operation ... and to consider a range of opposed-piston 2-stroke engines ... as possible replacements for B range petrol engines.

Eric Coy was involved with the development of the L60 Chieftain tank engine. He suggested that the only way of fitting an engine producing in excess of 600bhp into a smaller than usual engine compartment was to design an opposed-piston 6-cylinder engine. Tilling-Stevens engineers developed the pistons and the liners for the engine, and then it was passed over to Leyland to finish. However, the fate of this engine remains a mystery!

Although the multi-fuel version of the TS-3 was considered a great success, Cyril Corke recalls that, apart from prototypes, only twenty-six split-cab Commer CCs were ordered by the Army. Commer engineers spent much time testing the multi-fuel TS-3 in Norway, as well as on official test programmes with the Army at Farnborough, alongside BMC and Bedford. Although the Commer prototypes performed excellently in all respects, it was Bedford who became the favoured supplier to the Army with their TK-derived range of trucks powered by their 4.9ltr 6-cylinder multi-fuel engine, and that would remain the case for some years to come.

The TS-4: The Engine that Never Was

Although a 144bhp version of the 215cu.in engine was built, it never saw production. A turbocharged version was also built and Don Kitchen even patented the pressure relief valve but it, too, never saw the light of day. The TS-4 (4-cylinder opposed-piston 2-stroke) was the next logical step in the development of the opposed-piston engine for commercial vehicles.

If there were inherent technical problems with the TS-3, then the design of the TS-4 overcame them. In essence, the TS-4 was the engine the TS-3 should have been.

Development of the TS-4 started in 1964, with the assumption that the production of the engine would commence in 1971 or 1972. The intention of Product Planning was that the TS-4 would be used in the existing C-series chassis; the engine was still compact enough even though the additional cylinder took up more space. Eventually a new cab, known as the 600 and 700 Series, was to be introduced to take the TS-4. The additional cylinder enabled the cylinder displacement to be raised to 287cu in, developing 200bhp at 2,600rpm, which was 200rpm faster than that of previous 3-cylinder engines.

The basic structure of the TS-4 was similar to the TS-3, and where possible improved materials and strengthened components were used, as well as a higher capacity water pump, oil cooler and lubricating pump. Provision was also made for a bigger clutch and stronger engine mountings. The re-introduction of an in-line fuel pump was considered in order to achieve an engine life of 250,000 miles, as projected. The main structural changes involved: 'the fitting of through bolts at the front and rear wall of the crankcase and forming part of the rocker shaft attachment, thus preventing crankcase failure'. (On the 3-cylinder engine, studs had been used. Through bolts were used only between the liners.)

Due to the increase in engine speed, and stresses that would be present, a great many detail changes were made. After the design had been finalized and prototype and test-bed trials carried out, in May 1966, the engine was presented to

Two views of a standard version of a prototype TS-4, photographed at Maidstone; the front end (right) and the offside (below right). Apart from the extra cylinder, the distinguishing feature was that through bolts were fitted on the end bearings as opposed to the single stud fitting of the TS-3.

Product Planning. The decision was made to build more prototypes and initiate 'road rehearsal' tests with selected operators.

By 1969, the TS-4 was looking like an exciting and viable proposition to take Commer into the next decade, but this was not to be. Chrysler had taken over Rootes in 1967, and had no interest in continuing to spend valuable development cash on new, slightly esoteric, engines, when they already had their own engines available, and the project was eventually dropped.

Eric Coy retired in 1964. He was replaced by Heinz Stransky as chief engineer with Don Kitchen taking over as design manager, who saw the TS-3 project through to the end. Bill Garner was sent to Rootes' version of the Foreign Legion, Linwood, to sort out the Hillman Imp production. He was replaced by Harry Willshaw, who was general manager during the sixties. The design department was eventually moved to Whitley, near Coventry. Heinz Stransky and Don Kitchen were also relocated to Whitley. Kitchen eventually became chief engineer-power train, after the retirement of Cyril Pemberton, who had replaced the great A.J. Smith in 1971.

By the seventies, the TS-3 was struggling to keep up with legislative requirements as well as the marketplace, and by then truck manufacturing certainly was a very different ball game. However, the opposed-piston 2-stroke engine for commercial vehicles was, at the very least, a significant and bold engineering innovation that deserves a place in automotive history. The engine is a credit to the genius of Eric Coy and the Tilling-Stevens designers and engineers who created it.

If only the others had our guts

Instead of showing you a photograph of Commer Maxiload and CE models we're showing you the power behind them, the TS 3 Diesel It's a two-stroke, three-cylinder engine with two opposed pistons in each cylinder. And from a 3.52 litre capacity it develops the sort of power you usually expect from much larger engines. How do we get so much power from such a compact unit? By putting two opposed pistons in each cylinder instead of the usual one. Two-fisted power to give you more torque for tough jobs, more acceleration for fast jobs and extra miles per gallon on any job. Which leaves only one question to be answered. What about reliability and durability? Well, the TS 3 Diesel has been on the road for over 17 years now and has covered many millions of miles on all types of hauling assignments. Surely these facts speak for themselves. And if further proof were needed it comes from a 12 month/50,000 mile warranty. ☐ You rarely see engines featured in truck advertisements. Maybe because most engines haven't got the guts!

COMMER CHRYSLER UNITED KINGDOM

Commer We're sold on quality

The high-performance T S 3 Diesel is standard in Commer CE8 13 ton GVW models and Maxiload 16 ton GVW models

A last-ditch attempt in 1970 to promote the TS-3 opposed-piston 2-stroke engine, before Chrysler got their teeth into the old Rootes Commercial Vehicle Division.

8 Rootes and the Pentastar: The Sixties

George Martin ... asked us to go to Abbey Road Studios ...We recorded ['How Do You Do It'] in March ... and had to drive from Liverpool to London ... in our Commer van ...We got back at 2am. My mam, God bless her, had waited up for me and asked how it went. I said, 'Not too bad mam, at least the van got us home'

Gerry Marsden, lead singer of Gerry And The Pacemakers

In 1959, rock 'n' roll died ... Elvis Presley joined the army, Buddy Holly was killed in a plane crash, and Little Richard found God. Meanwhile, Britain's film and music industries were booming. A young teen idol named Cliff Richard was joining the pop-star ranks with his second hit, 'Livin' Doll', and Britain was preparing to export its own brand of rock 'n' roll to America, along with British-built Rootes' sports cars like the Sunbeam Alpine and the Minx-based Rapier 'sports coupe'. The 'Swinging Sixties' had arrived.

Attitudes during the sixties were, in effect, an antidote to the previous post-war period. By comparison to the fifties, the transition into the sixties was like a low-budget black and white 'B' movie suddenly changing into a 'Panavision' wide-screen 'Technicolor' spectacular. Most of Britain's motor industry was riding on the upwave of Britain's continuing prosperity. The 'mixed-economy' that had been created during the fifties led to an increase in consumerism during the sixties. This in turn enabled a wider cross-section of Britain's population to share in the nation's prosperity. There was, however, a downside to this newly found prosperity. The balance of power was rapidly moving from the side of the employers to the employees who

During the early sixties fleet sales for Commer and Karrier vehicles boomed, and Aer Lingus were enthusiastic Rootes' operators. This 1960 Hillman Husky was the estate car version of the Cob van. The Karrier Bantam behind it was one of many various Rootes' ground support vehicles used by the airline, which included Gamecocks and Walk-Thrus.

Demand for the old 'B' series (the BF van and the Superpoise ¼ton and 1½ton pick-up) continued to earn these models a place in the Rootes light van range until the mid-sixties. Here, four diesel BFD3024 1½ton vans, operated by Gibbs Mew & Co., stand outside the old Anchor Brewery, Salisbury in 1960.

provided the much-needed skilled labour, and in 1961, the Rootes organization found itself the victim of industrial unrest. A thirteen-week strike at British Light Steel Pressings in Acton had a catastrophic effect on the long-term survival of Rootes.

The Acton Strike

Although the BLSP dispute involved a smaller workforce than the strike involving 2,000 workers at the Pressed Steel Company in Swindon in 1961, it was to have more far-reaching consequences due to the length of the dispute and the number of other subsidiaries affected by it.

The principal products supplied by BLSP at that time were panels for the Humber Hawk,

The fleet of fourteen QX 7ton tippers in service with Robson Brothers of Haltwhistle, Northumberland in 1961.

Super Snipe and the Karrier Bantam; and cabs for the Commer forward-control series. It virtually halted Rootes' car production around mid-October and had similar consequences for Commer-Karrier.

The strike began at the end of August 1961 over a feared redundancy at the plant. New car sales had slumped during the year and Rootes had been stockpiling components at Acton. Militant members of the Acton workforce called for an unofficial strike until the management declared 'no redundancy' and started negotiating on a shorter working week and 'work-sharing' (similar to the scheme that had been started at Thrupp & Maberley, Rootes' coachbuilding concern, in October 1960).

The Rootes' management was not prepared to enter into any agreements at that point in time. Lord Rootes was of the opinion that to give in to the troublemakers at Acton would set a precedent for the motor industry, and the management, in effect, dug its heels in. Lord Rootes was not alone in his feeling about the situation, and he had wide support from the motor industry in general. The Acton plant had gained a reputation for having a militant workforce with a number of 'agitators'. Furthermore, neither the main engineering union or the skilled workforce supported the strike. A number of previous unofficial stoppages at Acton over petty grievances had already gained the plant a bad reputation from other subsidiaries.

Rootes had made a stand against unconstitutional action, but the cost to the company was immense: £3m in lost profits, and guaranteed wage payments to the Coventry plants in the earlier stages of the strike cost around £500,000. At the end of this long, drawn-out battle, there were no winners – only losers. Rootes lost production as well as badly needed profit, and striking workers lost their jobs, as inspection superintendent Norman Lawrence recalled:

> I was sent to BLSP to try and improve the quality of the cabs. I was up there every day for a month – this was about the same time [as], or before the strike. But they [the Acton workforce] weren't very happy about me going there. It finished us off here when the strike was

A vehicle attempting to either deliver to or collect from the BLSP factory at Acton during the strike that ruined Rootes.

on. [After the strike, the management] advertised in the local paper that if anybody wanted their job back, they could re-apply, but they knew who the troublemakers were. So they only had who they wanted ... to get the plant moving again without any further disruption.

Following the resumption of production, Lord Rootes made an announcement to the press in December 1961, expressing his gratitude to: 'the thousands of our employees who remained loyal

British Light Steel Pressings Ltd, Acton.

(Below) The Karrier Bantam continued during the sixties in both 'municipal' and 'industrial' versions.

to us throughout the dispute, even though it caused them and their families hardship.'

The Rootes' coffers had been seriously depleted, and the strike changed the direction of the organization. It could not have come at a worse time, as Rootes had major expansion plans, with the development of the Hillman Imp, as well as the new Commer models in the pipeline. The 1961 sales slump also compounded the problem. Figures released in November 1961 showed profits at the year-end, in July 1961, as being virtually sliced in half, to £2,911,652 from £5,863,852 the previous year. But the real seriousness of the Rootes group's financial problems was not revealed until 1962. Their profits had been wiped out, with record losses of £2m, and although 1963 did see a significant clawing back of profit, to just under £200,000, it was still not enough, and in 1964 Rootes had to sell a significant portion of their shareholding to the Chrysler Corporation of America. This had certainly not been in the Rootes' brothers' game plan.

New Decade – New Management

With the change of decade came a change of management. In 1960, Geoffrey Cozens retired, after twenty-three years at the helm. His place was taken by forty-year-old Rex Watson Lee, initially as director and general manager. It was not until 1962 that Watson Lee was appointed managing director of Commer Cars Ltd, and so assumed overall control of the Group's commercial vehicle manufacturing division.

As a Lt Colonel, Rex Watson Lee, being one of the youngest officers in the British Army, had a distinguished war record which earned him an MBE. He joined Rootes in 1948 as a student, working in the foundry, but his relationship with the Rootes' family went back beyond that. During the war Geoffrey Rootes and Watson Lee, as fellow officers, became good friends. They met up again after the war at Humber, when Geoffrey was MD of the Rootes manufacturing division and Watson Lee became his personal assistant. In 1956, Watson Lee became managing director of the Rootes parts division when the truck and car parts divisions were merged.

Simultaneously with the appointment of Watson Lee as MD of Commer, came the announcement that Geoffrey Rootes was to be made chairman and joint managing director of Humber, whilst also taking up the newly created post of managing director of Rootes Motors Ltd, the

Geoffrey Cozens accepts his retirement gifts with a handshake from Fred Lawrence on 26 August 1960, after twenty-three years as managing director of Commer Cars Ltd.

A rare late fifties photo of two Commer managing directors: Rex Watson Lee (centre), who succeeded Geoffrey Cozens (right), seen here probably at one of the Commer-Karrier sports days. With them is J.L. Dickenson, the managing director of Luton-based Skefko Bearings Ltd.

A few weeks short of his seventieth birthday Fred Lawrence retires after nearly fifty years' service with Commer. Fred is seen on the left of the picture with new Commer managing director Rex Watson Lee. Works director Don Burgess and Mrs Lawrence look on.

group's parent company. Geoffrey relinquished the post of chairman of Rootes Motors (Parts) Ltd, which was to be taken on by his cousin, Timothy Rootes (son of Sir Reginald), who was also made joint managing director of Humber.

In 1959, Cyril Pemberton was brought in from AEC as assistant chief engineer to A.J. Smith. He replaced H.E. (Bertie) Edwards, who had been Smith's assistant since 1952. Freddie Best would remain sales manager right through the sixties,

A Commer Wife's Viewpoint

It is easy to forget the important role that wives play in the running of big companies. Mrs Pamela Watson Lee is an example of a dedicated wife who accepted that she was married not only to her husband, Rex, but to the Rootes group as well!

When, for example, the parts operation was moved up to Birmingham, it was Mrs Watson Lee's job to make sure that managers' wives had a positive attitude towards relocation:

> If wives were happy about moving, then their husbands would follow, so I would help them find somewhere to live, and reassure them that towns like Solihull really were quite nice places.

Mrs Watson Lee also knew what it was like to uproot from an area and relocate, especially with young children in school. As she was well aware of the disruption moving caused, she was a good ally to the other wives. On one occasion during the late fifties though, she unwittingly almost prevented Rex from gaining promotion.

> Geoffrey Cozens asked me if I would like to go back to Luton ... I said, 'Certainly not, I am quite happy living in Leamington Spa'. Rex said to me later 'You nearly scuppered my career' [with that comment].

In the event, Rex was given the job of running Commer, and he and Pam moved to Woburn Sands, near Dunstable.

Being the wife of a Rootes' executive and good friends of the Rootes' family also meant that Pamela Watson Lee would be called upon to attend numerous functions, dinners and receptions, as well as presenting cups and awards, attending motor shows and entertaining visiting dignitaries:

> Geoffrey [Lord Rootes] used to use me as his hostess ... to entertain dealer' wives, when we had the motor shows ... and the American wives [in the early days of the Chrysler tie-up] ... and I remember once we had to entertain the Shah of Persia's sister, who spoke not a word of English ... and all I could say to her was. 'You have a family?' ... and she said, 'Yes', yes.' ... The next day, a taxi arrived all the way from London, and in the taxi was a bowl of red roses and two huge tubs of caviar. We had caviar parties for days after . ... Every friend we knew that lived in Woburn Sands [came]. That was really quite something.

(Above) Pamela Watson Lee presents a trophy to 'Miss Commer' at one of the Commer-Karrier sports days.

One of the many functions that had to be attended. Here Rex Watson Lee presents a trophy to parts manager Joe Newsome. To his left is Newsome's wife Nora, and on his right sits Pamela Watson Lee.

with Sid Cooper as assistant sales manager. Cyril Corke was made municipal sales manager in 1962.

One of the 'old brigade', Fred Lawrence, father of Norman, called it a day at Commer Cars when he retired, only a few weeks short of his seventieth birthday in November 1961. Fred had been with Commer for nearly fifty years! He had started back in the days of the RC 4-tonner at Biscot Road in June 1911 as a storekeeper. During the thirties, when Commer was strapped for cash, Fred used to collect money owed by dealers, so that the workforce could be paid. During the war Fred spent his time in the army, and rejoined Commer as chief storekeeper. He was made welfare and safety officer at the factory in 1946, and in 1954 became assistant personnel officer.

1960: the 1500/2500 ¾ and 1ton Van

Although Bedford, BMC, Standard and Ford had entered the 15cwt van market before Commer and therefore had a head start, when Commer launched the 1500 ¾ton van range in January 1960, it did not take long to catch up.

The Commer van shared some of its styling cues and general layout with competitors such as the Austin/Morris J2-M16 and the Standard Atlas. Both had closed-in wheelarches and both were well-equipped ¾ton forward-control vans with optional pick-up and passenger bodies, but there the similarities ended. The Commer 1500 was the first ¾ton van to be offered with a diesel option (BMC were still two years away with their 1.5ltr diesel). The Commer was also available in no fewer than sixteen body versions – a veritable chameleon.

The Commer body was designed and built by the Pressed Steel Company at Cowley. Its clean, uncluttered lines made it one of the most modern looking forward-control vans available to date. Other finishing touches like hideaway windscreen wipers and neat push-button door handles, inherited from the Commer Cob, made the overall appearance of the 1500 a winner.

The Rootes Maidstone stand at the Commercial Motor Show at Earls Court in September 1962 showing a ¾ton Series 2 'High Top' van. Just visible behind is a 'Canopy Pick-up' version.

The key to the versatility of this new vehicle was in the construction of the underframe. A flat platform unitary type sub-assembly offered the necessary strength and rigidity to build numerous styles of standard bodywork. The basic van style was available with sliding or hinged front doors, and an optional side-loading door. Other goods styles on offer were two pick-ups, a bottle float, a gown van, a dropsider, a high-top van, a bakers' van and a mobile shop. Passenger versions included a light bus, contractor's bus and a model built specifically for public-service-vehicle duties. An ambulance, station wagon and two and four-berth caravans were built around the bus version. Rootes Maidstone, under the guidance of body production manager Stan Buss, built the passenger versions, and four other bodybuilders built the more specialized versions.

Rootes, once again, utilized the resources of their subsidiaries to the full. The 4-cylinder 1,494cc ohv petrol engine was the Hillman Minx unit; the gearbox was out of the Commer Express; the back axle and prop shaft was Humber Hawk, and as development engineer Ken Cain remembers, the front suspension comprised of 'a front crossmember from the Sunbeam Alpine, and Humber Hawk wishbones!' The result was a van with modern independent front suspension. The diesel option was the Perkins 'Four-99' engine, an economical and reliable unit of 1,621cc capacity, developing 42.3bhp at 3,600rpm, and costing an additional £112. The basic van had an internal capacity of 210cu ft (5.94cu m).

The senior project manager for the ¾ton van range, and other new development projects at the time, was Neil Bentham. He was responsible for overseeing much of the pre-production development, which initially was at Coventry, but was quickly moved to Dunstable. The first prototype, known as the WTN 13, was built in 1959 at Luton. It was tested in Mexico, Spain and Kenya, which resulted in many changes being made during the development period.

The wide appeal of the new van was undeniable. There was a vehicle for every kind of trade or business. In these pre-Ford Transit days, the comfort, versatility and lively performance of the vans also found a new market segment: rock 'n' roll! Many young bands of musicians and their assorted guitars, drums and amplifiers piled into the back of a 15cwt van, to plod wearily up and down the road to fame and fortune (which more often than not was the newly opened M1). The job of providing transport between a gruelling round of live gigs would often be entrusted to a Commer 1500 van. Even the Beatles, in their early days, progressed from their famous hand-painted Austin J12 to a bright yellow Ford Thames bus and, eventually, a Commer 1500 bus. Another up-and-coming band from Brian Epstein's blossoming 'Northern Songs' empire was Gerry And The Pacemakers. They had been asked by George

A 2500 dropsider pick-up, photographed in March 1965, showing the grille design change that was implemented in 1962 for the Series 2 version. The bold chrome 'Commer' letters were a later addition.

Martin to go down to Abbey Road Studios to record their first single, the events of which are etched on lead singer Gerry Marsden's memory:

> We recorded the song in March [1963] and had to drive to London in our bloomin' old van, a Commer [1500] it was, yes I remember that van well. Before we even set off the engine was frozen solid and we had to sort that one out. Then halfway there, just outside Birmingham it was, we broke down. The spring had gone … It was thick snow and freezing cold and I had to crawl under this van and fix it [with] a wire coat hanger.
>
> We had left home at 6am for our big day, and got to London at 2pm. We were knackered and looked dreadful … Brian [Epstein] said, 'Go to the hotel and have a rest'. We slept until 5pm … went to the studio and recorded 'How Do You Do It' in four takes … heard one playback and drove back to Liverpool in THAT van.
>
> … My mam, God bless her, had waited up for me and asked how it went. I said, 'Not too bad mam, at least the van got us home!'

Gerry And The Pacemakers' Commer van had played an important role in their success. The record was a number one hit in April 1963.

The ¾ton van range was to have an incredibly long production life. The 1500 was joined in November 1962 by a larger capacity 1ton 2500 model, now with twenty-one different body versions. In September 1965, both the 1500 and 2500 versions were joined by an intermediate 2000 version, all of which were available with a Borg Warner 35 automatic gearbox option. Factory designations would change to 'PA' and 'PB', and ultimately it would end up as the 'Dodge Spacevan', after a production life of nearly three decades, with virtually no major design changes.

Not quite 'rock 'n' roll', but dance band leaders like Nat Temple worked just as hard as their pop group contemporaries, providing swinging live music in the tradition of the American jazz big bands. Nat's 12-seater bus was supplied by the Caterham Motor Company, one of the Rootes Group's main dealers in Surrey.

A lozenge-shaped grille and amber direction indicators identified the 1500 and 2500 vans from September 1965 when the Rootes 1,725cc petrol engine was fitted to replace the old 1,592cc unit. The diesel option was now the more powerful Perkins 4.108 engine. The 1500 model was also offered with the Borg-Warner 35 automatic transmission as an option. This 'PBCM 2500 Series' hinged-door van is shown outside the office block at Dunstable.

1961: the 'Walk-Thru'

The Commer Walk-Thru was a revolutionary vehicle, which no other British vehicle manufacturer has come close to imitating, then or since. It was designed as a no-nonsense basic door-to-door delivery van, very much on the same lines as the American vans that came into vogue during the forties. Its design concept is well summed up by Peter Lewis, who was quality inspector at Dunstable at the time:

> It was an economy, flat-sided, rivet-construction, easy repair, door-to-door delivery vehicle – a tin box with gauges ... The BF was a good panel van, but the Walk-Thru was belt and braces!

The original ideas for the Walk-Thru had been echoing around the corridors of Biscot Road since the early fifties, following a series of trips that Geoffrey Cozens had made to America and Canada with A.J. Smith in 1955 and 1959. It was probably during these trips that the idea for what was to become the Walk-Thru came together. Although it was A.J. Smith who conceptualized the design of the van, Geoffrey Cozens had compiled a very detailed report in 1949 on manufacturing techniques in the USA and Canada, which included the design and manufacture of door-to-door delivery vans. During January and February of that year, visits were made to various truck plants: the Ford plants in Windsor, Ontario, and the massive River Rouge plant in Detroit, where everything from factory lighting to assembly methods were studied. Production control at the Dodge plant in Detroit, and the material control section at Chrysler's Plymouth assembly plant were also given close scrutiny. The Studebaker CKD operation at South Bend, Indiana gave valuable insight into manufacturing for export. The most in-depth analysis that was made during the trip, however, was of the door-to-door delivery vans made by Dodge, Chevrolet, GMC and a small, but significant independent called Divco.

It was a combination of all of these vans that spawned the creation of the Walk-Thru. All of the North American examples were well-built, well-designed forward-control vans, but only the Dodge 'Route' and the little Divco could be considered genuine door-to-door easy-access delivery vans, and it was these vehicles that Cozens and his team became most interested in. In his report he concluded:

> Divco as a purely specialist machine has the best specification for door-to-door delivery work. It is

An early 1½ton Walk-Thru model seen in the old cattlemarket car park in Northampton, just round the corner from the supplying dealer Arthur Mulliner Ltd. The Walk-Thru was a no-nonsense delivery van that was developed on a shoestring budget, and proved to be a very profitable product for the Rootes Group. David Streeton was responsible for creating the front-end styling of the Walk-Thru.

A big square tin box on wheels. The Walk-Thru was designed as simply as possible, so that every bit of its 350cu ft (10cu m) capacity could be utilized.

equipped with suitable controls for sit or stand driving ... Quick operating 'jack-knife' doors, column gear shift, column accelerator.

Dodge have produced a good machine, with low step in, and a large, low, flat floor area. They have ... employed De Dion type rear axles, and a fixed differential unit, which has greatly assisted in keeping down the floor level.

The Commer 'Walk-Thru' was introduced in October 1961, at the Earls Court Commercial Motor Show. It was available in 1½, 2 and 3ton

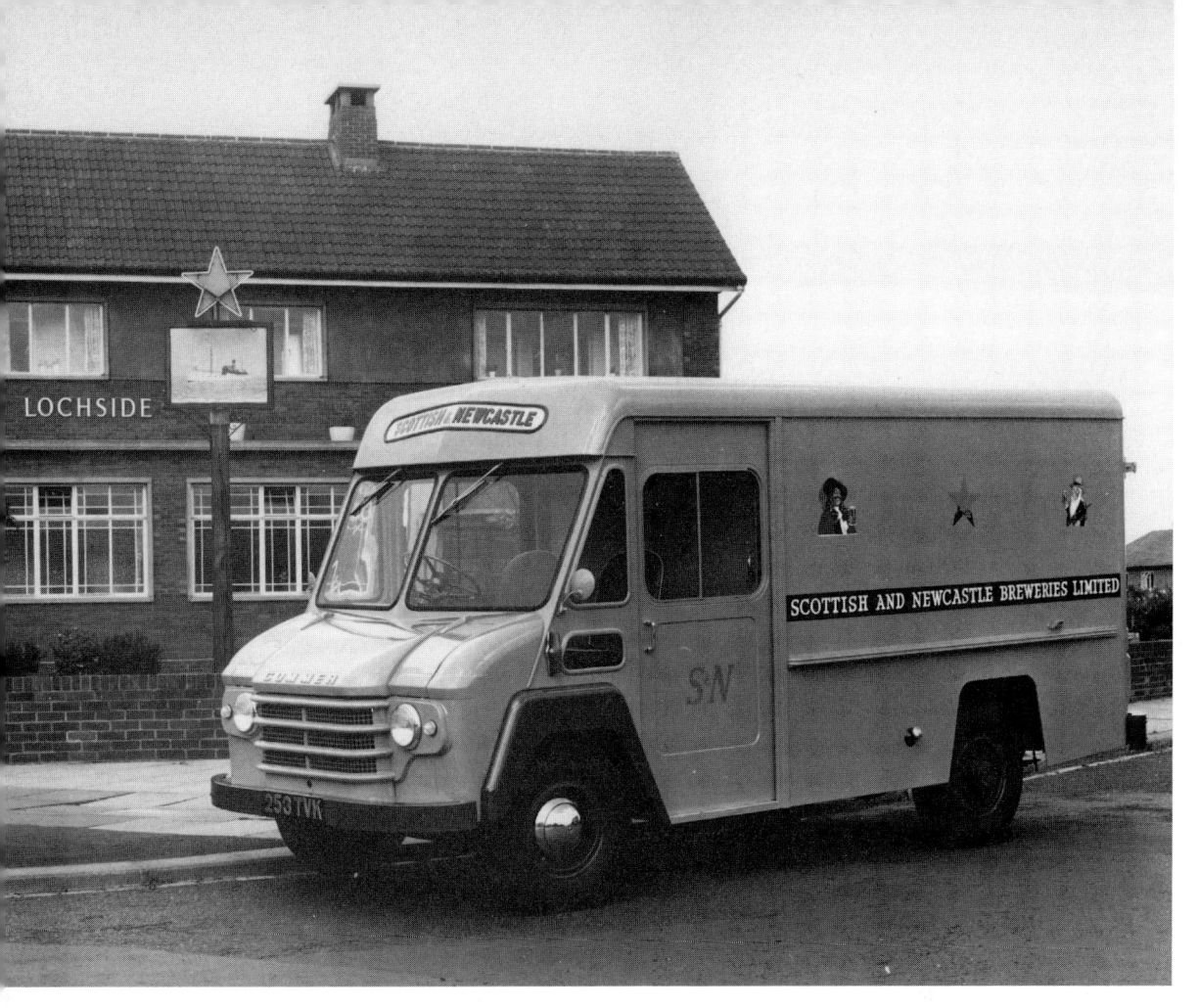

All bigger-engined Walk-Thru models, those fitted with the Perkins diesel or the 6-cylinder petrol unit, were given a projecting, curved radiator grille and bonnet, as seen on this 'Scottish & Newcastle Breweries Limited' 1½ton van.

versions with 4-cylinder petrol (4P.138) and light-diesel (0.138) engines in the 1½ and 2ton models, and the light-six (6P.181) de-rated Humber Super-Snipe petrol engine available in all models. A Perkins diesel (4.203) was the optional diesel. The basic van versions were offered on a variety of wheelbase lengths, as well as chassis/cab and chassis/front-end versions, to facilitate various body options. The chassis/cab versions utilized folding 'jack-knife' type doors, which were copied directly from the Divco.

However, it was very, very basic, and if any criticism was made, it would have come from drivers who had to put up with a noisy cab through lack of insulation, heavy steering, and an uncomfortable seat. The gearbox was a standard 4-speed synchromesh box with a floor-mounted lever.

The handbrake was mounted on the steering column. The Walk-Thru was not exactly big on creature comforts, but it was cheap and reliable, and for those reasons, operators loved it.

It was designed 'in-house' at Luton by Derek Scrivener and Doug Young, a new designer who had been brought in by A.J. Smith, over the head of Alec Single. There was, understandably, a great deal of animosity between the two designers, who had been thrown together by Smith. David Streeton concurs that there was 'a lot of friction between Alec Single and Doug Young at the time'. The body pressings for the front-end were made by the Wolverhampton-based firm, Willenhall Motor Radiator Co. Ltd.

Initially, a BF chassis was used to try out different suspension layouts. Ken Cain remembers

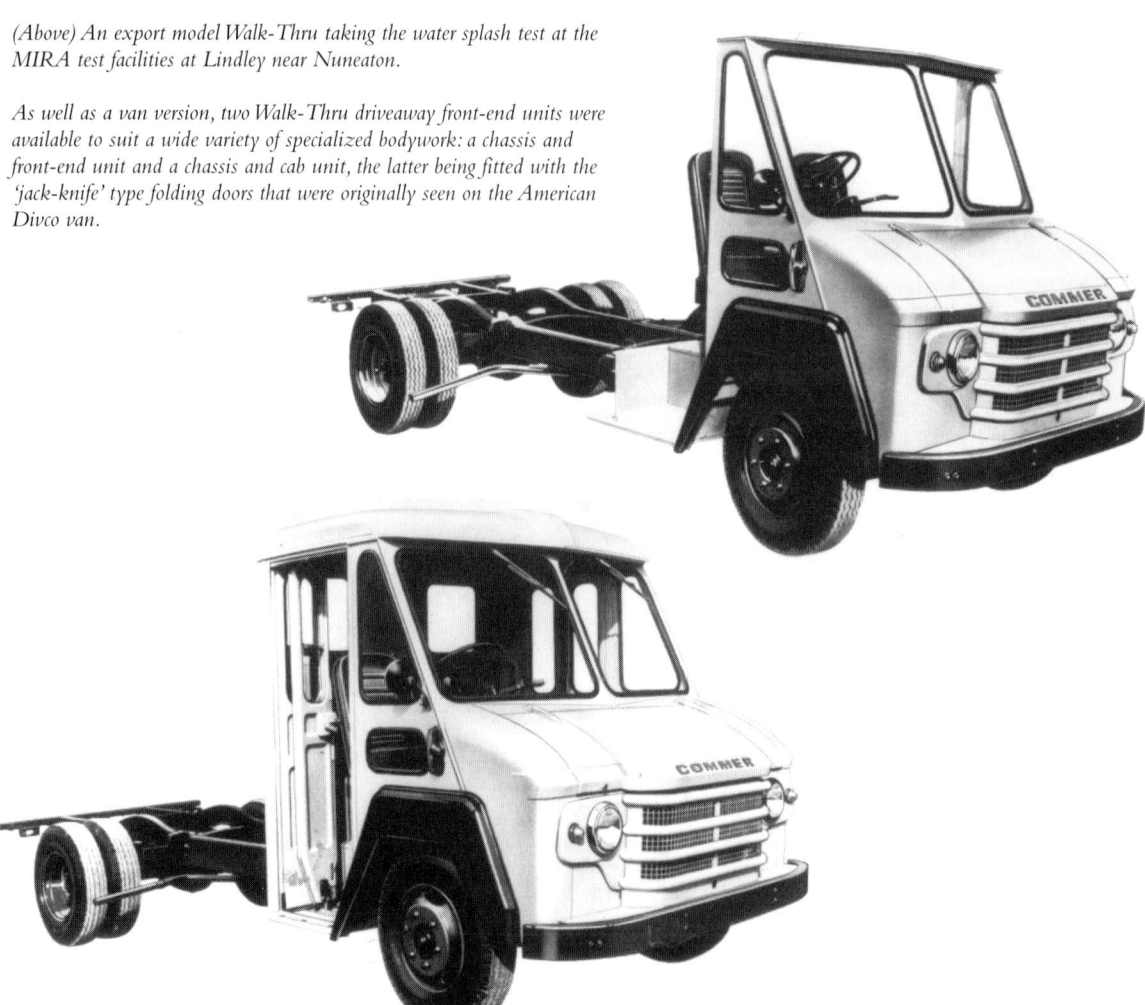

(Above) An export model Walk-Thru taking the water splash test at the MIRA test facilities at Lindley near Nuneaton.

As well as a van version, two Walk-Thru driveaway front-end units were available to suit a wide variety of specialized bodywork: a chassis and front-end unit and a chassis and cab unit, the latter being fitted with the 'jack-knife' type folding doors that were originally seen on the American Divco van.

For certain municipal customers the Karrier name was used. This Walk-Thru ambulance was built by Rootes Maidstone, and is shown on their stand at the 1965 Commercial Motor Show. The vehicle was supplied to 'Leeds and District Spastics Society'. Political correctness had not been invented in 1965!

that it all had to be changed when the Walk-Thru prototype chassis was built:

> We started it off with the same chassis as the BF, then changed to underslung springs, to get the back end down ... [but] it never did work ... the handling was so ... awful. So, we quickly went back to putting normal overtype springs on, and [that] overcame all our problems.
>
> We built three prototypes – a 30cwt, 2-tonner and 3-tonner. All this [was happening] at the same time as the CA and VA range [was being developed] and the PB van. It was a really busy time for us.

Like the PB van, the Walk-Thru would eventually wear a 'Dodge' badge. In the late seventies its place would be taken by the Dodge 50 Series. During the sixties, though, the PB and the Walk-Thru represented major contributions to the profits of the Rootes Group. All of the Commer-Karrier vehicles at this time were good sellers, which made the commercial vehicle operation very profitable. It was not surprising therefore, that there was a growing resentment from the workforce and management of the truck operations towards the car divisions, due to the disproportionate amount of investment that was put into cars compared with trucks and vans. As Peter Lewis says:

> The attitude was very much 'we make the profit, and they go and spend it!'

With the PB, Walk-Thru and the new forward-control C-series all being developed at the same time, the early sixties was one of the busier and more successful periods for Commer-Karrier. In 1960, nearly £4m worth of vehicles were sold in continental Europe. The European market, which didn't include the UK in those days, made up 23 per cent of all Rootes Group exports.

One of four Dodge Walk-Thru KB400s operated by Norwich Corporation in 1966. The supplying dealer, Reliance Garage of Norwich, designed and built their unique tipper bodies.

Volume Production at Dunstable

Demand for the new ¾ton van range had exceeded all expectations. In order to meet the demand a new production line was installed which effectively doubled the output of vehicles at Dunstable. It was the first Commer production line to adopt full-scale mass-production techniques.

The new line was also compact, taking up only 70,000sq ft (6,500sq m) of the 250,000sq ft (23,200sq m) of total factory space at Dunstable. The main assembly block measured 720ft (220m) by 330ft (100m) and had within it twelve bays, each 60ft (18m) wide. A new despatch department at the eastern end of the main block, which was completed in May 1959, itself had an area of 43,000sq ft (4,000sq m). To make maximum use of the floor space the six conveyors that had been installed were shaped like a double-S. A mezzanine floor contained the final colour paint shop, with continuous ovens operating on a return conveyor.

Commers always had a reputation for good build quality and finish, and the PB range was no exception. As well as a 'saloon car' paint finish, a number of anti-corrosive and protective finishes would be used during assembly. Latterly, wax-injection, an industry first on vans of this kind, was used on the PB range.

Two other separate assembly lines existed at Dunstable: One devoted to the assembly of larger Commer and Karrier trucks, and one for special-purpose and custom-built vehicles. Each line ran nearly 500ft (150m) in length, through the building from west to east.

By 1961, the final extension of 175,000sq ft (16,250sq m) was under way. This would allow for Walk-Thru assembly and for the remaining truck and van body production that had carried on at Biscot Road, to be moved to Dunstable.

Although the expansion of the Dunstable plant now meant that Commer could meet the anticipated demand for its vehicles and compete in what was getting to be an increasingly competitive marketplace, one perennial problem still existed: lack of skilled labour. Virtually every week *The Luton News* would carry adverts for skilled and semi-skilled jobs, such as fork-lift truck drivers, body builders, welders, body metal finishers, trimmers and vehicle

Assembled 1¼ton vans on the double tier conveyor, awaiting testing. In the background can be seen the trim line.

Luton – Number 2 Machine Shop Differential cases on multi-spindle drilling machines.

assemblers. Office staff were also needed – typists, telephonists, accounts personnel – the list went on. Both the Luton and Dunstable plants needed labour. Some of the posts had very specific criteria, most of which would be very politically incorrect today, such as: 'Male clerk aged 17–18'; 'female juniors aged 15–16'.

Due to the close proximity of Vauxhall and Bedford to Commer-Karrier, it is true to say that skilled motor tradesmen during this period could

One of the inspection stages on the newly installed Walk-Thru assembly line at Dunstable.

Walk-Thru body being lowered on to a chassis on the assembly line at Dunstable.

pick and choose their jobs according to who was paying the best wages – and they did!

Ironically, the labour situation could have been made even worse for Commer-Karrier had Rootes been given planning permission to develop the Dunstable site to build their new small car, the Hillman Imp. They had already been refused an Industrial Development Certificate to develop land opposite Ryton-on-Dunsmore, and so the next best option was Dunstable. From the Rootes' point of view, the problem of the difficult labour situation at Dunstable was greatly outweighed by the disadvantages of relocating to an area with an inexperienced and largely unskilled workforce. In the event, that is exactly what happened. Rootes were persuaded to build a factory at Linwood, Paisley in Scotland, which would prove to be a costly exercise fraught with problems.

The ill-fated Imp was in many ways a better car than its rival, the BMC Mini, but it was relatively short-lived. It also spawned the Commer 'Imp' van that replaced the Commer Cob in 1965, but the Imp was a poor replacement for the

During the incredibly busy early sixties period, advertisements for jobs at Commer Cars Ltd would appear in The Luton News *virtually every week. This one is from the March 10 1960 issue.*

Cob. Although the Imp was nippy and slightly more economical than the Cob, its unconventional rear-engine layout created impracticalities that operators of light delivery vans did not like. For example, the engine was only accessible through a load-floor compartment, which was no good if you had a breakdown and you were fully loaded. The presence of the engine under the floor also made the load floor high, and reduced the internal capacity of the van to 5cwt (250kg).

Commers Built in Rhodesia and Spain

The expansion of Rootes' commercial vehicle manufacturing was not just confined to Luton and Dunstable. In March 1960, a plant was opened in Salisbury, Southern Rhodesia (now Zimbabwe) to build the complete Commer and Karrier range from CKD assemblies from Dunstable. The new plant, which covered an area of 46,000sq ft (4,275sq m), was built at a cost of £100,000. It was intended that the new facility would serve the whole of Central Africa, which had enormous potential for new trucks and vans due to the rapid industrial development in the region. A new subsidiary had been formed to run the organization, Rootes (CA) (Pvt), Ltd, which was staffed by British and Rhodesian personnel. This was the first plant of its kind to be established by a British motor manufacturer.

Three years later, in October 1963, an agreement was made between Rootes and a Spanish company, Metalurgica de Santa Ana, for them to produce a 2ton version of the Walk-Thru. It was to be built at the MSA factory, in Linares, south of Madrid and would be known as the 'Commer-Santana Walk-Thru'. A new company was formed to handle the marketing of the van, Rootes Espana SA, with Brian Rootes as president. The vans were to be powered by either a 60bhp diesel or a 77bhp petrol engine made by

The last year of the Commer Cob van was 1965. It was replaced by the Imp van, but it was a poor substitute by comparison, its smaller size and unconventional layout not being conducive to fulfilling practical, everyday, small van duties.

(Below) The rear-engined Imp van may have been more economical than the Cob van as far as fuel consumption was concerned, but it still had the same inherent reliability problems of the saloon model. The fuel that the lady in the stiletto heels and white coat is pumping into the Imp is priced at 4s.11d. per gallon ... in other words, only £1.50 for a tank full of fuel!

'Commers For The Common Market': 'V' Series 7ton dropside trucks destined for Germany, being loaded at Regents Canal Dock, London, under the agreement between Rootes and Henschel Werke AG, the Kassel industrial undertaking, which included Walk-Thru vans. The agreement, made in September 1963, was meant to ensure sales of Commer vehicles in seven European countries, but it did not meet anticipated sales volumes for Commer.

MSA. The first Commer-Santana was unveiled at the 1963 Zaragosa Trade Fair on 1 October.

Rootes saw the venture as a way of getting into expanding markets that held restrictions on the import of built-up vehicles. In addition, there were opportunities to export Spanish-built vehicles to certain overseas markets that were closed to direct imports from the UK, but not to those from Spain.

While the Spanish idea was a sensible and logical step to take in order to obtain growth (Land Rover had set up a similar deal), on 6 September 1963, just prior to the Santana agreement, Rootes set up a deal with Henschel Werke AG which was to prove to be a disaster. Henschel, one of Germany's major producers of heavy trucks, and Rootes would establish a new joint sales and service organization to market Commers in seven European countries: Germany, France, Italy, Belgium, Luxembourg, Switzerland and

The Earls Court Commercial Motor Show 1962, Karrier and Commer stand. Note the BF 'Mr. Whippy' ice cream van in Karrier guise on the right of the picture.

Austria. Unfortunately, the deal did little to increase sales of Commer vehicles and proved to be a one-sided agreement, as Commer employees remember. Timothy Rootes instigated the deal, but as Ken Cain recalls: 'Tim Rootes really got his fingers burnt with that one'.

1962: The 'C' and 'V' Series

When the Bedford TK was introduced in 1960, it sent shock waves across the rest of the British commercial vehicle manufacturing industry. It offered operators a cheap, reliable truck in a very stylish package. The TK caused the same kind of a stir the Commer QX had done twelve years earlier, but by 1962 the QX was starting to look decidedly long in the tooth, despite well executed face-lifts and the fitting of the Perkins 6.354 diesel engine as standard equipment.

The first news of a replacement for the QX came in 1962 with a new Commer 8-tonner: the 'CA'. It featured an entirely new cab, designed and built by Sankey's in Birmingham, which was every

A 1962 CA 7½ton Unipower 6-wheeler conversion.

bit as stylish as the Bedford TK. Twin-headlamps flanked a horizontal-barred radiator grill, behind which lurked a TS-3 (3D.199) engine. The Commer 5-speed constant-mesh gearbox was used in the CA, and in March 1963 production of the Commer 5-speed synchromesh box commenced, which was then made available as an option. The new 8-tonner was available in two wheelbase lengths, either with a platform or dropsider body made by Rootes Maidstone, or a 6cu yd (4.6cu m) tipper version on the shorter wheelbase of the two. As with the QX, which continued to represent the 5 and 7ton payloads for Commer, the new CA 8-tonner was available with Eaton 2-speed axles and a Clayton Dewandre Airpak air-pressure servo, which boosted the Girling two-leading-shoe hydraulic brakes. (QX continued to use the Hydrovac system.) Cam Gears cam-and-peg steering gear was also used on the CA, and semi-elliptic springs at the front and rear.

As well as the 8-tonner, a new CA 7½-tonner was offered, which was in effect a combination of the QX 7-tonner and the new CA 8-tonner, with a choice of three wheelbases and petrol or TS-3 diesel engine options. New CA tractor units replaced the existing QX tractor units in the 10/11 and 12ton range, but it would not be until the following year, when the 'V' Series would replace the remaining QX models.

By 1963, the new Sankey cab was being fitted right across the Commer and Karrier range, and the QX had at last finished its fourteen-year tour of duty, with distinction. The Commer VA 4, 5, 6 and 7ton ranges filled in the gaps, along with corresponding Karrier Gamecock 4, 5 and 6ton chassis. Although the VA utilized the same body as the CA, its appearance differed by only having single headlamps. The TS-3 was not an option: instead either the Perkins 6.354 was fitted, or its 4-cylinder brother the 4.236, which was available towards the end of 1963 in the 4-tonner, as well as the 4,139cc 6-cylinder petrol engine (6P.252). A 4,752cc 6-cylinder petrol engine (6P.290) was available in the Commer 6-ton chassis, as was the new 5-speed synchromesh gearbox. The 4-speed constant-mesh box was standard equipment across the range, with the exception of the 7ton chassis which had the 5-speed synchromesh unit

A 1963 CA8 fitted with a 'Bulkflo' bulk feed delivery body.

(Below) An early 'VA' flatbed, complete with concrete blocks, used by the factory for testing. The Perkins-diesel powered 'V' Series differed visually from the 'C' Series by having single instead of twin headlamps.

fitted as standard. The VA was available in three wheelbase versions, including a tipper.

The Karrier Gamecock continued to be used for municipal applications, which included a seven-seat crew cab version, and the new Blenheim continuous loading refuse collector. The Bantam continued to use the old BLSP cab, as certain municipal requirements demanded that it would not die altogether. The new smaller Ramillies refuse collector, based on the Bantam chassis,

British Railways Bantam tractor units, and various airport vehicles (such as baggage and cargo loaders and aircraft servicing vehicles), all used the old cab right up until 1967 when both BLSP and Thrupp & Maberley were sold off.

In 1964, the CA became the 'CB', with only minor detail changes being made to specifications and appearance. The new maximum-gross class 14 and 16ton Maxiload with its up-rated TS-3 (3DA.215) engine and two-tone trimmed and padded cab offered the most significant changes. The following year the 'CC' models differed from the CB models only in terms of a further boosting of TS-3 power to 132bhp and a split-braking system, offered principally for the 24ton CC15 tractor unit. This unit had been introduced as a response to the 'Construction and Use' regulations, which required gross vehicle weights (g.v.w.) to be quoted by manufacturers in their vehicle specifications, instead of payloads. Introduced in 1964, these regulations virtually ended the prominence of the rigid 8-wheeler.

The Perkins-powered VA range continued, with the addition of an 8-ton 4-wheeler and a 12ton tractor unit. Both the CC and VA ranges were now available with 5 or 6-speed gearboxes. As with the C Series, the V Series designation would change as detail changes were made, and 'VA' became 'VB' in 1965 and subsequently 'VC'!

The C and V ranges continued to be a significant part of the Commer-Karrier (and Dodge) product range, through to the early seventies. Although a prominent player in the UK's medium to heavy vehicle market, it was generally

(Below) Subtle frontal styling changes were also in evidence on the new 'CC' Series and Maxiload range. The twin headlamps were lowered a couple of inches to the lower part of the grille 'lip', and the chrome 'COMMER' letters were now within the grille 'mouth'.

(Below right) The 'Luxury Plus' cab interior in the 'Maxiload', with seats trimmed in 'Balmoral Grey' welded leathercloth.

Its wider track and bigger wheels and tyres gave the 'Maxiload' a more muscular appearance than previous 'C' Series models. This CE16 Unipower three-axle rigid version was one of the first 20–22ton gross vehicles to be produced by Commer. It is finished in the distinctive blue and grey two-tone paint scheme of the sales department demonstration fleet.

acknowledged that the big Commers were competitively priced, but not always the cheapest trucks available. In 1963, the Bedford TK 7-tonner in standard dropsider form could be purchased for £1,359. An equivalent 7-tonner from the BMC camp, an Austin FJ K140 was the more expensive option at £1,695, while the CA 7-tonner on a 9ft 7in (2.8m) wheelbase would set you back £1,481. Buyers of Commers and Karriers knew, however, that they were getting a high quality, well-built truck that would last. As the advertising slogan stated: 'Whatever The Load, Commer Can Take It!'

Evidence of the quality of the C Series was borne out by the proving trials carried out by the Army during 1966. Norman Lawrence was involved in the trials with A.J. Smith and Jack Pringle:

> We built thirteen prototype CA multi-fuel TS-3 engined vehicles for the War Department [Fighting Vehicles Research & Development Establishment], the only vehicle(s) that the multi-fuel engine was put in. We were competing with Bedford [TK] and BMC. I had to go down to Farnborough and Bagshot, and we had a week to [trial] each vehicle. Our truck came out tops, with only one design fault. There was a horrible clanging sound [coming] from the front propshaft ... It was too close to the engine rear cross-member, and was hitting it. A phone call was made by A.J. Smith to Luton ... to check the drawings to see what the clearance was ... which was insufficient ... so they got a piece of flange to reinforce it ... to rectify it.
>
> The Bedford was breaking down all the time due to metal fatigue. They [Vauxhall-Bedford] reduced the thickness of the chassis frame to reduce weight. They had fitters and welders there ... We hadn't got anyone, apart from A.J. and Jack ... They still got the order though!
>
> BMC pulled out the second week ... Their engines blew up!

The FVR&DE had two TS-3-engined multi-fuel Commers on the approved supply list: a wide track 3/5ton 4×4, fitted with a 5ton power-

As with the C Series, the V Series also took on new front-end styling changes, to differentiate from previous models. Although their head office was in London, Electrolux, like Commer were a major Luton-based manufacturer.

(Below) As well as split-cab TS-3-engined multi-fuel Commers, a standard GS type 3/5ton truck with Marshall dropsider bodywork was also on the approved supply list for the Army.

An institution that died when employees became a 'marketable commodity' in the eighties was that of long service. Here, the loyalty and skill of employees that have contributed to the success of the company is acknowledged at the 1963 long-service awards dinner held in the Luton factory. Presentations were made by Geoffrey Cozens, former MD, to A.G. 'Curly' Toyer (bar lathe setter) for 40 years' service and for 25 years' service to Freddie M.S. Best (centre, front row, director and sales manager), A.S. Brightman (maintenance and electrical foreman), H. Janes (fitter assembler, chargehand, steering bench), J. Lake (rate fixer), H. Matthews (gear cutter), W.J. Pullen (assistant service manager), T. Reid (senior rate-fixer), A.E. Rooms (welder), J.E. Swann (heat treatment foreman), R. Turner (setter, stub line), D.R. Wright (works supervision foreman, Dunstable).

driven winch. This vehicle had a removable cab roof so that the whole vehicle, unladen, could be transported in a Hawker-Siddeley Argosy aircraft. The second was a standard GS type 3/5ton truck with Marshall dropsider bodywork.

1964: A Sad Year For Rootes

Despite the sales success of vehicles like the 'C' and 'V' forward-control series, and vans like the 1500/2500 and Walk-Thru, Rootes had not recovered from the financial bruising it had sustained as a result of the BLSP strike. Compounded with a drain on resources from the Linwood plant and the Hillman Imp, Rootes needed investment in order to keep up its expansion programme.

In June of 1964, the Rootes Group issued a statement to the press about a proposed acquisition by the Chrysler Corporation of America, of 30 per cent of the ordinary voting shares, and 50 per cent of non-voting 'A' shares of Rootes. The value of the offer was about £12.3m. The statement went on to say that: 'the Chrysler car and Dodge commercial vehicle operation in the U.K. would be combined with the Rootes Group as soon as possible'.

Rootes was no longer in a position to 'go it alone', but at least the Chrysler involvement meant that Rootes could implement its proposed development and expansion plans. When the agreement between Rootes and Chrysler was actually signed, the share acquisition for Chrysler was higher than first stated, at 46 per cent of ordinary voting shares and 65 per cent of 'A' non-voting shares.

Lord Rootes was clearly saddened by this turn of events, as John Bullock (Rootes' PR director), in his book about the Rootes' brothers recalled:

> Rupert Hammond [the accounts director with Rootes] told me later that Billy was far from happy about the deal even so, and had telephoned him late at night on the day they signed the agreement to tell him so and to ask if there was any way in which they could rescind the deal. Rupert Hammond recalled that when he told Billy that there was no way of going

Lord Rootes and Chrysler representatives on the Rootes stand at the 1964 Paris Motor Show following the announcement of the Rootes tie-up with Chrysler. Left to right are: Robert C. Mitchell, president and managing director of Chrysler International; Sir Reginald Rootes, deputy chairman of the Rootes Group; Louis B. Warren, a director of the Chrysler Corporation; Lord Rootes, chairman of the Rootes Group; Irving J. Minett, group vice-president, international operations, Chrysler Corporation; Geoffrey Rootes, managing director of Rootes Motors Ltd.

back on the agreement, he sighed and said, 'I just hope we have done the right thing, but I feel we may all live to regret the involvement with Chrysler. I wish we could do something about it, but I suppose you are right and there is nothing we can do now.'

In public, Lord Rootes, in his inimitable manner, put a brave face and a different gloss on the deal in an interview at the Paris Motor Show in October, with the BBC's Raymond Baxter, which also included Irving J. Minett, group vice-president, international operations, Chrysler Corporation. A transcript of some of the interview is as follows:

Raymond Baxter: What are your personal feelings now that you will have three American directors on your board?
Lord Rootes: Naturally I'm delighted because I've always stood for Anglo-American relations and the expansion of trade between our two countries, and the three directors joining us, I'm quite confident, are going to give us no end of assistance and we shall be a good team.

Raymond Baxter: This leads me to my second question, which is this. As a former chairman of the Dollar Export Board, what is your reaction to the increased American participation in British business, and an increasing tendency to control British business?
Lord Rootes: For over twelve years I have been visiting America with the object of getting British industry to invest in America; equally to get Americans to come and invest in England. I believe that it is through this co-operation of interest in industry that we shall be able to be more successful on both sides of the Atlantic.
Raymond Baxter: You have no fears then, sir, that we are losing our economic independence?
Lord Rootes: Not a bit, not a bit. I'm not an inward looking man – I look outwards.
Raymond Baxter: A technical question, Lord Rootes. Will any of your Rootes plants in Great Britain be turned over to Chrysler or Dodge production?
Lord Rootes: That has been made quite clear in the offer – that the boot is on the other foot; namely that Chrysler have been generous enough to say that we have the option of taking over the Chrysler and

The Dodge D300 used the 'LAD' cab, so called because it was also shared with Leyland and Albion. This 1964 Perkins diesel-powered version was probably one of the last 300s to be built at Kew before Rootes took over.

Dodge interests in Great Britain. This will be to the benefit of all concerned.

Raymond Baxter then asked some questions of Irving Minett:

Raymond Baxter: Do you envisage any new policy or policy trends?
Irving Minett: We do not expect the policies of the Rootes Group to change in any sense whatsoever as a consequence of this relationship. The Rootes management, the Rootes name, the Rootes product lines and the Rootes organization in Britain and the world will be maintained – but we hope it will be developed and enhanced and will experience important growth as the consequence of our new association.

In fact, Lord Rootes' worst fears were confirmed, and the deal turned out to be a poisoned chalice. Although Rootes was still technically independent, the hoped-for co-operation between the two companies did not materialize. The agreement was one-sided, and it was clear that Chrysler's ambitions did not include furthering the progress of Rootes. Immediately, cars began to appear with discreet little 'Pentastar' logos on the front wings, and all Rootes car and truck literature boldly displayed the 'Pentastar'.

With the winter of 1964, came the sad news of the death of Lord Rootes, on 12 December, aged seventy. Geoffrey Rootes succeeded to his title. Tributes were paid to the man who had help create the organization that bore his name, by distinguished personalities from within and outside of the motor trade. More significantly, he was respected by many of the employees in the Group. Fred Lewis recalls one of the times he met Lord Rootes:

> I used to attend the annual dinners at the Dorchester, and year after year, the dealers and staff went through and were greeted by Lord Rootes and Sir Reginald. Lord Rootes would greet everyone by name – He had a fantastic memory!

1965: Rootes Acquire Dodge

By the early part of 1965, Rootes had acquired Dodge Brothers (Britain) Ltd, and with it their manufacturing facility at Kew, Surrey. By the spring of 1965, Commers would be sold with Dodge badges on them, and Dodges with Commer badges on. The reasoning behind this was that Dodge had traditionally concentrated on the medium and heavy range market sector, while Commer had tended to specialize in the lower and medium weight range of vehicles. It seemed sensible to integrate the Dodge and Commer dealer networks to allow both to offer a wider range of vehicles.

In January 1965, Rootes signed an agreement with the Iran National Industrial Manufacturing Company of Tehran, to make Commer 2500 1ton vans, as well as the Hillman Super Minx and Singer Vogue. The deal added an additional 5,000 vehicles a year to Rootes' export figures.

After declaring a profit of nearly £2m in 1963–64, Rootes recorded a loss of £927,812 in 1965. The following year, a massive expansion programme costing £3m commenced at Dunstable. It included a 172,000sq ft (16,000sq m) extension to the existing assembly plant, with new assembly tracks and a new paintshop. A 71,000sq ft (6,600sq m) office block was also planned. The main aim was to allow Dodge production to be transferred to Dunstable from Kew.

In 1965, the Commer works director, Don Burgess died suddenly, aged sixty-six. He had been works director since the new Dunstable

Commer LA6 low-loader with the Dodge tilt-cab. Engine options were the Chrysler-Cummins V-6 or Perkins 6.354 diesels.

plant had opened in 1955. He was replaced by W.C. (Cliff) Toll. Also, in August 1965, Rex Watson Lee, as the commercial division's managing director, announced that F.J. Willard, the American-born boss of Dodge at Kew, would be taking on the role of managing director of Commer Cars and Karrier Motors, as well as his existing role as managing director of Dodge.

During the following few months, Chrysler tightened its grip on Rootes, and by the New Year of 1967, Rootes would find itself 'under new management'.

Dodge K700 'medium-range' truck with an all-steel 7 cubic yard tipper body. In order to give as wide a range of vehicles as possible to both Rootes and Dodge dealers, Commers could become Dodges and vice-versa.

(Below) The Dodge stand at the 1966 Commercial Motor Show, Earls Court, London.

9 The Chrysler Takeover

Chrysler's mistake was that they thought that a truck was just a car with a big boot!
Norman Smith, Commer Service Manager

As the sixties drew to a close, so the supply and demand curve on Britain's economic chart started to change direction. Demand was no longer outstripping supply, as had been the case in Britain during the post-war boom, and problems for truck manufacturers were compounded by increased competition from continental makes, such as Daf, Volvo and Scania. The problem was, however, far worse for the car sector which had to endure threats from European and Japanese imports. It was partly this situation that found Rootes unable to continue operating without further investment capital.

Chrysler Take Control of Rootes

The Group's loss on trading for the six months to January 1967 was reported as being in excess of £4.7m. The government subsequently gave Chrysler Corporation permission to acquire a majority 77 per cent shareholding in the Rootes Group. For Rootes, it was the end of the road.

An injection of £20m to add to their existing £27m stake in Rootes was promised by Chrysler.

The Rootes stand at the 1967 Tripoli Trade Fair: a Hillman Hunter and a Hillman Imp flank a Commer V Series dropsider.

The Chrysler Takeover

A reception was held at London's Ritz Hotel on 5 April 1967, to mark the retirement of Sir Reginald Rootes. From left to right: Rex Watson Lee, Mrs Brian Rootes, Rupert Hammond and John Bullock.

Nationalization had apparently been considered by the then Labour government under Harold Wilson, but it was rejected. Instead, an additional £3m was put in by the government, so that a 'watchdog' from the Industrial Reorganisation Corporation could be appointed to the Chrysler board to oversee the American company's activities. Bernard Boxall joined Sir Eric Roll, a former permanent under-secretary to the Department of Economic Affairs, Erwin H. Graham, vice president of Chrysler's European operations, Georges Hereil, chairman of Simca and W.J. Tate, from Chrysler, on the new board.

In February 1967, at the age of seventy, Sir Reginald Rootes retired as chairman of Rootes Motors Ltd. The following month Brian and Timothy Rootes resigned from the Rootes' board, although Timothy, Sir Reginald's son, remained divisional managing director of sales and distribution. Brian left the Group after twenty-seven years' service. Rupert Hammond, Rootes' financial director, who had reached retirement age, also resigned after thirty-eight years' service with Rootes.

Lord Rootes replaced his uncle, Sir Reginald, as chairman, and remained managing director until Gilbert Hunt took over as managing director and chief executive officer on 1 May 1967. Hunt joined the new Rootes Motors Ltd from Massey-Ferguson in Coventry where he had been managing director since 1960. Under Hunt, the car and truck divisions were quickly merged, and a new management structure put in place. On the truck side, A.J. Smith was made engineering-truck director, being responsible for Commer-Karrier and Dodge. Bill Garner returned from Linwood as manufacturing director for the Luton and Dunstable sites in September 1967. Rex Watson Lee became director of the sales division, which also presided over the parts division, with Joe Woodin as the parts director.

The next principal task for Rootes was to close the Kew plant and move Dodge production to Dunstable. Bill Holmes, who was transferred from Coventry in 1967 to Dunstable as Planning Manager, was involved in closing the plant down. Geoffrey Booth was a sales liaison manager at Kew and remembers the last vehicles to be made at Kew: '... forty-four Dodge 500-K1100 tankers for Esso, with Cummins V-8s and Allison automatic 'boxes with integral retarders'.

By the end of 1967, Kew had been closed and the land sold to a London property company,

Chrysler in Britain: The First Forty Years

Chrysler's involvement in Britain goes back to 1924, when it acquired the Maxwell Car Company, which built a range of touring cars in the States and supplied the British-owned subsidiary Maxwell Motors Ltd in London. Maxwell was already well-established in Britain, having formed a company in Great Portland Street, London, in 1919. The following year, larger premises at Lupus Street, Pimlico were acquired and in 1922 Maxwell Motors acquired 14½ acres (5.9ha) of land at Kew to build an assembly shop, offices, parts and service depots.

In 1924, when Chrysler took over the Maxwell Car Company in the States, and subsequently Maxwell Motors Ltd at Kew, it started to import built-up Chrysler cars from the parent company. The name of the company was changed to Maxwell-Chrysler Ltd, although it remained in British hands. In 1925, the name was changed again: to Chrysler Motors Ltd. The acquisition of Maxwell was the beginning of Walter P. Chrysler's new venture as an independent car maker. With the Maxwell designs he created the Chrysler '70', which was an instant hit on the American market. In 1928, Chrysler Export Corporation acquired the share capital in Chrysler Motors Ltd, and an American, C. MacAire, was appointed managing director in place of A. De la Poer, who had run the British concern from the start.

In July 1928, Dodge was acquired by the Chrysler Corporation. The following year, the Plymouth name was created and used on the Chrysler '50', and subsequently to represent Chrysler's 'low-priced' car lines. Another brand, DeSoto, was introduced by Chrysler the same year to fill in the market gaps between Chrysler and Plymouth. Walter P. Chrysler had, in effect, taken a leaf out the book of his friend and colleague at General Motors, Alfred P. Sloan, by creating car lines for different price brackets, as

continued overleaf

During the thirties, drivers who stopped at a café on the A3 Portsmouth Road out of London, could have their photograph taken by their vehicle, and collect it upon their return journey. Here, two chaps pose by their early thirties' Dodge Brothers 1–1½ton van.

Two 1935 Dodge 1ton vans with English-built bodies used by Selfridge's department store.

Chrysler in Britain: The First Forty Years *continued*

(Above) On the left of the photograph are two mid-thirties examples of the British-built Dodge semi-forward-control style of cab, and on the right a contemporary American-style Dodge tipper.

The cab styling of this Dodge 200 Series 5/6ton high-sided tipper shows the uncanny likeness to its contemporary, the Commer Superpoise.

Sloan had done with Chevrolet, Oakland (later Pontiac), Oldsmobile, Buick and Cadillac. The De Soto name was used on trucks for certain export markets, as well as that of Fargo, which was primarily used for heavy-duty trucks and coaches.

Dodge had started to build a reputation for innovative and reliable cars, however, long before Chrysler came along. Brothers John and Horace Dodge started building bicycles in 1899, after they left their birthplace in Niles, Michigan, to move to Windsor, Ontario. They progressed to building car components in Hamtramck, Michigan, prior to going into car production in 1914, where the first Dodge automobile was made. Both brothers died in 1920, but the name of Dodge continued to be associated with rugged, dependable cars and trucks.

In Britain too, the Dodge name was fast gaining a reputation for quality vehicles. In May 1922, Dodge Brothers (Britain) Ltd was formed as a wholly-owned subsidiary of Dodge Brothers Inc. The company's first factory was at Stevenage Road,

Fulham, in south-west London. There, the parent company's cars and chassis were brought in fully assembled. The first chassis imported were the 'No. 1 Passenger Chassis', which was adapted to carry a 15cwt van, the 'No. 6 Chassis', for Limousines, Landaulettes and other special bodywork, and the 30cwt 'Graham' truck, bodies for these being supplied by various outside coachbuilders. By 1924, the American-built Graham Brothers' truck chassis, with its Dodge powerplant and English bodywork was proving to be a popular delivery van, and contributed considerably to Dodge Brothers' total sales to the British market in 1924 of 1,552 vehicles. In May 1925, Dodge Brothers (Britain) Ltd moved to new premises at Park Royal, north-west London, which had enough space to accommodate a woodmill, body and paint shops and a chassis assembly line.

In the States, largely through the association of Dodge with the Evansville, Indiana-based Graham Brothers company, the volume of commercial chassis had grown to 20 per cent of total Dodge output. After the deaths of John and Horace Dodge, the company had been operated by the Dodge heirs until 1925, when Graham Brothers Trucks joined the Dodge company. That same year, Dodge was bought by Dillon, Read & Company, a New York banking firm, for $146m. On 30 July 1928, the company was purchased by Chrysler Corporation which, under the guiding hand of its founder, Walter P. Chrysler, was destined to become one of the world's largest motor manufacturing companies.

With the acquisition by Chrysler, it was decided to move Dodge Brothers to the Chrysler Motors' premises at Kew, in order to concentrate on a range of trucks for the British market, that would be known as the Dodge Kew range. At around the same time preparations were being made to assemble Plymouth cars on a separate line at Kew. During the thirties, production volumes of the 'all-British' Dodge truck range and the Chrysler car range continued to increase. The company went to great pains to point out the increasing amount of British components that were being used on the car range, which also had local names: Chrysler Kew, Richmond and Wimbledon.

During the war the factory made Dodge trucks for the Ministry of Supply, and components for the Halifax bomber. The post-war period saw more concentration on the production of trucks, although there was an increase in sales of American-built Chrysler cars and French Simca saloon cars during the sixties. Both were distributed from Kew.

The entrance to the Dodge works. The site became an industrial estate for a period of time during the seventies.

A Dodge 300 being inspected, and a 200 Series behind it, at the Dodge plant at Kew.

Among the last vehicles to be manufactured at Kew were a batch of 44 Dodge 500-K1100 2,800 gallon tankers for Esso Petroleum Ltd. They were fitted with Cummins V-8s and Allison automatic gearboxes with integral retarders.

ending what was in itself a colourful chapter in the Chrysler story in Britain.

1967: The Culture Clash

Within months of Chrysler gaining control of Rootes, a culture clash between the Chrysler management and the old Rootes management resulted in neither camp agreeing on the future direction of the company. The Yanks were intransigent and insisted that things were done their way, while the 'old-school' believed that they knew what the market wanted, and that they had been successful in satisfying that market for a great many years. Bill Holmes remembers one of his first encounters with the Chrysler 'system' when:

> ... A set of Policy and Procedure Manuals were dumped on my desk and I was told, 'This is the way we operate at Chrysler'.

A.J. Smith was dismissive of Chrysler to the point of contempt:

> Chrysler put in procedures and systems for the UK, but they were only relevant to the USA ... They made cars like shelling peas!

It is also important to bear in mind that the Rootes' truck operations had, by and large, been profitable, despite inadequate investment. It was the car side of the business that had drained Rootes' resources.

The effects of the different attitudes and aspirations of Chrysler management also started to permeate through to the workforce. For the first time, a usually co-operative workforce was starting to show signs of mistrust and militancy. Apart from the BLSP debacle in 1961, and a few minor skirmishes at Ryton, there had been no significant industrial relations problems at Rootes' production plants in Luton, Dunstable or Coventry, until Chrysler took over.

The Luton and Dunstable plants in particular had gained an enviable reputation for good workforce/management relations, but a series of minor disputes in the autumn of 1967 had started to affect

Export Dodge 500s being loaded on to ships for use by UNICEF.

the company, creating a volatile industrial relations atmosphere.

In October, the company was put on a four-day week, affecting about half of the 1,200 workforce. In response, forty workers in the toolroom staged a one-day sit-down strike, claiming that there was more than enough work to keep them busy for five days a week. In November, short-time working finished, but not before some of the Luton and Dunstable workforce had left to join Vauxhall, who were expecting to recruit 3,000 extra workers between November 1967 and the spring, in anticipation of the success of the new Victor saloon. The headlines in *The Luton News* for 2 November hailed: 'As the Vauxhall orders pour in – OVERTIME GALORE AND MORE JOBS'. Meanwhile, a token strike by 800 workers at Dunstable over storemen being given overtime by management, without consultation with union shop stewards, was supported by the entire hourly paid workforce of 894 men at Luton, who came out in sympathy with Dunstable.

Although management had agreed to review the pay of workers at Dunstable, in order to bring wages more into line with Vauxhall, pay negotiations did not progress quickly enough for the workforce, and during the last week of November fifty workers on the PB assembly line walked out. The dispute was over a claim for increased waiting time allowances. A few days later, 130 men were sent home following a work to rule by forty-four men in the body section. The *Dunstable Evening Post* on 5 December reported:

> Because of absenteeism in the trim and chassis sections of the plant, supplies of components to the final assembly line have fallen below the normal level ... Normally 185 van bodies a week are fed into the final assembly line. Mr Jack Button, works convenor of the Amalgamated Engineering Union at the Dunstable factory ... said that the men's piecework earnings were being reduced because of the shortage of bodies.

As one dispute followed another, an outside dispute involving the supply of Walk-Thru body panels from Willenhall Radiators compounded production problems at Commer. The dispute went on through to the New Year, resulting in more workers being laid off at Dunstable.

Various pay disputes continued to disrupt production until 1969, when a pay and productivity agreement was accepted by Rootes' workers. As well as pay increases, higher overtime rates, and improvements in holiday pay, all employees were put on a fixed hourly rate. In a press release in June 1969, Gilbert Hunt stated that:

> The successful conclusion of pay and productivity agreements at our plants, to match the investment in new production facilities, is vital to the Company's long term development.
>
> It is a significant advance in the motor industry and in the progressive reconstruction of Rootes.
>
> We always appreciated that the Coventry proposals would be most difficult on which to reach agreement, because of the tradition of piecework in the Midlands.

Sadly, life at Commer continued to get worse before it got better, and by the end of the first year under Chrysler, the company reported a loss of nearly £11m.

Rex Watson Lee did not see eye-to-eye with the American Chrysler management, and in November 1967 he resigned to run a car dealership in Ryde, on the Isle of Wight. He was, after all, a Rootes' man and could probably see the writing on the wall for Rootes. Another experienced Rootes' truck man, Cliff Toll, director and general works manager of the truck operations, also resigned at the end of November. He had been with Rootes since 1956, and went to join the British Motor Corporation Light Commercial Division in Birmingham.

The 'culture clash' that had prevailed also extended to product policy, and the Chrysler management held the view that the municipal range was not profitable. Consequently, Karrier

A high-lift cargo van on a Commer VC 5ton chassis.

(Above) An 18 cubic yard 'Dual Tip' Refuse Collector on a Karrier Gamecock WC5 chassis.

A Karrier Bantam 11–15 cubic yard 'Blenheim Junior' refuse collector.

became more of a model name, rather than a marque in its own right. To add to the confusion, the Karrier name started to appear on Commers if, for example, a vehicle was ordered and that particular operator was a 'municipal' customer. Similarly, the Karrier Gamecock was effectively a re-badged Commer utilizing the same Sankey cab.

One of the bones of contention for Rex Watson Lee had been Chrysler's inability, or unwillingness, to view the municipal product range as an important key to the success of Rootes commercial products in general. Cyril Corke was municipal sales manager until Chrysler took over, and was then sent to Bristol as regional sales manager handling cars and trucks. He was at the sharp end of the argument:

> Rex Watson Lee asked our accountant George Hopkinson to do a financial study, and he found it [the municipal business] to be very profitable indeed. The selling spin-off was that if a vehicle was good enough for the council, it was good enough for the lighter end of the market ... local tradesmen.

Other Rootes' managers shared the same opinion regarding the municipal business. Fred Lewis was one:

> The worst factor [when Chrysler took over] was when we ditched Karrier and lost all of the municipal business. At one time, Karrier must have had 80 per cent of the business ... Overnight, the business just faded. Dodge didn't fit into the municipal business.

The Cummins V-8 Engine: An Unmitigated Disaster!

Dodge at Kew had been associated with Cummins' engines since 1963, when a joint venture was signed between Chrysler Motors Ltd and the Cummins Engine Company Inc. of Columbus,

The ill-fated Cummins V-8 VALE engine.

Indiana to manufacture a range of diesel engines. These included the VAL and VALE 6- and 8-cylinder engines that were being developed by Cummins. Prior to this Dodge had bought in diesel powerplants from AEC, Leyland and Perkins. Dodge had produced their own 6-cylinder petrol engine at Kew, but when demand fell, the line was sold off to Chrysler Argentina in 1960.

A new company, Chrysler-Cummins Ltd, was formed on 19 August 1963, with the intention of providing a complete range of engines for all Dodge trucks. A 30-acre (12.2ha) site was acquired at Darlington, Co. Durham to establish manufacturing facilities.

The plan was that Chrysler would use their own engine, the Cummins V-8 VALE, in all future heavy Commer and Dodge models. It was also intended that the VALE powerplant would replace the TS-3, but Chrysler's plans backfired.

In theory the Cummins V-8 was a well-designed engine, and during development testing showed every sign of being a reliable unit, but in practice, the opposite was the truth. It was a high-revving engine, developing 170bhp at 3,000rpm and Commer engineers and service managers were rapidly made aware of its quirks and foibles, as a picture of questionable reliability became apparent. Geoff Booth recalls that 'The first prototype engines were very dry – no diesel mist or oil leaks', but David Bryant, a Dodge regional manager, had 'a 100 per cent failure rate' in his area, and problems were not only confined to the V-8.

> A man at Bury with a 500/K1100, for the first four months never got to London ... We had a spate of flywheel bolts breaking ... the crankshaft pulley/vibration damper to which the fan was attached used to come undone, and half [of] the pulley used to come off and hit the radiator.
>
> On the V6 VAL, the oil pressure relief valve exit hole was not big enough, so oil pressure soared during cold start-up, i.e. on frosty mornings, and used to blow the end off the oil pressure sender unit.

Problems with the engines were made worse due to drivers who were not used to coping with such a high-revving engine, and who did not adapt their style of driving accordingly. A.J. Smith was well aware of this aspect of the engine's characteristics:

> An ordinary commercial vehicle engine gave its peak torque at about 1,100 to 1,200rpm, but this Cummins engine didn't give its peak torque until 2,100rpm. When the revs dropped off, the driver [would] let it go too far, and he'd have to play old Harry with the gearbox to keep the vehicle going ... I told the sales boys, 'You should tell them that they can't drive this [in] the same [way] as the old ones'!

Journalist Ron Cater, when commenting in *Commercial Motor* about the Esso Petroleum order for Dodge 500s with Allison automatic boxes, had formed a similar view to that of A.J. Smith:

> I had forecast some three years earlier that the high-speed Cummins VALE engine would be more readily acceptable to the average British truck driver if it was coupled with automatic transmission.

The standard transmission that was fitted in the Dodge 500, as well as other problematical aspects to the vehicle, made the driving experience even worse. Norman Lawrence took the opportunity to make his feelings about the vehicle known to management:

> Chrysler phased out the TS-3 for the Cummins, which was a load of rubbish! The Dodge 500 series [had] a 6-speed crash gearbox, air-assisted two-speed axles, [and] no power steering – boy were they hard to drive. I took one out on test on the M1 ... My first recommendations were to get our own gearbox ... They put our own 5-speed 'box in, and with the Perkins engine and electric 2-speed axles, it was a good vehicle.
>
> The cab wasn't bad on the 500, but I got into trouble for making my suggestions [to management]. One day, I had to take Mr Watson Lee out on a test drive in the new CA887 long-wheelbase 8-tonner. My governor at the time was Mr Ron Dowthwaite, who said I had got to pick up Mr Watson Lee at his house at Woburn Sands at 8am, and take him to Bison Hill [where most of the Commer hill tests were carried out]. I was told, 'Don't speak to him unless he speaks to you'... Then when he asked me about the Dodge 500, I told him ..., but I got told off by Don Burgess when I got back!

John Horley was a supervisor on engine development and testing at Tilling-Stevens, and transferred to Dunstable when Chrysler took over:

> The TS-4 [4-cylinder 2-stroke] was shelved by Chrysler due to their involvement with Cummins ... The Cummins engine was a very troublesome engine. [It was] a high revving engine ... a new concept for a diesel engine, particularly of that size. It was eventually dropped, because of its unreliability, in favour of Perkins.

In July 1968, the decision was made to fit the Perkins V-8 510 engine as the standard powerplant in the Dodge 500 Series. It was available from January 1969, thus ending the short and somewhat ignoble career of the Cummins V-8.

With the Perkins unit in place and a number of other improvements that were made, the Dodge 500 Series went on to become a good seller, as David Bryant affirms:

> When the Dodge 500 came to Dunstable, Jim Pullen, the service manager, and Norman Smith, the assistant service manager sorted out all the problems. They were a good team ... and they turned it into the best-selling 16-tonner on the market!

The Ghost of Whitley Abbey

The fortunes of Rootes improved dramatically in 1968, when the company announced an operating profit of £927,000 for the six months ending 2 February 1968. Car sales had increased by 28 per cent, which had contributed to the books going back into the black, but much of the profit had come from the sale of buildings and land at Dunstable and the Dodge plant at Kew. Critics of the new management team just saw this as 'selling off the family silver'. The company did, however, appear to be turning the corner and there was evidence of real investment now being put into Coventry and Dunstable. Unfortunately, during 1968 the market share of the truck operation had reduced from 9.6 per cent to 7.9 per cent, no doubt due in part to the numerous technical and production problems encountered whilst incorporating Dodge into the Rootes' truck operations. Even so, by the end of the year, profits had leapt to £2.7m, and in anticipation of increased orders following the Commercial Motor Show, a recruitment drive started for about a hundred new employees to work at Luton and Dunstable, which included machine operators, assembly workers, welders and trimmers.

In June 1968, Rootes took a lease on a huge office block overlooking Dunstable's main shopping centre, with the intention of centralizing the car and truck engineering departments. Meanwhile, rumours had been rife about a proposal to move these departments to Coventry, but emphatically denied by management. As well as about 300 draughtsmen and design staff, 282 employees were transferred to the new administrative building at Quadrant House, from what was the old Commer headquarters at Biscot Road.

Rumour and counter-rumour continued throughout the year, until it was announced in March 1969 that, indeed, the Rootes' design and engineering teams would be moving to Coventry. Quadrant House was to be retained by the company, but a new 'Engineering and Technical Administration Centre' was to be established at Whitley, near Coventry.

In October 1968, Rootes purchased the 187-acre (76ha) site from Hawker Siddeley Dynamics for £1.8m. In Gilbert Hunt's announcement to the press at the Geneva Motor Show in March, he stated that, 'Whitley will be one of the best equipped technical design centres in the industry'. Rootes planned to spend £4m on establishing the new centre, over £2m of that investment being spent that year on adapting and equipping the site and the 470,000sq ft (43,660sq m) of buildings. By the end of 1969, it was intended that the centre would be

A 1967 Cummins-powered Dodge 500 K Series fuel-oil tanker by the River Thames, with one of the chimneys of Battersea Power Station providing part of the backdrop. An advantage the Dodge 500 had was that it enabled Rootes to offer a factory-built trailing axle or tandem-drive 6-wheeler rigid, whereas Commer 6-wheeler models had to be converted by Universal Power Drives Ltd. A 'Dodge-Unipower' option did, however, become available in the re-launched 500 K Series, along with the Perkins V-8 540 engine.

operational, with 1,600 employees working under Rootes' director of product planning and development, H.J.C. Weighell.

Although the site had been associated with aircraft research and development since 1923 when it was established by Sir W.G. Armstrong Whitworth Aircraft Ltd, and prototypes of many famous aircraft had been produced there, including the Whitley bomber, the site held mixed feelings for some people who worked there. The Whitley works was built on the site of the old Whitley Abbey, and was certainly shrouded in mystery, as well as having its own ghost! Roger Jenkins was a senior development engineer on the car side, who moved on to truck development during the Chrysler period:

> Whitley Abbey was haunted, and no company that [had] existed on the site had success there... [Also] the only maps that were available when the plant was extended after the war were Luftwaffe reconnaissance maps.

Administration staff continued to occupy Quadrant House at Dunstable until 1971, when they were moved to the Chrysler International offices at Bowater House in London.

With the re-launch of the Dodge 500 K Series and the completion of production facilities to accommodate the big Dodges, came the transfer of PB chassis frame manufacture to Dunstable from Linwood. All PB manufacture could now be controlled at one plant.

All efforts were on to try and stop the slide in sales of Rootes commercial vehicles, and this was reflected in the 1969 sales figures. The Society of Motor Manufacturers and Traders' figures for the year recorded 31,422 trucks being built, with the car operations putting out 172,647 units. As well as a high profile at the London and Scottish Commercial Shows, truck products were shown alongside Rootes cars at the Tripoli International Trade Fair in March 1968, and a display of fourteen vehicles at the Amsterdam Motor Show the previous month. Holland had always been one of Rootes' best export territories, with new vehicles being specified by the Dutch Government as a result of the show.

New appointments were also being made to ensure maximum sales of Rootes' products. In April 1968, Joe Campeau was appointed home sales director. The 43-year-old Canadian had held a number of executive positions with Chrysler Corporation, and had been with Chrysler Leasing before coming to Britain. A newly created post of marketing services director was occupied by John T. Panks, an experienced Rootes' sales manager and ex-Austin apprentice who had been general manager of Rootes Motors Inc., New York since 1954. In 1965 he went to head up the Rootes Export Division.

In 1969, Geoffrey Ellison was appointed director of sales and marketing, and Des Thompson took over from Bill Garner who went to Automotive Products. In October 1969, Rootes scored an export record. Almost 50 per cent of total production went for export, 32 per cent more than the previous year. Of that total, 10,732 vehicles were trucks. A large proportion of the export figure came from a contract with the Sudan worth £2.25 million, to supply 1,845 vehicles of which 1,420 were medium and heavy commercial vehicles. About 1,300 were CKD (completely knocked down) trucks for assembly at the Sudanese Government's Motor Transport Works, and the remainder, which included coaches, buses and tankers, were supplied with bodies from various other British manufacturers.

The home sales market for trucks also saw a boom in 1969. During April, May and June, Dunstable received record orders worth more than £6m. The biggest single order came from the National Coal Board, for 103 vehicles ranging from 15cwt vans to 28ton Dodge 500 artics. Other major orders included twenty-eight vans for Hertz, sixty-six vans for the Southern Electricity Board and twelve tippers for the Hoveringham Stone Company.

Against Chrysler's reluctance to concentrate on the specialized municipal business came a concession, a decision in 1969 to start up a new department to concentrate on supplying specialized 'bespoke' and non-standard vehicles. The department was known as the Special Equipment Operation, and was run by Roland Browne, with a full-time team of fourteen designers and draughtsmen. The SEO became a vital 'support unit' to dealers who were trying to meet their customers' needs in a rapidly changing commercial vehicle market. In a nutshell, if you could not supply the type of vehicle a customer wanted, somebody else would.

Roland Browne and his team became responsible for an array of non-standard vehicles bearing Commer, Karrier and Dodge badges: fire tenders; ambulances; airport service vehicles; special buses for export markets; the GPO vans based on the PB 2500 chassis; double-drive third-axle Unipower conversions; skip-container conversions; a tipper conversion with a Hiab crane and grab ... the list is long and, of course, includes municipal vehicles.

1970: Rootes Motors Becomes Chrysler UK

Rootes entered the seventies against a backdrop or economic recession and fierce competition. A general election with the lowest turnout since 1935 put a Conservative government under Edward Heath into power. The seventies would become synonymous with recession, takeover mania resulting in massive collapses such as that of the Slater-Walker empire, the three-day week, and the visible decline of Britain's manufacturing industry.

For Rootes, the success of the last two years was like turning a corner, only to find that you had ended up right back where you had started. Although the truck operation was still performing well, with 31,972 vehicles sold, the car side had taken an almighty punch in the stomach. The combination of low demand for Rootes cars, under-utilization of capacity in the car operations and massive pre-production costs of the new Hillman Avenger had put Rootes back in the red again. On 1 May 1970, the company announced that they had made a £7.5m loss in the first six months of the year, and that possible losses for the rest of the year could be between £10m and £11m. In the light of this, the decision was made to change the name of the company from Rootes Motors Ltd to 'Chrysler United Kingdom Ltd'. An arrangement was also made for a rights issue to raise £10.9m of new capital, in addition to a £5m loan, for five years, guaranteed by Chrysler.

In a statement issued to the press, Lord Rootes stated:

> Although my family founded Rootes, and has been closely involved with the business, I feel that the change of name is a logical step at this stage in the development of the company. The brand name of our cars and trucks, which are so famous, will remain the same.

The Simca 1100 van range was brought in from France as a light-duty van to replace the Imp. The standard model was based on the Simca 1100 Estate Car. Pictured here is a 'High Top' van version.

Introduced in 1973, and built at the Spanish Barreiros plant of Chrysler España, the 38tonne gross Dodge K3820P provided Chrysler UK with an entry into the heavy tractive unit market. Powered by a 270bhp 11.9ltr turbocharged 6-cylinder engine, it rapidly gained a reputation as being the truck for the 'motorway boy-racer'.

In addition to Rootes, Chrysler had also acquired a 35 per cent shareholding in the French Simca company in 1958, by acquiring shares that had previously been held by Ford. Chrysler continued to increase its stake in Simca by buying up Fiat shares in Switzerland until 1966 when it acquired a 76 per cent majority shareholding. Subsequently, in 1969, the Simca 1100 ½ton van was brought in to replace the Imp van, which soldiered on until mid-1972. In 1973, Chrysler, who also had a controlling interest in the Barreiros company in Spain, brought in their range of heavy tractive units, to give dealers the chance of offering a wide range of payload capabilities in vehicles from ½ton up to 38ton.

Overall responsibility for the UK operations now came from Chrysler International SA in Geneva, Switzerland. Chrysler had announced a new President of Chrysler International in January 1970: Philip N. Buckminster. He had been with Chrysler since 1958 as the first president and managing director of Chrysler International, and then went on to be assistant general manager of the Dodge Car and Truck Division in 1961, and had a short spell as general manager of the Chrysler-Plymouth Division, until 1965. As well as the UK, his new responsibilities included that of Société des Automobiles Simca, Barreiros Diesel SA, Chrysler Sanayi SA and Chrysler Benelux.

Now Chrysler International was in control, but having control and knowing what to do with it are two different things. Control of some of the marketing activities in Europe and other export territories meant that the marketing and sales people in the UK would not be dealing with certain territories that they had managed for years, as Norman Smith confirmed:

> In the Sudan they [Rootes] must have had in excess of 3,000 vehicles, and India was going great guns, but they pulled out when Chrysler took over.

The net result was that Chrysler lost ground in areas that had been export strongholds for the old Rootes organization. From 1971, truck production figures dwindled to 26,027, even though a modest net profit of £514,000 was made, but 1972 saw an even lower production figure of 24,419. The following year, sales virtually equalled that of 1971, but this was a high point; from then on, it was downhill all the way for Chrysler!

In August 1970, Chrysler sold off yet more of 'the family silver': 100 acres (40ha) of land at Dunstable to Brixton Estate Ltd, to be developed as an

(Above) Two Commer-based 'Lambourn Commander' nine-horse transporters, and a 'Mark II Travelmaster Four' were used by Britain's show jumping team for the Olympics in 1972. The three transporters were also used to take the team all over Europe to 'warm-up' events prior to the Olympic Games at Munich in September.

The last Commer line-up to feature the Sankey cab was in 1973. Only two of the seven-model range of two-axle rigid and tractor models were available with a TS-3 engine. The biggest tractive unit available was this single-headlamp VC12 version, powered by a Perkins 6.354 diesel.

industrial estate. In July 1973, Chrysler Corporation USA acquired a 100 per cent stake in Chrysler UK Ltd.

That Chrysler had over-estimated the potential of the European market is an understatement. This, combined with an economic recession and the massive investment in plant at Dunstable meant that production capacity would constantly be under-utilized. Roland Browne estimated that the market share for vehicles of 3½ton upward, during the Chrysler days 'went down from 15 per cent to 9 per cent'. Although much of this situation was due to the ineptitude of Chrysler management, this has to be tempered with the fact that the early and mid-seventies represented a low point in industrial relations at Dunstable. Stoppages were all too common, whether as a result of an internal dispute, or disputes at suppliers. During 1973, Perkins' stoppages put serious strain on Dunstable's ability to meet production targets, as did disputes at Lucas and Rubery-Owen two years later.

1974: Commando – The Last Commer

Development of the Commando started in 1968. It was the last 'official' Commer to be made, and was the last vehicle that A.J. Smith would be involved in. He retired in 1971.

The Commando range was designed to replace the ageing Commer and 'C' and 'V' Series and eventually the Dodge 500 'K' Series. Designed in-house by David Streeton, the Commando, or 100 Series as it was known, would comprise two-axle rigids in the 4.9 to 16ton gross weight range, with tractor unit derivatives up to 18ton gross. It was intended to be cheap to run and relatively simple to build, therefore making it competitive in the marketplace whether ordered with standard bodywork, or as a special order vehicle that would pass through SEO. All of these criteria were fulfilled by the design team. One chassis frame was shared by all models in the medium 7.38 to 9.7ton range, and one for the 11.2 to 14.5ton range, thus making it possible to 'tailor-make' a vehicle on the production line. The 'uni-structural' design concept of the chassis frame meant that over 4,000 variations could be offered to customers. Ken

A 1971 'styling approval' model for the 100 Series 'Lo-line' cab. 1973 on the number plate represented the anticipated launch date.

(Below) The Phase 2 Commando 103 prototype cabs were 2½in (6cm) wider than the eventual production cabs.

(Above) The Commer 100 Series Commando (launch date 7 February 1974).

The cab interior of the Commando.

Cain was one of the development engineers throughout the whole of the design and development period of the 100 Series:

> The 100 range had the easiest and cheapest chassis that Commer ever built ... and it was easy to maintain. Bedford was always a well-made, cheap vehicle, but reliability-wise didn't stand a cat in hell's chance compared to the Commer.

By 1970, various prototypes had been built and were being tested. A 'Phase 1' cab and a reworked 'Phase 2' cab were designed, the 'Phase 2' being 2½in (6cm) wider. It was this cab that was the proposed production cab, but due to development budget constraints, the earlier narrower cab was chosen for production. Prototype designations were: '102' for vehicles up to 8ton; '103' for 9.73 to 13ton; and '104' for 15 to 16ton. During 1970, extensive tests were made alongside the current Chrysler vehicles (the Commer CE8, the VC4 and the Dodge K850), as well as the current competition vehicles (the Ford D550 and D700, the Bedford TK and the BMC Laird LR1300). Evaluation reports and

The Perkins 6.354 became one of the most reliable and economical proprietary diesel truck engines available, and consequently was the most popular powerplant for the Commando.

As far as petrol engines went, the Chrysler V-8s were the industry standard, and although the utterly reliable 318cu in block had been propelling Chrysler, Dodge and Plymouth cars around since the late fifties, it was not an economical unit for a truck in seventies' Britain.

testing at the Motor Industry Research Association test facilities at Nuneaton were carried out over a six-month period during the year.

Conceptually, the 100 Series was not a million miles away from the range that entered production in 1974, with the exception of the adoption of a narrower, re-styled cab. Chief body engineer David Streeton and his team had done a wonderful job on creating one of the most stylish tilt-cabs on the market.

Although the Commer Commando was well accepted by press and operators, the Chrysler influence was starting to show. The constraints that designers and engineers had endured during the development of the 100 Series was evident in certain aspects of the Commando. These are well born out by comments made by Norman Smith, who was at this time a fleet service representative visiting operators, and dealing with the second new 'Commando' model of his career:

One of Chrysler's mistakes was [that they thought] there's no difference between a truck and a car ... A truck is only a car with a big boot!

From the seventies onwards we were controlled by car people who didn't understand trucks. For example, a simple thing like a throttle ball-joint on a car – it stays put with a spring clip ... and they thought that if it would do for a car, it would do for a truck, but, if you get a diesel vibrating, it's only a matter of time before the ball-joint springs off. The consequences of a breakdown in a truck are far greater ... Reliability is number one!

Even car components, like car door handles, were used on the Commando. During early *Commercial Motor* road tests, criticism was made of flimsy trim and fittings; for example the discovery of 'a bent throttle treadle' at the end of the test of a G1611 tipper, and comments such as 'The bottom of the radiator is protected by a very thin and pathetic looking guard, and I doubt if it would last five minutes'. The other main criticism of the early models was lack of power steering, and excessive noise from the turbocharged Perkins T6.354 engine.

Easy maintenance and access to the engine was praised, as was the excellent fuel consumption, and the higher trim level on the de-luxe 'Hi-Line' cab. Tipper models had the more basic 'Lo-Line' cab trim. The Commando range consisted of eight models and six engine options. The G08, G09 and G10 series up to 9.7ton g.v.w. had either Perkins 4.236 or the 6.354 diesel units, or a petrol option of the legendary Chrysler LA 318cu in V-8, with a

The Simca 1100 eventually became the Dodge ½ton range. A pick-up version, seen here outside the main entrance to the Dunstable plant, was added to the range in 1976.

4- or 5-speed gearbox. The G11 had the additional option of the Perkins T6.354 diesel, the uprated Perkins 6.354-2 or the Mercedes-Benz OM 352 engine and a 6-speed gearbox option. For the G13 up to the G16, the petrol V-8 was not offered, and the G18 tractor unit used the Perkins T6.354 as its standard powerplant.

As the range developed, the Commando would make a name for itself as a reliable and cheap to run truck, but not before initial market share was lost – all because of the 'bean counters'.

1975: the Government Rescue Plan

As early as 1970, rumours had been floating around the industry that Chrysler 'wished to divest itself of its European manufacturing operations'. Philip Buckminster, speaking at a press review during the 1970 Geneva Motor Show, claimed that a 'false and malicious rumour had circulated around Europe in February' and subsequently made an 'unqualified denial' of any such possibility.

In truth, Chrysler was starting to feel uncomfortable about its long-term future, and was putting a brave face on its economic vulnerability. Chrysler's problems during the early to mid-seventies stemmed from the problems with its domestic car market. Chrysler was still trying to sell big cars in the USA to a market that wanted alternatives to the V-8 engined gas-guzzlers that had been the trend during the fifties and sixties. The 1973 oil crisis had buyers turning to imports from Europe and Japan, and the muscle-car market in which Chrysler, along with GM divisions like Chevrolet and Pontiac, had been very successful during the sixties, had all but dried up. GM, and Ford to a lesser degree, had suffered during the early seventies by not reacting quickly enough to what people really wanted, that is, compact, fuel-efficient cars, but they were big enough to take a few body blows – Chrysler was not. During the mid-seventies Chrysler had added to their problems by rushing their new compacts, the Dodge Aspen and Plymouth Volare, onto the market.

They were under-developed and badly made, and they cost Chrysler dearly. By 1975, Chrysler Corporation was in very serious trouble.

In Britain in 1975, Chrysler United Kingdom lost £16m in the first six months of the financial year, but that was peanuts compared with the massive losses from Chrysler's US operations: $231m in nine months. On 29 October 1975, Chrysler's chairman John Riccardo held a press conference in Detroit to announce that Chrysler Corporation could no longer afford its loss-making overseas plants and was considering disposing of them. In November, Riccardo came to London to have talks with re-elected Prime Minister Harold Wilson and his new Industry Chairman, Eric Varley. Riccardo's proposal was blunt: either the Government take over Chrysler UK, or it would be closed! Eric Varley was not inclined towards Riccardo's ultimatum, but apparently Wilson took a different view. What followed was a period of intense negotiation that resulted in the Government agreeing to back a rescue plan for Chrysler UK. On 5 January 1976, the plan was signed and the conditions agreed on. Chrysler became the first company ever to enter into a financial agreement and rescue plan with the Government.

The plan received its fair share of criticism, not least from Government opposition. An article in the *News Of The World* on 12 December 1975, headlined: 'CHRYSLER RESCUE A FRAUD, SAYS TOP TORY'. Commenting on Shadow Industry Secretary Michael Heseltine's 'to-the-point' style of heckling, the article went on to state that: 'The rescue would need at least another £100 million ... to relaunch the firm as a profitable and viable venture' and that the Government's calculations were over-optimistic. Heseltine claimed that 'the five "new" models on which the deal was based would just be face-lifted versions of existing cars'.

Whether flawed or not, the deal went ahead, and in February 1976 a report was issued by Chrysler UK's managing director Don Lander outlining the details of the £162m rescue plan. The government agreed to lend Chrysler £55m up to the end of 1979, half of which was to be guaranteed by Chrysler Corporation, and bank loans of £35m to reduce the usage of other short-term borrowings, which would also be guaranteed by Chrysler. New investment would be made at Ryton, so that the new Alpine could be produced there. Chrysler Corporation also agreed to write-off loans to Chrysler UK for £19.5m.

Much of this activity was obviously aimed at the car operations, but what did the deal hold for the truck side? Firstly, £1.5m was to be spent at Luton over the following three years to refurbish and replace machine tools. A further £2.7m had

Cyril Corke, truck sales director, Fred Mulley, Minister of Transport, Geoffrey Ellison, sales and marketing director and Gilbert A. Hunt, managing director Chrysler UK at the Earls Court Show 1974.

Don Lander (left) inspects a new Commando truck at the Frankfurt show.

been allocated to replace the existing paint shops at Dunstable with one consolidated paint shop incorporating both an electro-phoretic primer process and an under-seal facility. New and existing model development had also been included in the new investment. Detail improvements for the Commando and an extensive re-vamp for the PB van were to be completed by 1977, and a new light truck range to replace the Bantam and Walk-Thru was to be in place by 1979. Maidstone was the concession to new investment at Dunstable, and was to be closed, and work moved to Stoke and Luton.

With the new agreement came new management. Canadian Don Lander had replaced Gilbert Hunt as managing director of Chrysler United Kingdom, who was made chairman. Lander subsequently went on to become vice president for Chrysler Europe. His place was taken by fellow Canadian George Lacy in October 1976. Gordon Pfeiffer replaced Geoffrey Ellison as sales and marketing director. Cyril Corke had been made truck sales director in 1973, and continued to run the sales operation with Brian Mac Mahon, who had overall responsibility for car and truck sales. A new engineering director on the truck side also came on the scene: Peter Willmer.

In April 1975, Arthur (Beau) Brandon retired, after fifty-one years' service with Commer, latterly as chief engineering designer for special equipment operations. In January 1976, Fred Lewis retired, after spending over forty years in Rootes and Chrysler parts operations. Although his brother Harry had retired in 1968 after fifty-one years' service, members of the Lewis family would continue to be represented in Dunstable's truck operations with Harry's son Peter, who had been apprenticed in 1962. Fred Lewis' retirement also coincided with the end of Commer trucks. In August, Chrysler made the decision to give all Chrysler commercial vehicles one name: Dodge. The lineage that had started with the first Commer Car in 1906 had finished exactly seventy years later.

10 Recession and Demise: The French Phase

*Dodge 50 was a tough little beast that did its job ...
It wasn't just a big van, it was a small lorry!*
Peter Lewis, Warranty Returns Manager – Renault VI

The rumblings of recession that had been felt in the mid-seventies were by 1978 developing into a full-scale avalanche. The market for cars and trucks, worldwide, was collapsing. The American automobile industry was on its knees, and soon GM and Ford would join Chrysler in the queue on Capitol Hill for government money. Chrysler's new chairman Lee Iacocca went cap-in-hand to the US Government in order to save Chrysler from extinction. In 1978, Chrysler's losses in the USA were the worst ever.

Less than a year after the UK government rescue plan had been signed, Chrysler were trying to 'jump ship' again. To add insult to injury, John Riccardo was still blaming Chrysler's UK operations for the majority of their troubles, when the problems in the UK, although serious, were nowhere near the catastrophic situation of the parent company. In his autobiography, Iacocca comments that he was astounded at the situation that confronted him when he came to Chrysler:

> Chrysler didn't really function like a company at all. Chrysler in 1978 was like Italy in the 1860s – the company consisted of a cluster of little duchies, each one run by a prima donna. It was a bunch of mini-empires, with nobody giving a damn about what anyone else was doing.
>
> Nobody at Chrysler seemed to understand that interaction among the different functions in a company is absolutely critical. People in engineering and manufacturing almost have to be sleeping together. These guys weren't even flirting!
>
> They were babes in the wood when it came to international operations. I began to think that there were Chrysler people who didn't even know that the British drove on the left-hand side of the street!

In 1978, Chrysler wanted out, and the Government, under new Labour Prime Minister Jim Callaghan, also wanted Chrysler out. A new saviour in the form of Peugeot-Citroen, who had made a bid for Chrysler's European operations, entered the scenario, but angry PM Callaghan wanted the takeover by the French 'to go through only on the toughest of terms'. *The Luton News* reported him being furious because John 'Flamethrower' Riccardo (as he had been nicknamed) appeared 'once again to be holding a pistol to the Government's head'.

Enter Peugeot-Citroen

On 10 August 1978, an agreement between PSA Peugeot-Citroen and Chrysler Corporation was announced. Subject to Government and other approvals, PSA would takeover the principal European operations of Chrysler, in a bid worth £117m. On 16 August, Chrysler UK issued a statement to employees about the takeover, the main points being that PSA intended to 'carry on the Government/Chrysler Corporation agreement of 5th January 1976', and that there would be 'no major changes in management'. The deal was approved by the Government on 28 September, even though seven days prior to the agreement, Industry Secretary Eric Varley was still trying to

Bill Holmes (second from right) shows a group of dealers from Newcastle and Scotland the new Commer Commando on the assembly line.

make a stand on his demand for guarantees for the £162.5m lent to Chrysler, and lawyers had set about trying to find a way through the 'tricky legal situation' presented by the takeover.

Although PSA refused to give any assurances over future jobs at Chrysler, which had been a major factor in the rescue operation in the first place, on 1 January 1979, PSA Peugeot-Citroen took over the European operations of Chrysler Corporation. The registered names of all three Chrysler companies changed to 'Talbot Motor Company Ltd' on 1 January 1980.

The decision to get rid of the 'Commer' name was not popular with managers, but despite this 'Dodge' continued as the only badge on commercial vehicles, whilst Chrysler cars were called 'Talbot' as of 10 July 1979. 'Karrier' would re-surface occasionally on certain vehicles for the municipal market.

Although much of the engineering expertise within the company had retired along with the Commer name, which included A.J. Smith, Beau Brandon and Cyril Pemberton, there were still talented engineers and managers available to carry the torch into the next phase of the company's history. With the takeover by Peugeot-Citroen came the appointment of 53-year-old George Turnbull in June 1979 as chairman and managing director. Turnbull was considered to be a legend in the motor industry. He joined Standard Motors after graduating from Birmingham University and rose to be deputy chairman before the company became part of British Leyland. In 1973 he became managing director of BLMC, and went on to set up virtually the whole of the South Korean motor industry when he became vice-president of Hyundai. By 1976, his services were sought by the Iran National Manufacturing Company in Tehran, and he oversaw much of the Chrysler UK business before the call came to return to England.

A contemporary of Turnbull who was to prove instrumental in reorganizing the manufacturing side of the company, was Bill Holmes:

> I came out of the Navy after National Service ... and I joined Motor Panels, who did the SS Jaguar, and the first pressed steel body for the Armstrong-Siddeley and Daimler Conquest, in 1951. Then I went to Standard Motors, and funnily enough I worked on the next drawing board to George Turnbull. It's a small world, but I didn't meet him again, except occasionally socially, until he came to work for Chrysler. I was on the Operations Committee in Coventry and he looked at me across the table and said, 'Good God, it's bloody Bill Holmes!' – and I said, 'Yes, shall I leave now?' and he said, 'You'll leave when I bloody tell you to leave!' He was quite a character.

Like many of the engineers at Commer who had spent much of their working lives with the Rootes Group, Holmes joined Humber in 1956 and went on to work for various Rootes operations before coming to Dunstable:

> I had a roving commission for quite a while. There was a zinc and lead die-casting operation whose line

of business was coffin furniture – die-cast handles etc. and they wanted [to make] the handles for car doors etc ...The company was Hills Precision. I had to work for that company while retaining my own job.

I then went to Singer, and then over to Tilling-Stevens at Maidstone. I acquired all these names as I went on – Humber; Hills Precision; Singer; Tillings-Stevens, Commer, [then Dodge and Renault] without even changing my job.

In 1967, Holmes was transferred from Coventry to the Truck Division at Dunstable, as planning manager, where he redeveloped the plant to enable Dodge 500 production at Dunstable. He then became manufacturing engineering manager of Luton and Dunstable as well as Maidstone. In 1976, Holmes was made plant manager, and later that same year, truck manufacturing director.

The truck operations were, once again, to be marketed separately under Talbot. The potential for exciting and innovative developments in trucks and truck manufacturing lay ahead for Holmes and the new Talbot Motor Company, but the unknown quantity that would throw spanner after spanner into the works was the French.

The Americans having left, the Dunstable management soon realized that another set of problems was presenting itself under the Talbot banner. Peugeot and Citroen were car companies, and had no expertise or desire to be associated with trucks, so why buy a car company that had a sizeable truck operation attached to it? One of the incentives for the Chrysler acquisition had been to get Simca 'back in the fold', but it soon became clear that, even though PSA Peugeot-Citroen did invest in the Barreiros plant at Villaverde in Spain, most of the emphasis was placed, yet again, on cars. History was repeating itself.

However, the truck operation had the funding from the Government rescue plan. Without this, it might have folded. In the event, a new cab trim line was installed for the Commando, and provision made for production of a range of Dodge 500 heavies, which included a 28ton 8-wheeler, in January 1977. In May, a new light-van assembly line went into operation and in October, the PB got its promised improvements, resulting in a more comfortable, quieter and smarter Dodge Spacevan. In September 1977, a 20ton version of the 100 Series Commando G18 tractor unit was introduced. The new model provided an extra ½ton payload over the 500 Series K.2011.P tractor unit, which was discontinued, together with the K.2211.P model.

Peugeot-Citroen

In 1974, Citroen was in trouble, and Michelin, the majority shareholder of Citroen, asked for the co-operation of the Peugeot Group, in order to rescue Citroen who had been hit by a crisis in 1973. At the time, Citroen had been engaged in a vast rationalization programme, whilst trying to modernize its model range. So, in December 1974, Peugeot took over Citroen to form PSA Peugeot-Citroen. With the two like-minded companies working together, profits rose, and by 1978 they were a financially strong organization, and hence in a position to acquire Chrysler.

The Commando Hi-Line cab. David Streeton and his team did a great job creating one of the most stylish tilt-cabs on the market.

In September 1977 a 20ton version of the G18 tractor unit was introduced: the 100 Series Commando G.2011.P. This model effectively replaced the Dodge 500 K Series 20 and 22ton tractor unit models.

(Below) The 100 Series became an ideal vehicle for Roland Browne's Special Equipment Operations department to convert for fire brigade use.

With the Commando range overlapping at the bottom end of the 500 Series range, and the revised versions of the Spanish-built 300 series K3820.P 38ton tractors at the top end, this signalled the start of the phase-out of the Dodge 500.

The Dunstable site also acquired two leased buildings: a unit on the adjacent Fairview Industrial Estate for 100 Series and subsequently the 50 Series frame manufacture, and a similar unit on the Woodside Industrial Estate, at the rear of the main plant. This was used to make Alpine car trim.

Another part of the rescue plan provided investment for development of a new electric van. Based on the Dodge KC60 Walk-Thru, the

The Dodge 'Silent Karrier'. A group of the Walk-Thru-derived electric vans photographed at Wembley Stadium.

van was developed in conjunction with Chloride Batteries, to be a quiet, pollution-free and economical vehicle.

The prototype was tested during 1977 by National Carriers, and seventy Dodge 'Silent Karrier' vans were built the following year. Powered by an electric motor with 160volt high-energy lead-acid batteries, the vehicle had an operating range of 45 to 55 miles (70 to 90km), with a top speed of 40mph (64km/h). The vehicle was evaluated by W.H. Smith, Rank-Hovis, Unigate Dairies, as well as local councils, but sadly the Silent Karrier was not a commercial success. Not only was it slower than an equivalent diesel Walk-Thru, it was more expensive to run. The Walk-Thru was also seeing its last days out, as it was soon to be replaced by the new Dodge 50 Series.

June 1978 marked another 'end-of-an-era' for Dunstable: production of the last Karrier Bantam. After thirty years of continuous production, the Bantam was also making way for the new Dodge 50. Present at this auspicious occasion to see the last Bantam off the line were some of the 'old boys' who had been invited back to Dunstable for the occasion. A.J. Smith, Sid Cooper (ex-sales manager), Harold Sharp (ex-production control manager) and Freddie Best (ex-sales and marketing director) joined Cyril Corke, Bill Holmes and Doug Everden (programming manager) to witness the event.

1979: Making a Silk Purse Out of a Sow's Ear – Dodge 50

The Dodge 50 was inherited from Chrysler as another part of the government rescue plan. The 50 Series was based on the American-built Dodge B300 Tradesman truck and van range. As part of the deal the British version was to utilize the American model's cab panels, which was fine, except for the fact that the two trucks were catering to entirely different markets. The shape of the front end was not conducive to manoeuvring in tight confines, as Norman Smith, Commer's service manager, points out:

The 50 Series had terrible blind spots ... It would be alright out in the Wild West, you weren't worried about the odd foot here and there, but when you've got to aim your vehicle with an inch either side ...

Development engineers certainly had their work cut out trying to make something out of this sow's ear. What resulted was a range of well-built, highly versatile trucks and vans that for the next fifteen years would prove to be the best in their class. The Dodge 50 was, as Peter Lewis who went on to run the spare parts operation at Dunstable describes it: 'A tough little beast that did its job. It wasn't just a big van, it was a small lorry!'

The first prototype model was made in 1977, and it was launched in April 1979. The range consisted of models in five different payload groups, starting at the 'S35' and 'S46' for 3.5 and 4.5tonnes gross, the 'S56' (5.5tonne g.v.w.), and 'S66' (6.6tonne g.v.w.). An 'S75' (7.5tonne g.v.w.) was added in 1980. They were available as a drive-away front-end version, chassis cab, or as one of two van versions: a short and long wheelbase high-capacity integral van. The high capacity van, which was drawn-up at Dunstable by David Streeton's team, effectively solved a lot of the driver visibility problems of the chassis cab versions. As the vans were a 'high-top' design, they benefited from having a huge virtually upright windscreen, which also resulted in a more spacious cab.

All models were available with either the 4-cylinder 3867cc Perkins 4.236 diesel, or the 6-cylinder 4ltr Perkins 6.247 diesel engine, sourced from Perkins at Peterborough or Perkins Japan. An American-built Chrysler 3685cc 6-cylinder petrol unit was available in all models except the S75, and the smaller S35 and S46 models were also available with the French 4-cylinder 1981cc petrol engine. All models had options of 4- or 5-speed Luton-built gearboxes.

The body pressings initially came from Chrysler USA, but were subsequently made at Linwood. When Linwood closed, manufacture was transferred to Willenhall Manufacturing. Axles made at Luton and chassis frame pressings made by Rockwell-Thompson would be assembled at the Fairway unit for final assembly in the main plant next door. High Capacity Van panels were brought in from Howard Tenens Ltd.

The 50 Series was based on the American Dodge B300 Tradesman van range. The smaller B100 Tradesman shared body panels with the B300 and what was to become the UK-built 50 Series.

Recession and Demise: The French Phase 201

(Above) This 1978 Dodge CB400 Karyvan shows how the styling of the 50 Series chassis cab evolved.

Dodge 50 Series styling exercise.

Despite the fact that initially the 50 Series would have looked more in keeping delivering goods to Wall-Mart in downtown Minneapolis, rather than the Gas Board showrooms in Peckham High Street, two very important factors made the 50 a success. Firstly, it was extremely well built. Ford's nearest competitor was the 6-cylinder 'A Series', but it was no match for the 50 Series in terms of ruggedness, and consequently Ford lost much of their sales to Dodge. Secondly, the Dodge 50, like the Commando and the PB, was versatile. It could be ordered with options that tailor-made it to customers' requirements. For this reason, big fleet operators like East

The Dodge 50 Series front view displayed more than a hint of its American parentage.

Midlands Electricity, British Gas and the National Coal Board loved it.

Much of the credit must go to Bill Holmes, who created a flexible assembly system for the 50 Series, as well as the installation of Europe's first cationic electrophoretic paint plant. The paint deposition system differed from conventional 'anionic' methods of painting in use at the time, by using the body to be painted as the cathode instead of the anode, thus the paint is attracted to it by reversing the current. The 182,000ltr tank could take bodies up to 230in (5.75m) long and 98in (2.45m) wide. With this system, salt-spray tests resulted in paint lasting up to four times longer than with anionic systems, as well as giving a shinier finish. This system was brought to Holmes' attention during the Chrysler days:

> Our paint plant was an old carbon deposition system going through a booth. We were able to buy the

Dodge 50 Series S46C High Capacity van (1979).

(Above) A 50 Series cab in the new electrophoretic paint booth.

It was intended that the Dodge 50 would cater for lighter municipal applications, and the Commando chassis for more heavy-duty requirements. Shown here is a 50 Series S56C refuse collector (top) and a Bradley Municipal Vehicles Ltd BMV 5000 rear-loading refuse collector body on a 100 Series G10 chassis (bottom).

A Dodge 50 Series on the assembly line at Dunstable (1979).

(Below) 50 Series body in white (Dunstable, 1981).

electrophoretic deposition paint plant ... and the history behind that is a coincidence. I went over to Chrysler, Windsor [Ontario, Canada] and saw the plant there. It had been operating for about three weeks ... getting the bugs ironed out, but I saw enough to satisfy myself that it was what we needed. It was commissioned in 1978, and all car and truck plants now use this system.

Between 1976, when the paint plant was being installed, and 1979, Holmes completely reorganized the assembly operations to suit the new models that were coming on-line:

Because of the length of the building we had to assemble in, I had to pick the chassis up and bring it round to the driveline, and then drop the chassis on top ... We were one of the first to do it the right way up. Everybody else was dropping springs and axles on to the chassis, and then having a turnover fixture. Both Leyland and Bedford had costly facilities, whereas we didn't. We had some very good innovative engineers.

Renault Vehicules Industriels

Both Renault and Berliet have pedigrees equal to that of Commer or Dodge in terms of pioneering truck design. Marius Berliet built his first car in 1894, and by 1917 Berliet was a thriving company manufacturing a range of lorries, charabancs and omnibuses. To give an idea of the size of Berliet during this period, in terms of employees and production, it was about 30 per cent bigger than Ford in Detroit!

By 1923, Berliet had established a plant in Britain, alongside the River Thames at the Richmond Bridge Works, Twickenham, a business which quickly grew to produce well over 2,000 vans, trucks and buses per year, half of which were for export.

In 1955 the truck manufacturing combine of SAVIEM (Société Anonyme de Vehicules Industriels et d'Equipements Mecaniques) was created, which included Renault and the other French heavy commercial vehicle manufacturers of Latil and Somua. By 1974, the crisis that had hit the French car industry had also hit their truck industry. As Peugeot had taken over Citroen, so Renault had to take over Berliet. In 1978, Renault Vehicules Industriels was created, this being the legal fusion between Berliet and Saviem.

Everything was so bespoke ... Flexibility was a strength of the company. During the '79 recession, for example, we could slow the chain down accordingly, because the station lengths were fixed station lengths. We had a very co-operative workforce ... the dispute level was very low [during this period]. The boredom factor had a lot to answer for in the car industry.

Renault, Berliet et Saviem

Within a few short months of Talbot being formed, it became clear that the French were not interested in the truck manufacturing side. The widely held opinion is that the French Government coerced Renault Vehicules Industriels to take the trucks away from PSA Peugeot-Citroen, leaving it free to concentrate on building Peugeot cars at Ryton.

In January 1981, Renault Truck Industries Ltd and PSA Peugeot-Citroen combined to create Karrier Motors Ltd. A tenuous link with the past was made by using the old Singer Motors Ltd company registration number, so that in effect the dormant Singer Company was just renamed.

Into the Eighties

In 1979, there had been rumours that Dodge might join up with Daf, but this did not materialize. Dodge production had hit a low point, at 16,334, and it was still losing money (£20m in 1978), but the rest of the British truck sector was also feeling the pinch. Foden was virtually broke, and in 1978), Leyland had closed its AEC Southall plant and moved production of the Marathon to the Scammell plant at Watford.

Allied to this, imported competition was on the increase: Mercedes-Benz, Daf, Volvo, Scania, Magirus-Deutz and MAN were all starting to have an impact on the shrinking UK market. Even Japanese Hino trucks were being imported via Ireland. By 1980, British truck manufacturers no longer had a stronghold on the home market. This, combined with an unhealthy attitude towards investment in manufacturing in 'Thatcher's Britain', as well as a shrinking market, made long-term survival less and less probable.

Recession and Demise: The French Phase

Under the newly formed Karrier Motors Ltd, all trucks would display the Renault 'diamond' trademark on grilles, as well as the 'DODGE' badge. Both Dodge and Renault products would now be sold side by side. The seventy-six UK dealerships run by Dodge were joined by Renault's thirty main dealerships. The new deal only covered vehicles over 3.5tonne, and so the little Dodge (Simca) ½ton van would be sold through Talbot car dealerships, in line with Renault and Peugeot light van policy. The Spacevan was due to be phased out in 1981, but in the event it would not die, mainly because of the huge GPO contract. The last Spacevan was

Commando cab-trim line, Dunstable (1980).

Commando final assembly on track 3, Dunstable (1980).

The first of the last ... this 1977 Spacevan PB style would remain until 1983. For twenty-three years the PB was the 'bread and butter' earner for the company.

(Below) The PB van had always been a favourite amongst motorhome builders like Martin Walter and Dormobile. This CI Autohomes Trailblazer was based on the 2000 Series Spacevan, and was another model available from Dodge dealers through the SEO department.

produced at the end of shift at 3.30pm on 17 February 1983.

In 1984, the first Dunstable-built Renault, the G260, made its debut, having won the 'Truck of the Year' award the previous year. A revamped Commando 2, with new front-end treatment by Ogle Design of Letchworth, would now be sold alongside its other new stablemates: the Renault G170,

A GPO Dodge Spacevan heads a line of Spacevans on final assembly.

the R310 and R310 Turboliner. The 50 Series had firmly established itself as Britain's best-selling range of non-HGV commercials above 3.5tonne, but 1983 was turning out to be one of the worst years on record for the already besieged commercial vehicle manufacturing sector. It was, perhaps, a precursor of things to come: four years later the 'Crash of 1987' would see the most calamitous drop in the world stock markets since the war.

By 1983, Karrier Motors Ltd was known as 'Renault Truck Industries Ltd', under new managing director Herve Guillaume, who had replaced Laurent Brisset in August 1981. Brisset had taken over from George Turnbull when Karrier Motors was formed.

It was becoming clear that a close and harmonious relationship with their UK subsidiary was not necessarily on the cards. If the Americans a decade earlier had been difficult to communicate with, then the French were proving to be impossible.

David Streeton, chief engineer–body design, echoes the feelings that were held by much of the management and the 1,500 or so workforce at the time:

> The early days of handling the French was very difficult. There was a ... lot of headcutting, as they were getting in French sales people etc. ... The whole place was going mad ... the sales director would be gone, then the marketing director gone ...!

Many members of the management team at Dunstable found that the level of communication with the French was far worse than it had been with the Americans. Decisions were made by Renault management without consultation with British management, which only enhanced the already uncomfortable relationship between the two factions. Bill Holmes confirms this:

> The French were myopic and arrogant ... During the Chrysler days I went to the plant in Windsor, Ontario, and we found ways to cross-fertilize [ideas] from Canada and the US to the UK, but [with] the French [we] couldn't ... They couldn't understand that we did

(Above) A Renault G170 draw-bar unit, operated by Potter's of Wellingborough, seen here at Castle Ashby, Northamptonshire.

have talent. We didn't have the same problems with Chrysler management.

Cyril Corke echoes Holmes' opinion in a similarly non-compromising fashion:

> Under Guy Corniege, Renault were incompetent ... They didn't know what they were doing. The Americans were far more tolerant than the French.

Although Chrysler International had decided to take on some of the old Rootes' export territories themselves, Renault management decided that all exports should be handled by Renault in France. Holmes is of the opinion that this decision was a major factor in harming sales of UK-built trucks:

> Over 50 per cent [of our production] was always for export ... they stopped that – half our product ...! We lost face, and [our] reputation. Holland, for example, was a very big customer of ours and the French said, 'Sorry, you will not have an export division', so they just eliminated it. Although we were in a position to

Cyril Corke could sell trucks to anyone! Here he talks to Labour MP Michael Foot at an Earls Court Commercial Motor Show during the early eighties.

know financially how we were doing because we were a profit centre, the ability to create profit was removed from us.

The next thing they said was that they didn't like the fact that we were supplying the UK Government, because there could be a conflict if products were exported to certain countries ...

These decisions taken arbitrarily at the onset really pulled the rug from under our feet.

Roland Browne, head of special equipment operations, could see both sides and felt the French were badly handled by the British management:

> Our first problem in the eighties was that we had a management team that had been with the company for quite a long time. With some of those people we had a personality problem in as much as they wanted to tell the French how to do [things] and because they knew better. That came over very strongly, to the point where in the end, the French just didn't ask.

There was, however, more tangible evidence of French xenophobia developing with regard to quality issues. Similar vehicles were made in Caen and Dunstable. Bill Holmes and David Streeton were on the receiving end of Renault's criticism of the British-built vehicles.

Bill Holmes:

> We had better de-merit terms [than the French factory] but they took it that we were cooking the books ... They didn't want us to compete with their French or Spanish operations.

David Streeton:

> I would visit the French factories – Lyons and Caen ... They were forever criticizing our quality, i.e. it wasn't good enough. I would go over to find out why we were down on quality. They were de-meriting us on windscreen wipers, for example. There was only two threads showing through the nut, so we didn't put the washer on, so more than two threads showed, and we got de-merited for not putting the washer on! I was bashing my head against a brick wall. So, I asked one of the French management for help. We went down the line [at the Caen plant] and he took pictures as he went ... They had the same problems as us. They were trying to prove that the English couldn't build to the same quality standards as the French.

Renault's main business objective, above all else, was to ensure the survival of the French truck manufacturing industry. This remit did not necessarily extend to manufacturing subsidiaries outside France that had been foisted on them by the French Government. From Renault's point of view, the UK operation was something that they had inherited, and probably hoped would just go away. After all, the French plants and the Spanish operation could provide the product range for the market that they wanted to sell into, in other words the lower volume, but more profitable, heavy truck market. This also meant that Renault had a different type of dealer network to that of Dodge.

Combined with conflicts of opinion as to what type of vehicles should be in the range, this made the job of selling the existing product range all the more difficult, as Cyril Corke remembers:

> Our strengths were in the light end of the market, i.e. 16ton downwards, and you were dealing with local men, and local men want local service. Renault were into big dealer type networks...You need more, smaller dealers [to service the type of customer base that Dodge had] ... and now our dealer organization has been decimated.

Even though Renault were providing a range of existing 'home-grown' vehicles for the heavy end of the market, there were problems that had to be addressed before they would be accepted into the British market. Most of them had been developed for the French market, which had different demands. Roland Browne explains:

> Between 1981 and 1985, we started taking some of Renault's heavy product. We had some technical problems – mainly brakes fading, and the French insisted [that] there was no problem, and it wasn't until we got some of their senior test people and actually drove around the country ... They'd never seen anything like the M1 ... In France, once you get out Paris, it's like

Two shots of the Tuffnells' fleet, showing their G08 Commando 2s with revamped front grille treatment, incorporating a bold 'DODGE' badge, alongside others with the original frontal design that launched the Commer Commando in 1974. By the eighties, Tuffnells were operating 110 Dodge Commandos, plus three Volvo FL10s, and a 'Renault' diamond had been added to the Commando 2's grille. This style carried on until 1987.

driving in Scotland. They couldn't believe you could go from the south of England up to Liverpool and be in traffic jams all the way. They had no concept of the [number of] times you actually braked! It took a long time to sort out [those] problems.

If the G260 type, which had a very good engine, had had a cab change, it would've competed with the [Volvo] F7, F6 and the F10, but it was [built with] the ten to fifteen year old Berliet cab.

A more amusing example of the French/English culture clash came about when the new re-vamped Commando 2 was launched in 1981. Sales manager David Bryant took a party of fleet operators to Le Touquet for the launch. Renault had hired a hotel in a bay overlooking the sea:

> A voice came over the tannoy, 'Gentlemen, look out to sea'. There was music, lights, fireworks ... and a

Towards the end of 1983, a new Dodge G24C 100 Series 6 × 4 lightweight became available.

cross-channel hovercraft came up the beach ... the doors opened, and the ramps came down ... [and out rolled the new Commando 2]

Laurent Brisset, the managing director of Karrier Motors/Renault, and Guy Corniege asked these hard bitten fleet operators if they thought the show the UK factory had put on was good? 'Well of course it was good, we had a lot of practice in 1944!', came the reply.

Since 1981, there had been a slow, but progressive improvement in the financial situation of the company, but 1986 saw a reversal of this trend, and now, for the first time, talk of plant closure began to look like an option. In the light of this, Bill Holmes devised a plan and put it to Renault management for consideration. In December 1986, a confidential report was sent to Phillippe Gras, president of Renault Vehicules Industriels. In the report, Holmes outlined the feasibility of what amounted to a management buy-out of the UK manufacturing operation, the main points of which were:

An alternative strategy [to closure] was ...To separate the Dodge and Renault business operations in such a way as to enable Renault to continue to trade in the UK as an importer of built-up vehicles without damage to its image and reputation ... and Dodge to develop in its own right as a British manufacturing company.

The method of putting the proposal into practice was:

To sell the Dodge part of the business to a new company formed by the management consortium, which has obtained the support of a leading merchant bank for a leveraged buy-out offer.

Holmes had the support not only of fellow directors, but also of suppliers. Perkins had agreed to supply engines, and a major British truck manufacturer (who was not named) agreed to supply vehicles and/or components for the heavyweight market. Sadly, the proposal was not even considered by Renault, and dismissed 'out of court'.

Recession and Demise: The French Phase

In 1984, Holmes was asked to close the old Biscot Road plant. The closure was determined by the sale of land, and land prices were booming. Biscot Road, the place where Commer started, became a housing estate with blocks of flats, which if visited now would give no clues as to its former identity.

Commando Versus Midliner

In 1987, the Commando went through a final facelift, and although it was by now an old design, its smart new full-width grille and diamond emblem belied its age. There was still life left in the old 100 Series yet, but another battle was about to ensue. All vehicles by this time were badged 'Renault'. Any reference to 'Dodge' or 'Dodge-Renault' had disappeared. Both the Commando and the 50 Series were getting a bit long in the tooth, but decisions made regarding future products only served to worsen an already shrinking market-share situation for Renault. It was their intention to replace the Commando with a Dunstable-built Renault 'Midliner'. This was very unpopular with the Dunstable management, who foresaw problems that the French management either could not, or would not, see. Roland Browne was both a supporter and critic of the marketing decisions made by Renault:

> I don't believe that the decisions with regard to the product range were wrong, only that they came at the wrong time ... we needed them in 1981 ... to update their vehicles. I mean, the Midliner was quite old [then].
>
> Renault had been a heavy vehicle manufacturer ... They foresaw that although [this market] represented only 40 per cent of the volume, it [also] represented 70 per cent of the cash!

Commando 2: as well as three tractor units and a 6 × 4, variations on the Commando 4 × 2 rigid chassis theme went from 8 to 16ton g.v.w. in eight versions.

COMMANDO

Turbo INTERCOOLER

Built in Britain. By Renault.

OPPOSITE PAGE: *The Last Commando: The 1987 Commando sales brochure.*

THIS PAGE: *One of the few Midliner Fire Tenders, operated by Avon Fire Brigade.*

Their failing was that they didn't try to hold on to what they had and [then] expand into the big market. [Instead] all efforts went into that and allowed the other markets to dwindle. At one stage, we had 45 per cent of the fire tender market with the Dodge 100/Carmichael. Before Midliner came out, our market share actually equalled Dennis one year, who always had [at least] 40 per cent of the market.

With the Perkins engine, it actually suited the brigades well. We had built up a rapport with them ... We were the sole suppliers to Avon Fire Brigade for a number of years. When the Midliner was introduced, they hung on and on for eighteen months, and we were still another year away from offering a fire tender.

We walked away from the market, but they [Avon] did eventually have a Midliner, and they would put it up against a Volvo or Dennis and they believed it performed equally as well ... It performed as well as the super Dennis low-level tender on the 30 degree tilt test. We got within 2 degrees of that with a conventional vehicle! It was good, but too late.

Many other managers felt that, although the 100 Series was an old design by comparison to other vehicles on the market, to get rid of it at this point in time and replace it with the Midliner was financial suicide. In many ways, the 100 Series was as good as, if not better than, the Midliner. Roland Browne's comments about not looking after what was, in effect, their core business is exemplified when the opportunity to grasp another niche market was thrown away. In 1986, with bus deregulation, a new market for mini/midi-buses appeared:

> The Dodge 50 Midi-buses with Reeve-Burgess coachwork ... Perkins engine ... Allison auto box. We had the market, although we had [some] technical problems, but we cleared those problems [up]. Mercedes had the same ... The market went down, but we should've still had a residual of 500 vehicles per annum, but Mercedes had a product that kept in touch [with the market], and because our priorities were in other directions, we lost out.

In Renault's financial report for 1987, it actually stated that, '1987 was the first time an operating profit had been achieved (£6.5m loss to £600,000 profit) from sales of mini/midibuses ...' and that 'the share of the market was 8.7 per cent, with sales of 5,856 vehicles'. The following year showed a decline in market share to 6.8 per cent, with 4,639 registrations, but they claimed higher profitability due to sales of the Renault heavy truck range. In 1989 profit increased to £3m, but 1990 saw an apparent market freefall, which had reduced by an astounding 20,689 units, of which Renault took 6 per cent of market for trucks and buses over 3.5tonne g.v.w. – a paltry 2,927 units.

Built in Britain: Renault Midliner

Despite technical problems as well as assembly problems, the decision was made to go ahead with Midliner production at Dunstable in 1989. This was the last straw for Bill Holmes, who had reservations as to whether it was possible at all to assemble the Midliner at Dunstable without costly new fixtures, and still appeal to a market in which 100 Series been doing perfectly well for nigh on two decades.

Renault had other plans though, and decided to get their own manager, Michel Piganiol, from Renault's department of Methods and Industrial Planning, to oversee the implementation of Midliner production. Holmes decided that enough was enough, and resigned from his position as industrial operations director in January 1990, after thirty-two years' service.

The British-built Midliner, as Roland Browne points out, was too late to capture the market it was aimed at, although it was a good vehicle, with rigid versions offered from 6.5tonne to 14.5tonne

By the time the the Midliner cab came to Dunstable it was by no means a new design. The Saviem JK75, the predecessor to the Midliner, had been available to UK operators since the late seventies.

A Midliner S140 Curtainsider pictured outside the administration building at Dunstable.

A Midliner S160 chassis cab fitted with a 6/7 man crew cab. The Midliner proved to be an ideal roadside recovery vehicle used by motoring organizations like the AA (September 1990).

g.v.w., for solo and drawbar operation, and tractor units up to 21 tonne g.c.w. A choice of a five powerplants, starting with the Perkins Phaser 125 130hp 6-cylinder naturally aspirated diesel, and more powerful Renault 5.5ltr turbocharged engines developing 140 and 160hp, and then two Renault 6.2ltr turbocharged and intercooled engines developing 200 and 230hp. All Midliners were fitted with either a ZF 5-speed or 6-speed synchromesh gearbox.

The Midliner, by the early nineties, presented a good range of vehicles, but too much time had elapsed for the range to be integrated into what was a very competitive marketplace, and it was not the success Renault had hoped it would be. By the time the range had been fully constituted, the competition had caught up and were overtaking it. The Midliner had missed the boat.

Will the Last Vehicle off the Line Please Turn the Lights Out …?

In 1991, Renault bought Mack trucks in America. By 1992, their incredible range of Magnum tractor

Renault VI Ltd, Boscombe Road, Dunstable (1994).

units were doing well, but the UK economy was in deep recession. In their financial report for 1992, it stated that only 1,275 vehicles were sold, representing their lowest ever market share of 4.1 per cent. During 1992, the decision was made to stop vehicle assembly at Dunstable. On 14 December 1992, the company's name was changed to Renault VI United Kingdom Ltd to indicate a new start as a vehicle importer, as opposed to a manufacturer. Assembly of British-built Renault trucks stopped officially on 31 March 1993.

Although there had been a progressive shedding of the workforce since the mid-eighties, the majority of the production personnel were made redundant in March 1993, with a further batch of redundancies exactly a year later for

A Magnum tractor unit and a Maxter 8-wheeler await their turn for the special adaptations and modification section (June 1994).

The Vehicle Engineering Centre responsible for modifications to vehicles is now located at the 'Renault Trucks Chiltern' dealership in Luton Road, Dunstable. In June 1994, any special equipment was still fitted 'on-site' at Boscombe Road.

The 50 Series lent itself ideally to midi-bus coachwork, in what was an emerging new market. By the eighties, Renault were starting to lose out to Mercedes-Benz and Iveco.

This Renault 50 Series S56-90 was powered by the Perkins Phaser 90 naturally aspirated diesel. The bigger models in the range had the Perkins Phaser 110T engine and the option of a Torqueflite 3-speed automatic transmission.

development engineers who were seeing out existing projects.

The last Renault Commando was built at Dunstable on 4 October 1989. It was a G13 Rigid. The last Midliner to be built at Dunstable was on 29 March 1993. It was an M160 13-tonner and was sold to a dealer on Guernsey, Channel Islands. The last Renault 50 was built on 22 March 1993, and went to Kent Truck Services in Faversham, Kent.

The manufacturing plant, including the electrophoretic paint plant, was sold off to China, and ironically, quality manager John Milnns remembers two of the last 50 Series going to China!

The Dunstable operation continued to handle adaptation and modification work on all Renault models, but after nearly forty years, the site that had echoed to the noise of the manufacture of some of the most innovative and ingenious commercial vehicles went quiet.

Many of the managers and workforce had been with either Commer, Karrier, or Dodge for years. Some had spent their whole working lives with the same company. Some were at retirement age, or happy to take early retirement. Some would have to find new jobs. They had all experienced a period in British vehicle manufacturing that will never be seen again. One of the

This 50 Series driveaway front-end unit was probably for a midi-bus conversion as it is fitted with a 24volt battery system.

The Renault 50 Series Reynolds-Boughton 4 × 4 conversion. Many of these vehicles were purchased by gas, electricity and water utilities, and custom-built to their requirements. The 50 Series was still a market leader despite its dated looks. Its popularity in the late eighties remained high due to its versatility, economy and excellent build quality.

(Below) The administration building at Dunstable in October 2001 and the Renault Premium – at last Renault had achieved their goal of producing world-class vehicles for the heavy end of the market.

secretaries who was present when the axe fell told me: 'It was a sad day when the plant closed, but it's awful seeing men that you have worked with for a long time actually in tears!'

The UK operation of Renault Trucks, for the time being at least, retains its headquarters at Boscombe Road, and with the introduction in 1996 of the French-built Premium truck range, they are at last building high-quality, world-class trucks that rank amongst the best, but one item of nomenclature is missing: 'Built In Britain'.

Bibliography

Books

Adeney, Martin, *The Motor Makers* (Collins, 1988)

Bullock, John, *The Rootes Brothers – Story of a Motoring Empire* (Patrick Stephens, 1993)

Childs, David, *Britain Since 1945 – A Political History* (Routledge, 2000)

Dyer, James and Dony, John (editor), *The Story of Luton* (White Crescent Press, 1977)

Forty, George, *World War Two AFVs and Self-propelled Artillery* (Osprey, 1996)

Georgano, G.N., *The Complete Encyclopedia of Motorcars, 1885–1968* (E.P. Dutton, 1973)

Hutton, Will, *The State We're In* (Random House, 1996)

Iacocca, Lee, with Novak, William, *Iacocca – An Autobiography* (Guild Publishing, 1985)

Kennett, Pat, *Berliet* (Patrick Stephens, 1981)

Lumb, Geoff, *British Trolleybuses 1911–1972* (Ian Allan, 1995)

Munro, Bill, *Carbodies – The Complete Story* (The Crowood Press, 1998)

Robson, Graham, *The Cars of the Rootes Group* (MRP Publications, 1990)

Sked, Alan and Cook, Chris, *Post-War Britain – A Political History* (Penguin Books, 1993)

Sloan, Alfred P., *My Years With General Motors* (Sidgwick & Jackson, 1963)

Turner, H. A., Clack, G. and Roberts, G, *Labour Relations in the Motor Industry* (Allen & Unwin, 1967)

Magazines and Periodicals

The Commercial Motor

Motor Transport

Rootes Review, October 1965

Index

AEC 47, 136, 182, 205
Akroyd, Norman 48, 67, 69
Alvis 63, 64
Armstrong-Siddeley 196
Armstrong-Whitworth 125
Armstrong-Whitworth Aircraft Ltd, Sir W.G. 185
Arton, J.H. 45
Austin 36, 58, 62, 118, 148, 149
Austin, Herbert 29

Bayard-Clement 22
Bedford 58, 62, 138, 190, 205
Bentham, Neil 149
Berliet 22, 27
Best, F.M.S. (Freddie) 95, 99, 135, 146, 168, 199
BMC 136, 138, 190
Booth, Geoffrey 174
Bragg, Gerald 32, 55, 89, 99, 107
Brandon, Arthur (Beau) 93, 194, 196
Brisset, Laurent 208, 212
British Leyland 196
British Light Steel Pressings 77, 87, 92, 102, 142–5, 178
Broadbent, Gerald 109
Brown, Alec 127
Browne, Roland 185, 186, 188, 210, 215, 216
Bryant, David 182, 183, 211
Buckminster, Philip N. 187, 192
Buick 29, 176
Bullock, John 168, 174
Burgess, Don 146
Burrell, Ted 21

Cadillac 29, 176
Cain, Ken 153, 162, 189
Chevrolet 62, 151, 176, 192
Chrysler 139, 145, 168–70, 172–4, 175–7
Chrysler-Cummins Ltd 182
Chrysler España (Barreiros) 187, 197
Chrysler International S.A. 187, 209
Chrysler United Kingdom Ltd 186, 188
Clay, Tommy 130
Clayton & Company 45
Clayton, Herbert Fitzroy 45
Clayton, Reginald 45
Clyno 36

Cole, R. Barry 6, 15
Commer, models:
2½GA 34
3PG 32
4G 34
4GN 33, 35
5P 37
6TK Invader 37, 38, 42
15cwt De Luxe Van 41, 42, 43
30GP 32
40LG 33, 34
1500/2500/PB 148–51, 155–7, 171, 185, 186, 194
Avenger 90, 102, 103, 108, 109, 131, 134
B-series (Superpoise) 114, 116, 123
B3 42
B20 42
B30 Raider 40, 42
B40 Centaur 40, 41, 42
BF 108, 114, 122, 124, 142, 153
C Series 131, 134, 135, 136, 137, 138, 162–7, 188, 189, 190
C5FT 94
car-derived vans (8cwt, Supervan, Cob, Express, Imp) 40–3, 56, 67, 80, 109, 111, 114–18, 159, 160
Commando 81, 84, 194, 196
Commando 100 Series 189–92
F4/F6 34
G2 42, 43
G2 Corinthian 42
G3 43
G6 38, 39
LA6 171
LN5 58, 59
N Series 44, 54, 55, 57, 59, 61, 83
N4 34
N4/N6 34
N5 58, 59
NF6 Avenger 38, 39
Pug 42, 44
Q2 77
Q4 61, 62, 77
Q15 77, 91
Q25 77, 78
QX 80, 86, 87, 88, 89, 92, 95, 99, 102, 104, 107, 108, 109, 110, 120, 122, 123, 124, 131, 132, 137, 142

Superpoise 57, 58, 60, 61, 78, 80, 81, 91, 92, 95, 99, 100, 102, 103, 107, 108, 109, 116, 123
V Series 161, 162–7, 180, 188, 189, 190
Walk-Thru, 141, 151–5, 156, 158, 179
Commer Cars, models:
2G 30
2P 30
3P 30
3P Goods 30
BC Brackley 16, 18, 21
BC type 9, 12, 16, 22, 24
CC Leeds 15, 16, 30
Commer Tri-Car 20
Commer-Simonis 18, 19
County motor coach 9
HC type 8, 9
KC Luton 16, 30
Kerry-type Torpedo charabancs 17
LC type 9
MC Braintree 16, 18, 30
Norfolk Convertible Country House and Estate Car 11, 15, 18
PC Manchester 16, 17
RC Bridgewater 16, 22, 24, 27, 28, 29, 30, 31
RC Subsidy type 'A' 23, 24
RC type 16
SC type 8, 12
WP-1 11, 17, 30
WP-2 17
WP-3 17
YC Barnet 16, 18, 19, 30
Commer Cars Home Guard 73–4
Commer Exports 15–16, 79–86
Commercial Car Hirers Ltd 13, 31
Commercial Cars Ltd 30–1
Cooper, Sid 55, 148, 199
Corke, Cyril 95, 99, 148, 181, 193, 194, 199, 210
Corniege, Guy 209, 212
Courtney, Eric 67, 70, 74, 76
Coventry Climax 136
Coxhead, Ernest L. 20, 29
Coy, Eric 125, 126, 127, 139, 140
Cozens, Geoffrey 55, 74, 89, 107, 145, 146, 151, 168

Daf 173, 205
Daimler 63, 196
Dean-Averns, R. 45
Delahaye 22
Dennis 15, 22
Dimmock, Ernie 23
Divco 151, 153, 154
Dodge 58, 151, 152, 194, 197, 206
50 Series 155, 195, 199–205, 208
200 Series 176, 177, 203
300 Series 170
500 Series 174, 178, 179, 183–5, 189, 197, 198
Aspen 192
B100 Tradesman 200
B300 Tradesman 199
CB400 Karyvan 201
Commando 100 Series 197, 198, 211–15
K700 172
Silent Karrier 199
Spacevan 197, 206, 207, 208
Walk-Thru 198
Dodge Brothers (Britain) Ltd 171
Dorman Engines 40
Dunstable Factory 105–7, 156–9, 171, 206, 218

Edgerton, Hon. Wilfred C.W. 29, 31
Edwards, H.E. (Bertie) 93, 146
Ellison, Geoffrey 185, 193, 194
Everden, Doug 199

Faller, Fred 31, 55, 68, 78, 93
Fiat 187
Foden 205
Foden, Wilf 74
Ford 67, 92, 118, 149, 151, 187, 190, 201
Ford, Henry 29
French, Vic 106

Garner, Bill 130, 139, 174, 185
General Motors 29, 35, 130
Gibbs, George 55
Gill, Eric 134
GMC 151
Goddard, F.G. 55, 73, 74, 75
Golby, Roland 127
Government Rescue Plan 192
Gras, Phillippe 212
Great War 22–5

Index

Guillaume, Herve 208
Guy 63, 80

Halford, Julian A. 6, 7, 8, 11
Halley 18
Hammond, Rupert 168, 174
Hancock, Charlie 76
Hathaway, Fred 25
Hattersley, H.W. 45
Haydon, D.P. 55
Heath, Harold 55
Hillman 35, 40–2, 79, 82, 86, 92, 113–16, 139, 141, 145, 158, 168–9, 171, 186
Hills Precision 197
Hino 205
Holmes, Bill 174, 178, 196, 197, 199, 202, 208, 209, 210, 212, 213, 216
Horley, John 183
Humber 31, 32, 33, 35, 36, 38, 40, 92, 114, 127, 130, 142, 143, 149, 153, 196, 197
Humber Armoured Cars 63–5
 Coventry Mk 1 64, 65
 Karrier KT4 63
 Mk 1 Armoured Car 63
 Mk 1 Scout Car 63
 Mk 2 Armoured Car 63
 Mk 3 Armoured Car 64
Hunt, Gilbert A. 174, 180, 184, 193
Hutchinson, Horatio G. 6, 29
Hyundai 196

Iacocca, Lee 195
Iveco 219
Ives, Stan 109

Jenkins, Roger 185
Jowett 92

Kadenacy design principal 125
Karrier 22, 37, 44
 Bantam 56, 57, 80, 85, 100, 102, 105, 107, 110–12, 143, 144, 181, 194, 199
 Chaser 6 47
 CK-3 57, 58, 66, 80, 83, 84, 85, 103
 CK-5 57, 58
 CK-6 76
 Cob 47, 50–3
 Colt 53
 Fourteen 104
 Gamecock 102, 103, 104, 118, 124, 141, 181
 Karrier-Transport Loadmaster 101–3
 Karrier-Yorkshire RSC 101, 103
 KL type 46
 Mechanical Horse 50–3, *see also* Cob
 Monitor 47
 PB60 47
 Road Railer 47
 RSC 57, 80
 W6 46
 WO6 47
Karrier Cars
 'A' type 45
 'B' type 45
 WDS type 45, 46
Karrier Motors Ltd 44
Karrier Motors Ltd (1981) 205, 206, 208
Karrier Motors (Successors) Ltd 44
Karrier–Clough trolley omnibus 48
Keep, Col. Thomas B. 31, 54, 55
Kitchen, Don 130, 139, 140

Lacre 18
Lacy, George 194
Lander, Don 193, 194
Lawrence, Fred 73, 93, 104, 145, 146, 171
Lawrence, Norman 71, 76, 93, 106, 143, 166, 183
Lewis, Fred 55, 73, 76, 86, 113, 148, 182, 194
Lewis, Harry 55, 93, 194
Lewis, Peter 151, 155, 194, 195
Lewis, Sid 55
Leyland 18, 22, 46, 47, 136, 182, 205
Limon, Wally 64, 80
Lingar, Joe 23
Linley, Charles M. 6, 11
Linley Patent Change-Speed Gearbox 10, 30
Longbottom, Fred 55, 68, 76
Lorraine-Dietrich 22
Lowe, J.R. 69
Luton Factory 19, 20, 22, 23, 41, 60–2, 70–2, 74–6, 91, 93, 120, 121, 122, 157, 159, 213

Mac Mahon, Brian 194
Magirus-Deutz 205
MAN 205
Marsden, Gerry 141, 149, 150
Marsh, Percy 93, 95
Maudslay 22
Mercedes-Benz 205, 219
Merryweather 18
Minett, Irving J. 169
Mitchell, Frank H. 6, 11
Mongiardino, Joe 23
Morris; Morris-Commercial 58, 117, 118
Moth, J.C. 13

Nevil, S.S. 13
Newsome, J.J. (Joe) 113, 147

Oldsmobile 176

Panhard 95
Panks, John T. 185
Payne, George 87, 108
Pemberton, Cyril 140, 146, 196
Perkins Engines 58, 82, 99, 116, 131, 149, 151, 153, 163, 164, 165, 173, 182, 183, 188, 191, 200, 212, 215, 217, 220
Perks, W.W. 17
Peugeot 22
Pfeiffer, Gordon 194
Piganiol, Michel 216
Plymouth 151, 191, 192
Pontiac 176, 192
Post-War in Britain 1946–51 79
Post-War Slump, 1920s 27–9
Pringle, Jack 166
PSA Peugeot-Citroën 195–7

Reeves, W.J. 68
Renault 197, 206–21
Renault models:
 50 Series 215, 219–21
 Commando 214, 220
 G60 211
 G170 207, 209
 G260 207
 Magnum 218
 Maxter 218
 Midliner 213–17
 Premium 221
 R310/R310 Turboliner 208
Renault Truck Industries Ltd 205, 208
Renault Vehicles Industriels (inc. Berliet, Saviem) 205, 212
Renault VI United Kingdom Ltd 218
Reo 95
Riccardo, John 193, 195
Rolls-Royce 136
Rootes, Brian 99, 112, 159, 174
Rootes, Geoffrey 135, 145, 146, 169, 186
Rootes, Reginald 35–7, 67, 80, 99, 135, 169, 171, 174
Rootes, Timothy 146, 162, 174
Rootes, William 35–7, 67, 78, 80, 86, 89, 99, 143, 168, 169, 170, 171
Rootes (CA) (Pvt) Commer Ltd, Rhodesia 159
Rootes España SA (Commer Santana) 159, 162
Rootes Export Division 185
Rootes Group 79, 196
Rootes Ltd 35, 37
Rootes Motors Inc., New York 185
Rootes Motors Ltd 92, 145, 186
Rootes Securities Ltd 37, 54, 92

Saviem 216
Scammell 205
Scania 173, 205
Scrivener, Derek 109, 153
Seaman, Bill 130
Seeley, Bill 20
Sharp, Harold 199
Sherwin, Manny 99
Shuff, R.G. 67, 69, 70
Simca 174, 187, 192
Simonis & Company, Henry 18
Singer 112, 113, 171, 205
Singer, R.T.A. 106
Single, Alec 93, 109, 153
Smith, Arthur J. 80, 89, 92, 93, 109, 134, 140, 146, 151, 153, 166, 174, 178, 183, 189, 196, 199
Smith, Norman 55, 67, 81, 128, 130, 133, 173, 191, 199
Squires, Alf 76
Stafford, Robert 29
Standard 117, 148, 196
Stoke Aldemoor Factory 92, 124
Stransky, Heinz 139, 140
Stratton, George, R. 55, 68, 76
Streeton, David 109, 153, 189, 191, 208, 210
Studebaker 95, 151
Sunbeam 36, 37, 77, 141, 149
Sunbeam-Talbot 92
Sunbeam Trolleybus Company 80

Talbot Motor Company Ltd 196, 197, 206
Tansley-Witt, H. 31
Taylor, Aldersey 6, 11, 15
Thomas, Mr 29, 30
Thompson, Des 185
Thornycroft 15, 22, 80
Thrupp & Maberley 143, 165
Tilling-Stevens Motors Ltd (TS Motors) 44, 95–9, 130, 133, 197
Toll, W.C. (Cliff) 172, 180
Townsend, A.E. 69
Turnbull, George 196, 208

Underdown, Harry Charles Baillie 6, 8, 11, 19, 20, 29

Vauxhall 35, 118, 179
Vauxhall-Bedford 74, 105, 106
Volvo 173, 205, 211
Vulcan 95–9

War Office Subsidy Scheme 22
Watson Lee, Pamela 147
Watson Lee, Rex 113, 145, 146, 147, 172, 174, 180, 181, 182
Weighell, H.J.C. 185
White, Hector 93
Wilkes, E.G.M. (Ernie) 69, 108
Willard, F.J. 172
Williams, Laddie 32
Willmer, Peter 194
Willshaw, Harry 139
Wolseley 22
Woodin, Joe 174

Young, Doug 153